Open
Secret

Open Secret

THE GLOBAL BANKING CONSPIRACY THAT SWINDLED INVESTORS OUT OF BILLIONS

Erin Arvedlund

PORTFOLIO / PENGUIN

PORTFOLIO / PENGUIN
Published by the Penguin Group
Penguin Group (USA) LLC
375 Hudson Street
New York, New York 10014

USA I Canada I UK I Ireland I Australia I New Zealand I India I South Africa I China
penguin.com
A Penguin Random House Company

First published by Portfolio / Penguin, a member of Penguin Group (USA) LLC, 2014

Library of Congress Cataloging-in-Publication Data

Arvedlund, Erin, author.
Open secret : the global banking conspiracy that swindled investors out of billions / Erin Arvedlund.
pages cm
Includes bibliographical references and index.
ISBN 978-1-59184-668-0 (hardback)
1. Bank fraud. 2. Banking law—Criminal provisions. 3. Commercial crimes. 4. Global Financial Crisis, 2008-2009. 5. LIBOR market model. 6. Interest rate futures. I. Title.
K5223.A78 2014
364.16'8—dc23
2014021118

Printed in the United States of America
1 3 5 7 9 10 8 6 4 2

Set in Sabon LT
Designed by Alissa Rose Theodor

While the author has made every effort to provide accurate telephone numbers and Internet addresses at the time of publication, neither the publisher nor the author assumes any responsibility for errors, or for changes that occur after publication. Further, the publisher does not have any control over and does not assume any responsibility for author or third-party Web sites or their content.

To my father-in-law
John A. Beattie Jr.
1927–2014

Cast of Characters

Wall Street Journal

 Mark Whitehouse—journalist

 Carrick Mollenkamp—journalist

Bankers Trust International

 Evan G. Galbraith—inventor of the floating-rate note

 David Clark—broker

U.S. Treasury

 Timothy Geithner—Treasury secretary, 2009–2013

 Henry Paulson—Treasury secretary, 2006–2009

 Robert Rubin—Treasury secretary, 1995–1999

 Jacob Lew—Treasury secretary, 2013–present

 Robert Steel—Treasury undersecretary, 2006–2008

Manufacturers Hanover Limited

Minos Zombanakis—inventor of the formula for LIBOR

Citigroup

Scott Peng—Interest rate strategist

UBS

Marcel Ospel—group chair

Marcel Rohner—CEO

Tom Alexander William Hayes—trader

ICAP

Darrell Read—broker

Daniel Wilkinson—broker

Colin Goodman (aka Lord LIBOR)—broker

Michael Spencer—founder and chief executive

Federal Reserve Bank of New York

William Dudley—president, 2009–present

Timothy Geithner—president, 2003–2009

Federal Deposit Insurance Corporation (FDIC)

Sheila Bair—chair, 2006–2011

British Bankers' Association (BBA)

John Ewan—managing director

Angela Knight—chief executive, 2007–2012

Marcus Agius—chair, 2010–2012

Bank of England

Mervyn King—governor, 2003–2013

Paul Tucker—deputy governor, 2009–2013

U.S. Federal Reserve

Benjamin Bernanke—chair, 2006–2014

UK Parliament

John Mann—Labour minister

Barclays Capital

Robert E. Diamond—chief executive, 1996–2012

Rich Ricci—co–chief executive officer, 2000–2013

Jerry del Missier—chief operating officer, 2000–2012

John Varley—group chief executive, 2004–2011

U.S. Securities and Exchange Commission (SEC)

Mary Jo White—chair, 2013–present

Brevan Howard

Alan Howard—co-founder

Royal Bank of Scotland (RBS)

Tan Chi Min—trader

Scott Nygaard—head of short-term markets for Asia and Edinburgh-based RBS

Paul Walker—head of money market trading

Sim Suh-Ting—executive director and head of regulatory risk and compliance (SE Asia)

Deutsche Bank

Anshu Jain—co–chief executive

U.S. Commodity Futures Trading Commission (CFTC)

Gary Gensler—chair, 2009–2014

Vincent A. McGonagle—director of the Division of Market Oversight

Stephen J. Obie—acting director of the Division of Enforcement

David Meister—head of enforcement

Bart Chilton—commissioner, 2007–present

Jill Sommers—commissioner, 2007–2009

Mark Wetjen—acting chairman, 2013–2014

Timothy Massad—chairman, 2014–present

Long-Term Capital Management (LTCM)

James G. Rickards—Wall Street lawyer and hedge fund investor

J.P. Morgan Chase

Paul Glands—trader

Rabobank

Piet Moerland—chairman, 2009–2013

New York University

Rosa Abrantes-Metz—professor and director in antitrust, securities, and financial regulation practices of Global Economics Group

U.S. Department of Justice

Lanny Breuer—head, Criminal Division, 2009–2013

MF Global

Jon Corzine—CEO and chairman, 2010–2011

James Koutoulas—hedge fund manager and MF Global customer

Contents

Prologue

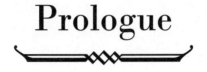

Tom Alexander William Hayes looked the part of the unremarkable British man. He sported short, dark blond hair,
slightly wide-set eyes ringed with brown circles, a white button-
down dress shirt, grayish blue V-neck sweater pilling on the
back, and black trousers over black leather slip-on shoes. Like
most Londoners commuting around town, he carried an um-
brella, as that autumn day it was drizzling.

A private man by nature, Hayes remained largely in seclu-
sion at his home in Surrey, with his wife and one-year-old son.
He had stayed behind closed doors for good reason: On the
days he did go out into the world, television cameras and pa-
parazzi followed him like buzzards.

This particular day, October 21, 2013, was no exception.
Outside the gray, modern-style courthouse, photographers waited

to snap photos of him entering and leaving the building. Hayes offered no answers to their questions, yet one word seemed to hang over the proceedings as if written in London's cloudy sky.

It was an acronym, one that consisted of five letters: L-I-B-O-R. Shorthand for London Interbank Offered Rate.

That little word—and its complex financial ramifications—represented countless billions of dollars in allegedly illegal gains *and* the means by which Hayes might lose his freedom.

Hayes had grown up in London, a middle-class lad with a gift for math and computers (a classmate called him an "incredibly smart geek"). His college record was such that employers flew him first-class to their offices for interviews, and, long before he became the poster boy for the largest financial scandal in London in anyone's memory, he accepted, in 2001, a position as a junior trainee at the Royal Bank of Scotland.

At RBS, his specialty was derivatives, the financial instruments that, with the advent of electronic trading in the 1990s, represented finance's new magic. Derivative agreements are contracts that specify an exchange of cash or other assets owned by one party for the second party's assets within some time frame. Hayes's talents aligned nicely with Wall Street's growing appetite for derivatives. The market included options, swaps, and other transactions priced off of interest rates, commodities, and a variety of other underlying assets, and Hayes demonstrated a particular knack.

Hayes didn't favor Savile Row suits as some of his well-paid coworkers did; for him, the dress code was post-college casual—jeans, pullover shirts, and sweaters. Fast food sufficed for Hayes, rather than the thousand-dollar dinners celebrated by some in finance.

In 2006, he accepted a new job, leaving RBS to work for the global banking power UBS (known in earlier days as Union Bank of Switzerland). That spring his new employer posted him to Tokyo, and his promising career—he hadn't yet turned thirty—took off, as he quickly became one of the most powerful derivatives traders in Tokyo.

In Japan, Tom Hayes gained a reputation for one particular proficiency: He proved skilled at betting on the difference between the lending rates offered by banks overnight in buying and selling derivatives. He hedged the tiny differences in the LIBOR, set in London, and the Tokyo overnight rate, set by the Bank of Japan. His ability to play the rate game came to mean millions in profits for UBS, elevating him from merely a trader to a recognized corporate asset, one whom the bank entrusted with immense sums in UBS assets.

Outside brokerage firms and other banks took note and, in 2009, he jumped ship, lured away by Citigroup—and a pay package that more than doubled the cool $2 million or so he took home annually at UBS. One of his new bosses proclaimed him "a star."

Within the financial world, Hayes's ability to make the market's numbers move his way mystified his rivals. Tom Hayes had truly arrived.

———

Southwark Crown Court sits between London Bridge and slightly east of Shakespeare's Globe Theatre. The drama unfolding with Hayes as the central actor, however, was of a distinctly twenty-first-century sort.

By the time he entered the courtroom in October 2013, the only thing different about him was the exhaustion clearly etched on his face. Hayes still wore his dark blond hair short, but on that autumn morning Hayes's wide-set eyes had bags, as if he had slept poorly. Though his expression was impassive, his demeanor was glum. He had been the first man arrested in the international scandal that had roiled the banking business.

Since 2008, businesspeople around the world had encountered the word "LIBOR" as they ate breakfast and surveyed the morning news. They had learned that LIBOR, established four decades earlier as a convenience in the early days of variable interest rates, had morphed, in effect, from a gentlemen's agreement to a vehicle for outright theft. In Britain, the United States, and elsewhere, journalists reported, LIBOR had become subject to widespread—and illegal—manipulation.

Hayes had drawn the special attention of authorities in the United States and the UK. They were eager to serve up the scalps of the men who had rigged the LIBOR, and the U.S. Department of Justice in particular spun a narrative in which Hayes was the principle protagonist, the figure most responsible for rigging the LIBOR. In a long and detailed complaint, filed the previous December, the FBI asserted (among many other allegations) that, in the months between November 2006 and August 2009, Hayes had sought to alter the LIBOR rate on 335 out of 738 business days. The agency cited emails and a plethora of documents. To the Americans, he was the mastermind.

Hayes knew the truth was a great deal more complicated, that the years-long fixing of interest rates couldn't be done by just one person; it took a village of traders, brokers, and go-betweens arrayed around the globe, along with bribes, soft threats, and hard financial rewards to push LIBOR up or down. But with the American prosecutors aiming squarely at him, Hayes's legal problems included the risk of extradition to the United States for trial.

As he anticipated his day in court, extradition was a prospect that not only Hayes but his countrymen found disquieting. The British public were outraged when three bankers for Enron (David "Bermie" Bermingham and two colleagues, known collectively as the NatWest Three) ended up being tried, convicted, and incarcerated in American prisons rather than in their home country ten years earlier. At the time, many Britons had actually protested the extradition of the men to America.

Thus, Tom Hayes had ample reason for looking grim on what was to be his offer of a plea, guilty or not guilty. This was a hearing, not a trial, but he'd had to relinquish his passport. Despite having no place to go, however, he was by no means without leverage.

One avenue was the press. The previous January, he had texted the *Wall Street Journal* with a tantalizing message: "This goes much higher than me." It had been a key public comment, one awash with implications for former bosses and colleagues. It implied that Hayes hadn't acted alone but had fiddled interest rates with the full knowledge and perhaps the blessing of his bosses. It also made him more sympathetic. The public was hungry to understand more, to learn the identity of other banker perpetrators, to get the whole story. A plot turn that implicated higher-ups just might improve his odds.

A proven manipulator of information, Hayes might also use what he knew to good advantage with the courts. In recent months, prosecutors in London had been gaining ground on their U.S. counterparts; the LIBOR scandal was an embarrassment to Britain. Serious Fraud Office chief David Green had pushed the rate-rigging investigations in London into overdrive, assigning sixty people on his staff to move the case through to an indictment phase. If Hayes was as important as the Americans said he was, could he be persuaded to cooperate with British prosecutors?

On that dreary morning, no one but Hayes knew exactly how much information he had to trade. Bankers, journalists, and lawyers alike feared and hoped that he would offer the names of others who had helped him rig the LIBOR rate. His naming of names could extend beyond the banks where he had worked to other financial institutions, including rivals and interbank brokers, where friends and colleagues worked. If so, that would be bad news indeed for many big banks, and not only those already embroiled in the controversy.

Potentially more explosive was his knowledge of higher-ups—possibly much higher—on the corporate ladder who were co-conspirators in the scheme to rig interest rates at UBS and Citigroup. He'd already hinted as much: Three days after his dismissal in September 2010, an angry Hayes (his firing had come just a few weeks before his wedding day) wrote a letter to a Citigroup human resources executive, ominous in its implications for higher executives. "My actions were entirely consistent with those of others at senior levels," Hayes had written "[and] . . . senior management at [Citigroup Japan] were aware of my actions."

In less than a decade, the fortunes of Tom Hayes, derivatives whiz kid, had earned him millions in bonuses and the status of certifiable star in the world of finance. As this book goes to press, it isn't clear whether he will land behind bars. His future almost certainly depends upon a different set of skills than those that made his fortune: With his trial expected to begin in January 2015 in London, its outcome hinges on his capacity for negotiating the British legal system and, possibly, the American justice system in the future.

To understand LIBOR, its workings and its crisis requires getting to know the other essential players in New York and Washington, in London and Tokyo. Though he may be the most visible villain in the drama, the story began well before Hayes. In the chapters that follow, you will learn about dozens of men and women on Wall Street and in the City of London. Together, they, like the balls on a billiard table, repeatedly collided, transforming their fortunes and careers and the lives of us, the unwitting investor, in a rigged game they knew was an open secret. The ricochet patterns that emerged are crucially important, as they have altered the global financial landscape.

CHAPTER 1

Is LIBOR a Lie?

In April 2008, Mark Whitehouse and Carrick Mollenkamp had almost given up bothering to go home to sleep. The schlep from the London bureau of the *Wall Street Journal* often didn't seem worth it when they knew they'd have to turn around and come back again after just a few hours of rest. Instead, the two American reporters regularly camped at the bureau's offices in central London, accommodating the time lapse that separated Greenwich mean time and the *Journal*'s New York deadlines. The long evenings spent at the London office only accentuated the sense that the paper's main offices on the other side of the Atlantic resembled a hungry beast, always ravenous for another batch of copy.

The night of April 14 promised to be another long one as they waited for their work to be digested.

Though Mollenkamp and Whitehouse had already filed their stories for the next day's editions, their New York bosses, as usual, kept them waiting. The London bureau folks had to be at hand until the final edit was completed, usually around seven p.m. New York time. That meant midnight in London. But as the darkness fell over the British capital, the Americans abroad had time to mull over the story they were breaking and that, they hoped, would break big. They wondered and worried and dared to hope—this one could just be the sort most reporters come across once in a lifetime.

Nearing forty years old, Mollenkamp already had a solid track record. He had joined the *Journal* in 1997, rising swiftly to become one of its top reporters. During a several-year stint in Atlanta, he'd covered the Southeast and, in particular, Big Tobacco. Though he hadn't been persuaded to give up cigarettes (he remained a devoted smoker), his reporting gained him a promotion to cover the banking world in London's financial district.

In the banking crisis at hand, he believed he'd uncovered something important. He and Whitehouse were still thinking through what it could mean, what might follow. The subject—interest rate machinations in international markets—was complex and involved some deep financial history.

After all, the story had begun to unfold around the time he was a young boy.

In 1969, another American in London had a brainstorm while bathing (in sixties Great Britain, showers were rare indeed). As one colleague remembered years later, "There is no historic plaque affixed to the door at No. 13 Pelham Crescent in London, yet it was in the bathtub at this house that Evan Galbraith is said to have invented the floating-rate note."

A man comfortable on two continents, Evan G. Galbraith had moved back and forth between business and public service since the 1950s. He had gone to Yale (his contemporary William F. Buckley would be a lifelong friend) and graduated from Harvard Law School. He served on active duty in the U.S. Navy from 1953 to 1957, attached to the CIA. In 1960 and 1961 he was the confidential assistant to the U.S. secretary of commerce before moving on to the private sector, where he quickly became a high-level businessman. Having been a director of Morgan et Cie in Paris in the 1960s, he moved to London, where he worked for Dillon Read in the 1970s. He held positions on several corporate boards, including Groupe Lagardère in Paris, and he was later chairman of the board of the New York subsidiary of Louis Vuitton Moët Hennessy, the luxury goods giant.

"I've lived in Europe probably twice as much as any Foreign Service officer existing today," he once said. "I've lived in Europe twenty years. I've lived in France now ten years. I've lived in England eleven years. I have had business transactions in thirty-five different countries, and I'm not rare. There are a lot of us out there." Galbraith confided that there were many businessmen like himself who engaged in high-level negotiations and dealings; in his case, he would later shift streams again, becoming a diplomat (he served as U.S. ambassador to France during the Reagan years). Galbraith never expected that his fame in financial circles would be linked to the rate he dreamed up in the tub for U.S. dollars, but *Institutional Investor* magazine would later memorialize him as the father of the floating-rate note.

It came about during the Nixon administration, when Galbraith worked at Bankers Trust International, which was considered an innovator; that reputation would gain luster thanks to Galbraith. A year after his big idea, Galbraith found a way to put it to work. When the Italian state electric company, Enel, came to the market in 1970, Galbraith helped convince Guido Carli, governor of the Banca d'Italia, that the interest rate on $50 million in notes should be reset, at six-month intervals, at 0.75 percent over the interbank rate. (The year 1970 would be a notable one in the history of finance in another way too, as it also saw the creation of money market funds, created to offer investors better returns than bank savings accounts while providing a higher degree of safety.)

The idea that a company or a person would pay an interest rate reset every six months, rather than a fixed rate for the term of the loan, sounds today like no big deal. After all, many home mortgages, student loans, and credit card contracts now function this way. But in 1970, the idea was revolutionary. With inflation skyrocketing, variable rates seemed to make sense. Galbraith's idea was well adapted to the moment.

A British colleague fresh out of university, David Clark, remembered the moment years later. Clark had been drafted onto the Enel bond-offering team with the much more senior Galbraith because he knew about foreign exchange and was young and eager. "I was twenty-two years old and I was one of the traders there. They pulled me into the team for the first floating-rate note." He may have been young, but he knew even then that the Enel deal, made on May 20, 1970, represented a momentous shift. "It was the beginning of a new era. We knew it was big. It was stunningly simple."

The team had to attach a name to this variable rate, and the one assigned to it, which Bankers Trust wrote into the prospectus, was "London Interbank Offered Rate." Until that closing, Clark had never seen such a rate specified in print, though he had heard it casually quoted between traders at London banks. But now, recorded in a public document, the concept—which soon enough would be referenced by its more colloquial nickname, LIBOR—had been granted official status.

Mollenkamp's life in the City, London's much older version of Wall Street, involved socializing with traders and bankers alike. He had a way with people, in particular Brits, in part because he was so damn American. He was prone to drinking bourbon along with his daily cigarette and espresso habits. He had a gentle Southern drawl and his gray pinstripes seemed to put people at ease. Plus he had the manners of a gentleman. He and his finance sources liked to relax in bars around Canary Wharf, which was where, after his arrival in London in December 2006, he started hearing talk about the fiddling of a key interest rate.

The months leading up to April 2008 had been busier and more soul-killing than any Mollenkamp could remember in his career. The tension had risen in summer 2007 when the French bank BNP Paribas broke ranks and halted redemptions for three of its investment funds. Then the quantitative hedge funds began losing boatloads of money in August. In March 2008 Bear Stearns collapsed, or rather fell into the arms of J.P. Morgan in a U.S. government–engineered bailout. Suddenly, banks around the world—not just in the United States but also in the United Kingdom and Europe—were trying not to be the next Bear Stearns. Portfolio managers and chief risk officers everywhere were trying to sell mortgage-related assets, loans, and anything they deemed risky. They were willing to mark down painfully to shed it all. The situation was, in the words of one economist, like "trying to pour an ocean through a thimble."

As Mollenkamp slaved away covering the banking crisis, he was grateful to have an ally at hand. Mark Whitehouse had his own sterling reporting credentials, and an MBA to boot. He'd covered Russian business and reported on Boris Yeltsin's drunken dance in and out of the Kremlin. During Whitehouse's Moscow stint, he'd aroused the fury of the city's mayor with his stories about city corruption and of politicians enriching themselves at the expense of ordinary business owners. He and his Russian wife, Alla, had lived through Russia's default and ruble devaluations before settling into Western life in a transition country— close to Europe, but not too American. They thought London cosmopolitan, filled as it was with immigrants from all over, including a large Russian community. They'd arrived thinking it was the best of East and West.

Instead, the developed world in 2007 and 2008 was starting

to feel a lot like the third world, engorged on debt. Governments were bailing out centuries-old banks, and it seemed like a different currency was devalued every week. All of it had been prompted by the crack in the U.S. housing market, where for years anyone with a driver's license and a pulse could get a $500,000 mortgage. But when housing prices stopped rising and mortgage holders stopped paying, the ripple effect was felt across Europe and Asia.

But Mollenkamp had been hearing other noises, other complaints. His sources moaned that the cash market—the market for loans between such giants as the American multinational Citigroup and Swiss giant UBS—was wobbly. The talk was of a funky interest rate, something called the London Interbank Offered Rate, or LIBOR, which had emerged over the years as the market's reference point.

Mollenkamp knew it was the main interest rate that pulsed through the banking community in the City, but, strangely, it didn't seem to be reflecting the chaos of the times. Or perhaps, he'd wondered, the bankers were suppressing the number, trying to make it lower than it was supposed to be? Apparently, Mollenkamp learned upon asking around, the manipulation of the LIBOR rate was an open secret in the City's banking community. Rumor had it that Barclays had complained to higher-ups at the New York Federal Reserve about the LIBOR. Though some academics and analysts seemed aware of the situation, no one wanted to say it too publicly.

"So who cares?" Mollenkamp asked his buddies at the bar, trying to draw them out.

A lot of people, they told him. Banks in London weren't just banks in London anymore. They were global entities starting to teeter amid the credit crisis, and no bank wanted to send a signal to the rest of the market that it was in trouble. If word got out, the rate at which they needed to borrow money would suddenly get more expensive.

No one wanted to be the next Bear Stearns, which had been gobbled up for less than a tenth of what it had been worth only months earlier. The very real prospect of financial disaster put everyone on edge.

Back in the 1970s, floating-rate loans made immediate good sense to the oil companies. Drillers in the North Sea, for example, needed huge amounts of money in long-term loans of, say, $100 million for what might be a ten-year project. But banks were afraid of lending that kind of cash since no one knew where interest rates were going in a world where inflation was hitting double digits.

As David Clark, the bright young man at Bankers Trust, remembered, "The great skill of the market was to respond." Again, Evan Galbraith had done his bit. Not only was his timing suited to the volatility of the times, but it also felt as if a quarter century of economic history had conspired to make it the perfect moment.

At the close of World War II, a new international monetary system had been agreed upon at an economic conference of forty-four countries held in Bretton Woods, New Hampshire.

The new currency regime established values for the currencies of International Monetary Fund (IMF) member countries in terms of gold or the "U.S. dollar of specified gold content." Under the terms of the Bretton Woods understanding, foreign monetary authorities were to intervene in the markets to maintain the value of their currencies within 1 percent of the dollar par value. They would intervene in dollars and, in exchange, the U.S. Treasury stood ready to sell gold to the central banks or buy it from them at the official price of thirty-five dollars per ounce. One effect of Bretton Woods was to establish the dollar as the principal reserve currency and, aside from gold, as the principal reserve asset of the world's monetary system. Sterling remained a reserve currency, but it was only a minor one outside of British Commonwealth countries.

Soon after the war, U.S. Secretary of State George Marshall outlined a plan to halt Joseph Stalin's advance of communism into Western Europe. Marshall's goal: to enable the postwar economy in Europe to recover so that countries outside the Soviet bloc would be able to pay for their own military capabilities. One solution was to address the so-called "dollar famine," and so, starting in 1947, Marshall managed to shift dollars abroad. It was the first in a series of economic moments in which very large quantities of American currency moved outside the boundaries of the United States.

The outflow of dollars increased again in 1963, when President John F. Kennedy imposed a 1 percent tax on dollar accounts; according to economic historian Martin Mayer, that had the "monstrous" effect of flooding Europe with still more U.S.

dollars. With the dollar holding sway as the world's dominant medium of exchange, foreigners had to keep borrowing dollars. But they couldn't borrow them in the United States, so they borrowed from the stashes in Europe. That meant that a large pool of dollars swirled around Europe. American currency was held by Soviets fearful that the Americans would forcibly seize the cash over old lend-lease debts; some was hoarded by Arabs afraid that their assets could be frozen in the event of a Middle East war. Other dollars were held by businesspeople who found it easier to use the one currency accepted around the globe.

Kennedy's tax also had the unintended consequence of distinguishing plain-vanilla dollars from those dollars held in Europe, and the latter gradually came to be known as Eurodollars. Since the 1963 tax made repatriating dollars to the United States more expensive than keeping them abroad, London rapidly emerged as a hot spot for trading in Eurodollars (not to be confused with the euro currency, which wouldn't come into being for another few decades). Banks outside America still needed a way to borrow and lend in dollars, and London soon overtook the United States in dollar trading, leading to the creation of the Eurodollar market.

The next U.S. president also helped drive dollars to London, as a new rule of thumb became apparent in international money markets: The more barriers to lending dollars that the U.S. government devised, the higher would be the interest rates the banks (American and foreign) paid for dollar deposits to be kept and lent abroad. With his heavy spending for the Vietnam War, as well as the costs of antipoverty and other Great Society programs, President Lyndon B. Johnson exacerbated weakness in the U.S. dollar. His guns-and-butter spending created such huge deficits that the dollar began to slide against other currencies. One result was the decision by his successor, Richard Nixon, to end Bretton Woods. In the first six months of 1971, Nixon put domestic price controls in place and stopped American gold sales.

As was the pattern, however, the resulting economic tremors caused European central banks to focus on the dollar, and they put more than $10 billion in Eurodollars into private banks. The Eurodollar market heated up even more in the wake of the oil shock of 1973, when the Organization of Arab Petroleum Exporting Countries (OPEC) proclaimed an oil embargo. A few years later, the 1979 Iranian Revolution caused another oil crisis. Overnight, oil prices quadrupled, which led to a flood of OPEC earnings entering the Eurodollar market and its London-based underwriters like Bankers Trust. The Arabs needed somewhere to park their oil riches, so Western European nations began floating huge dollar-denominated bond offerings, and the oil producers promptly reinvested their billions in Eurodollars.

Even the British cabinet had taken advantage of the Eurodollar's interest rates, noting in 1973 that raising funds for housing could take the form of borrowing with a Treasury guarantee: "It could either be a Eurobond issue—like the recent National Coal Board issue—or a Eurodollar syndicated rollover loan, like the Electricity Council. Eurodollar rates are at present several percentage points lower than British interest rates and with the possibility of $20 billion of OPEC money coming in may fall further."

The impact on the overall market was great. Again according to Mayer: "This gigantic dollar-denominated Euromarket became the engine for recycling the money OPEC extorted for oil. Eurodollars became the medium for the Third World debt."

None of the changes moved the dollar off its pedestal and—even without the anchor of the gold standard—the dollar remained the reserve currency of the world. On the other hand, trading increased in an already buoyant Eurodollar market, where London was the major financial center. Perhaps most important, the immense trove of Eurodollars had entirely escaped the jurisdiction of the U.S. Federal Reserve.

The transnational character of the dollar wasn't limited to the Old World. Global capital in dollars dispersed to the East too, especially to cities like Hong Kong. And as the U.S. regulators tried to control dollars flowing out, the faster dollars left the country. According to Ron Chernow's *The House of Morgan*, J.P. Morgan's Walter Page told then assistant secretary of the Treasury Paul Volcker (at this time serving the Nixon administration) that the old rules risked "the end of the American banking system." J.P. Morgan wanted to be able to accept those dollars outside the United States even though U.S. regulations forbade them from doing so. "You will throw us out of Europe and Singapore and Japan," Page said. Volcker rewrote the regulations on the spot.

The more they asked around, the clearer it had become to Mollenkamp and Whitehouse that LIBOR wasn't quite what it seemed. Their insight wasn't an entirely new one in 2008, and it wasn't the result of the credit crisis precipitated by the mortgage outrages in the United States. It had started many years before. What was new, Mollenkamp suspected, was that it had gotten out of control. Like the little white lie that grows by degrees to become a dangerous, all-consuming untruth, LIBOR was beginning to seem unwieldy as a sequence of convenient untruths only added to the economic destabilization happening all around the world. And this was a gigantic problem, since LIBOR was the interest rate to which *billions* of dollars in contracts and *trillions* of dollars in loans were pegged.

As the journalists looked into the London night, they understood that what they were discussing would call into question the trustworthiness of LIBOR. It had begun as a convenient benchmark for British banks to set adjustable rates at a time after fixed interest rates became less useful. By pegging lending rates to LIBOR, which was supposed to represent the rate banks charge one another for loans, banks sought to guarantee that the interest rates their clients paid never fell too far below their own cost of borrowing. It made good business sense, of course. Their small clients borrowed at prime rates, and their best clients borrowed at a cheaper, lower LIBOR rate. It had worked so well that the British Bankers' Association (BBA), which issued the LIBOR numbers, had eventually trademarked the interest rate and marketed it abroad. The Chicago Mercantile Exchange popularized LIBOR among its floor traders of interest rates and futures. The BBA began publishing rates set for fifteen different loan durations, from overnight to one year, and in ten currencies, including the pound, the dollar, the euro, and the Swedish krona.

By April 2008, the LIBOR had come to have the importance in finance of atomic time, of the longitude and latitude of the hemispheres. LIBOR rates were used to set the terms of more than $350 trillion in derivatives contracts such as interest rate swaps, which companies all over the world—including U.S. mortgage guarantors Fannie Mae and Freddie Mac—used to protect themselves against sudden shifts in the difference between long-term and short-term interest rates. There was a great deal of money involved. In the abstract, those trillions equaled about $45,000 for every man, woman, and child on earth. In more concrete terms, with the overheated housing markets of the United States and European countries, families everywhere had been borrowing adjustable-rate mortgages (ARMs) with a low teaser rate that ticked up to LIBOR plus a hefty premium.

The problem was that there simply wasn't anybody watching over the process. There was no guardhouse, there were no regulators standing over the rate-setting process, Mollenkamp discovered. That led to the realization that what they knew about LIBOR was akin to learning the equator is really supposed to be five hundred miles farther north or south than they'd always been told and that everything based on our understanding of the equator—where it was on every map, every chart—was suddenly in question.

"Carrick was talking to bankers all the time," Whitehouse

recalls of those nervous, hectic days. His beat was the Square Mile, as the City of London financial district is known. What he heard again and again was that the "world's most important number," as many moneymen called it, was put together on an *honor* system. Unlike the composition of, say, the S&P 500 Index, or the FTSE 100, there was little transparency about who was setting LIBOR. Neither the Bank of England nor the toothless regulatory body known as the Financial Services Authority (FSA), the British version of the U.S. Securities and Exchange Commission, claimed to oversee the rate.

It had become obvious to Mollenkamp that the "system," if it could even be called that, was easily manipulated. That was serious enough in the good times, when a new crisis wasn't lurking around every corner. But it was a whole lot worse with economic disasters emerging daily. Whitehouse had begun to think of the banks as the equivalent of bookmakers taking bets on the World Cup or the Super Bowl. After all, if the bookies in all the casinos in town knew one another, wouldn't they try to move the line on all the big games and rip off the betting public? Wasn't it human nature? If there was money to be made and opportunity makes a thief, who wouldn't try to change the rate to their advantage?

Galbraith may have conceived the idea, but Minos Zombanakis claims to have given the floating rate its handle, namely the LIBOR itself.

Zombanakis was a pioneer in trading Eurodollars. In particular, he worked the syndicated-loan market after January 1969, when Manufacturers Hanover Limited, his employer, became a major player in the market. With Zombanakis helping drive it, the market grew rapidly, expanding from an estimated $2 billion in 1968 to almost $22 billion in 1973.

One of Zombanakis's key contributions was the formula he devised whereby a group of large, so-called reference banks within each syndicate would report their funding costs shortly before a loan rollover date. Then the weighted average, rounded to the nearest 0.125 (one-eighth) percent (plus an allowance, or "spread," for profit), became the price of the loan for the next period. The formula was widely adopted, although over time the practice became to strip out the highest and lowest outliers. The approach remained broadly similar many years later, when Mollenkamp and Whitehouse got wind of the LIBOR rumors.

In the early days, according to Zombanakis, the system worked well because there was no incentive to lowball rates, as this would have left a bank out of pocket. After all, banks were lending money at those rates rather than borrowing. In the same way, Zombanakis remembered, any bank that submitted an unreasonably inflated interest rate would be thrown out of the syndicate, costing the bank potentially valuable relationships. "In the early days it was very much like a club," said Stanislas Yassukovich, veteran banker of the brokerage firm White, Weld & Co. and a former chair of the UK's Securities Association, a forerunner of Britain's Financial Services Authority. Often the only force keeping ambitious and hungry bankers in check was the governor of the Bank of England, who would express his displeasure with any transaction by "raising an eyebrow" and summoning a bank's manager if he saw anything untoward going on in the marketplace.

But the convenience of LIBOR made it, over a period of years, broadly popular in the wider marketplace. Within a few years, LIBOR had evolved from a measure used to price individual loans to a benchmark for deals worth hundreds of billions of dollars a year. In 1969, Zombanakis arranged an $80 million loan for the Shah of Iran, beginning a cross-border financial market with London as its global financial center.

In 1984, the British Bankers' Association stepped in to formalize LIBOR. The BBA had no special powers or regulatory function; it was a trade-friendly group of about two dozen big-name banks in London. But each day the BBA would poll a group, or panel, of banks on what interest rate they would charge for various loan lengths and currencies; the actual question posed to each bank was, "At what rate do you think interbank term deposits will be offered by one prime bank to another prime bank for a reasonable market size today at eleven a.m.?" The responses were used to calculate the rate that the banks would then cite as that day's rate. In January 1986, the BBA's first official LIBOR rate was published in three currencies: the U.S. dollar, the British pound sterling, and the Japanese yen.

The explosive growth of Eurodollar business made LIBOR

important, but another innovation, the swaps market, made LIBOR an even bigger factor in the marketplace. A swap is simply two parties exchanging interest rates. On Wall Street, a swap is a type of derivative contract involving two investors exchanging the cash flows thrown off by specified investments for a set period; no principal changes hands, but, typically, one company has a fixed interest rate while the other has a variable rate, typically based on LIBOR. After the initial interest rate "swap" between IBM and the World Bank blazed the trail in 1981, credit swaps proliferated. Total outstanding swaps reached $682 billion in notional value in 1987, $6.2 trillion in 1993, and, by one measure, $250 trillion by 2013 in the United States alone. To put it another way, swaps came to account for about one-third of all derivatives in the world, or about $600 trillion to $700 trillion. In comparison, the world's GDP—the dollar amount of every good and service produced around the globe—is only $50 trillion.

By the time the two *Wall Street Journal* reporters tuned in to the LIBOR story in 2008, it had become the reference rate for most of the swaps market, 70 percent of the U.S. futures market, and nearly half of U.S. adjustable-rate mortgages.

But that certainly hadn't been Galbraith's intention. Nor Zombanakis's: Like many banking veterans, he complained that the whole point of LIBOR was lost when it became a funding benchmark for everything from corporate borrowing and commodity trading to home loans and credit cards. "We started something which was practical and convenient. We never had in mind that this rate would spread to mortgages and things like that."

Most certainly, however, it had. Data from a sample of Ohio borrowers revealed that subprime mortgages were based on LIBOR far more often than prime mortgages were. Before 2005, about two-thirds of the subprime adjustable-rate mortgages that originated in any year in Ohio were linked to LIBOR, with most of the remaining loans linked to Treasury rates. By 2007, nearly all subprime ARMs were linked to LIBOR. According to the Federal Reserve Bank of Cleveland, fewer than one in five prime ARMs was indexed to the rate in 2000; by 2008, the ratio was roughly one of every two. The widespread use of LIBOR was paralleled in other areas, as a long-established benchmark for interest rate swaps, foreign exchange options, and forward-rate agreements.

Yet the alignment wasn't always apt, pointed out David Clark. "You could rightly question whether LIBOR was the right benchmark to use for subprime property debt in Florida—which it clearly wasn't," observed Clark, who remained a keen observer of the financial markets long after his days with Galbraith at Bankers Trust. "In the absence of a properly functioning unsecured interbank cash market, is LIBOR the right way to value off-balance-sheet items? The answer is probably no."

So why did LIBOR become so widely popular? Academics argue it was a "stickier" interest rate than, say, the prime rate in the United States. The U.S. prime rate—the basis for most consumer lending by American banks—changes only when the bank rate changes, not on a daily basis in response to market conditions as does the LIBOR. That meant prime had essentially become a fixed rate. Depending on a firm's time horizon, prime rates might serve as a fixed rate for a loan, but, with the spread over the base rate added, prime had become a more expensive choice over the long term.

Academics argue that LIBOR became the standard for loans above $1 million. Small businesses borrow first at prime because it is usually higher than LIBOR and they are considered riskier borrowers, explained Patricia A. McGraw of the Ryerson University School of Management in Toronto, Canada, in a paper comparing prime versus LIBOR.

Ironically, the spreading use of LIBOR solidified the dollar's status as the reserve currency of the world. "As a reserve currency, you can run deficits forever," said a former Federal Reserve employee. "The LIBOR became significant to the dollar as a reserve currency—because it created a sense of trust."

Indeed, the nexus between the U.S. and UK dollar markets was symbolized by the LIBOR. It was peculiar, though, as the world's most important private short-term dollar interest rate was determined in London, and, as the IMF noted, "Only three of the sixteen banks on the panel are U.S.-based."

For a long time, the LIBOR worked properly, although its underpinnings consisted of little more than good faith. The honor system for LIBOR simply worked. As Evan Galbraith's old colleague David Clark put it much later, "Everyone back then behaved correctly." And as a result "a generation of people in finance grew up using" LIBOR.

But, as Mollenkamp discovered, LIBOR's free-form nature made it ripe for abuse.

Rumor had it that London bankers were fibbing about their own creditworthiness. In September 2007, Wrightson, the research arm of interbank brokerage ICAP, reported allegations that one-month interest rates were being underquoted relative to actual borrowing rates. But how were they doing it? Mollenkamp, having long wondered how the damn thing worked, found a source to explain it to him.

When the BBA bank members each morning submitted the rate at which it could borrow funds in a reasonable size at various maturities (from overnight to twelve months) in the open market, it was usually some junior-level boy fresh out of university sitting on the money markets desk—or "cash" desk, as it was known—who got stuck with the drudge work of typing in what amounted to his bank's best guess. With no basis in real transactions, Mollenkamp learned, the process was more like guessing what your house would sell for today, even though not a single home on your block had sold in the past month.

In a small room across town staffed by Thomson Reuters, the information and data giant, two other young men waited for their computer screens to light up with each BBA bank submission for the day.

For each currency and maturity, Thomson Reuters tossed out the highest and lowest quartiles of rates, then found the simple average of those that remained. Rate contributions were nonbinding, in that the banks were not obliged to prove that they did—or even could—borrow at those percentages. Indeed, it had the air of a gentleman's agreement.

Whitehouse couldn't believe what he was hearing. An interest rate used around the globe—again, as the basis for countless mortgages, student loans, credit cards, and interest rate derivatives—was little more than guesswork? Not only that, Whitehouse observed, but the process was so informal that every banker submitting the daily rate knew what every other banker was submitting. They chatted by phone and email every day prior to LIBOR's eleven a.m. setting. And it was transparently obvious that the collective motive was to keep things looking good for them and their pals.

"I was deputy bureau chief, and Carrick said he had sources saying LIBOR wasn't a true number," Whitehouse recalled. "I remembered having spoken to traders about it before, and they explained to me that 'it's just what the banks say it is.' So when Carrick came up with the idea, we knew it would be a good story."

A recent piece of financial history suggested what a big deal LIBOR was. The prior summer, American car manufacturer Chrysler and its finance unit had borrowed $20 billion from banks as part of the automaker's acquisition by Cerberus Capital Management. The $20 billion in loans was indexed to LIBOR interest rates, meaning its interest costs would move up and down as LIBOR rose and fell. It was subject to little scrutiny by senior executives, not to mention regulators. With that kind of money on the table, even tiny changes in interest rates could amount to great piles of money in somebody's bonus.

Mollenkamp continued to ask around borrowers too. He spoke with Lou Barnes, owner of Boulder West Financial Services, a Colorado mortgage bank. Barnes carried three LIBOR-linked mortgages of his own, worth more than $800,000 in all. Because his loans reset after several years, he wasn't particularly worried about being hit. But he did worry that many other U.S. consumers had fortunes tied to an interest rate that few understood and that had all the science of medieval alchemy. "They don't know how to pronounce it," Barnes told the paper. "They don't know what it means."

Mollenkamp found that others had been raising questions about LIBOR as far back as November 2007. Then, at a Bank of England meeting, UK banks, the firms that process bank trades, and central bank officials had discussed the recent financial turmoil and freeze in interbank lending. The minutes of that meeting revealed that "several group members thought that LIBOR fixings had been lower than actual traded interbank rates through the period of stress."

The situation spooked those in the know. Suddenly, no one trusted anyone, and no bank wanted to lend to its neighbor bank in case there was a run. The panic among the executives had become palpable.

Mollenkamp also came across a now infamous Citibank report titled "Is LIBOR Broken?" Published on April 10, 2008, the in-house report on potential LIBOR problems was the work of Scott Peng, an interest rate strategist at Citigroup in New York. Peng was highly educated, one of a new breed of quantitative experts, scientists, and general turbonerds working on

Wall Street. Peng had a bachelor's degree in nuclear engineering from Texas A&M and a PhD in plasma physics from MIT.

Peng's was a scathing note to his clients, calling out the traders who were setting LIBOR and, in effect, accusing them of rigging the interest rate the world looked to as a reference.

"LIBOR at times no longer represents the level at which banks extend loans to others," he wrote. "If any bank submits a much higher [LIBOR] rate than its peers, it risks looking like it's in financial trouble. So banks have an incentive to play it safe by reporting something similar—which would cause the reported rates to cluster together."

Peng continued: "LIBOR is by far the most popular floating-rate index in the world," and the BBA, which cobbled together the figures, was right to call LIBOR "the world's most important number." In fact, he added, the interbank rate "touches everyone."

Most people didn't realize its significance—at least not yet.

Peng explained that LIBOR had "evolved far beyond its humble roots as an interbank lending rate. LIBOR touches everyone from the largest international conglomerate to the smallest borrower in Peoria: it takes center stage in every interest rate swap." By the time of Peng's report in 2008, derivatives had become so ubiquitous that small towns and big cities used them to hedge their municipal bonds.

Mollenkamp and Whitehouse recognized that the LIBOR rate-setting process, which had been engineered ad hoc by a few men in London, had quietly wormed its way into financial products everywhere. Students borrowing money for school paid back their loans at a rate pegged to LIBOR; credit-poor home-owners in America paid monthly mortgages at LIBOR plus a premium, depending on their expected ability to repay; and corporations issued bonds in many currencies around the world at the LIBOR rate.

It all added up to the biggest and scariest question of all:

Since LIBOR wasn't the product of market forces, was it being manipulated at will?

In his report, Peng certainly suggested it could be. As an interest rate strategist, he thought the rate for short-term money (funds loaned for ninety days) should be much higher, that the three-month LIBOR should be up to 0.30 percent higher than traders were setting it. Peng speculated that some banks were understating the rate for a number of reasons. One was to conceal the full extent of the liquidity problems that these banks were encountering, since no bank wanted to look like it was in trouble. His second explanation was even more damaging: that traders at each bank were gaming the rate for their own positions. And Peng added, ominously, that if LIBOR wasn't working anymore, "the long-term psychological and economic impacts this could have on the financial market are incalculable."

Although 0.30 percent doesn't sound like a lot, in practice even a tiny increase in LIBOR made a difference for corporate borrowers like Chrysler and its $20 billion in loans or for moms and dads in small towns across the world working to stay financially afloat. For example, an extra 0.3 percentage points would add about $100 a month on a $500,000 adjustable-rate mortgage, or $300,000 in annual interest costs for a company with $100 million in floating-rate debt.

On the day that Mollenkamp and Whitehouse filed their first LIBOR story, the LIBOR rate for three-month dollar loans stood at 2.716 percent. Peng's estimates suggested that "the world's most important number" should have been higher, closing in on 3 percent to be real and accurate.

Mollenkamp noticed the uncomfortable parallels between the ups and downs of the LIBOR and, say, throwing a game of football. Match fixing—when the outcome of a game is determined in advance—is used by gambling rings to make money off bets they know they will win. Sometimes they bribe the players, sometimes the referees, but matches are rigged to propel a team into higher or lower ranks to earn more revenue.

Could it be that Peng was right and London bankers were playing a similar game?

In the case of LIBOR, the growing worldwide financial crisis was beginning to reveal its depth. By April 2008, jitters had made many banks unwilling to extend loans to one another for more than one week, and as a result the rates quoted for loans of three months or more were often speculative, because there was little to no actual lending. "It amounts to an average best guess," Don Smith, an economist at ICAP, the London broker of interbank loans and derivatives, told the *Journal*.

It all added up to the newspaper article that, by midnight, the editors in New York released for publication. Mollenkamp's story ran on April 16, 2008, headed with these ominous lines: "Reliability of key rate called into question; fears that banks aren't reporting their true costs of borrowing could be affecting LIBOR rate—and global loans."

Mollenkamp and Whitehouse had done their job. By morning, countless other inquiring minds were asking: Were bankers in London mounting a price-fixing campaign to artificially raise and lower the price of money at will?

CHAPTER 2

Yanking the Yen

In Tokyo, Tom Alexander William Hayes was considered the king of manipulating interest rates for profit. While at Swiss banking giant UBS, he and a ring of traders at eight other banks—including HSBC, Royal Bank of Scotland, Deutsche Bank, J.P. Morgan, Citigroup, as well as brokers at ICAP and RP Martin—allegedly colluded to manipulate the yen LIBOR rate. For Hayes, LIBOR was the goose that kept laying golden eggs.

Starting in July 2006, Hayes worked as a senior yen swaps trader at UBS in Tokyo. There, as during the previous five years at the Royal Bank of Scotland (RBS), he traded in derivative products that referenced yen LIBOR with counterparties in New York and elsewhere in the world. He was so successful that he would later leave UBS, in December 2009, lured away to Citigroup with a $5 million job offer and a position as a senior yen swaps trader in Tokyo.

The way he made money is worth a closer look.

Over an eight-year period starting in 2001, Hayes made some twelve hundred requests to five brokers to rig Japanese yen LIBOR, emailing around the financial centers of the world, to New Zealand, London, and Hong Kong. Because these trades were primarily settled based on the published yen LIBOR, the profitability of Hayes's trading positions depended on the direction in which yen LIBORs moved.

His broker of choice for many of these trades was ICAP, a UK-based dealer. Usually when Hayes used that company to broker a trade, his counterparty to the trade was another client of ICAP. In practice, that meant that ICAP, in assisting Hayes at both ends, shortchanged other clients.

Darrell Read worked for ICAP as a derivatives broker on the yen medium interest rate swaps desk in London in 2007, during which time he reported to Daniel Wilkinson. Read's primary responsibility at ICAP was to broker interest rate derivatives trades that were settled based on yen LIBOR rates. A significant portion of Read's compensation was derived from earnings on trades brokered for his and the firm desk's biggest client, one Tom Hayes.

At about that time, Colin Goodman also worked at ICAP as a cash broker on the Euro Yen Cash desk in London. In addition to his cash-brokering responsibilities, Goodman distributed an email—the so-called daily "SUGGESTED LIBORS" email—on most business days to individuals within ICAP, as well as to outsiders. Significantly, some of those were employed at various yen LIBOR contributor panel banks, some of which were headquartered in New York.

Although Goodman did not report to Wilkinson or Read, he was paid a bonus that flowed through the yen swaps desk and he regularly communicated with them ahead of time about the substance of his daily email—and, as it happens, about Hayes's trading positions. It was Read and Wilkinson's job to accommodate Hayes's requests and promote Hayes's trading positions.

It was a closely interrelated matrix of people, each of whom was in a position to pull certain LIBOR strings for the others.

By 2006, the influence of ICAP's daily email was considerable in the world of LIBOR, and these men knew it. In an email dated March 9, 2006, Wilkinson bragged to a senior manager at ICAP, "The market at the moment is so volatile that banks are becoming dependant on ICAP for LIBOR calls." They also knew where their priorities lay. On August 13, 2007, Read assured Hayes, "If you get hurt its going to hurt me as well, you are not in this relationship on your own."

Similarly, Read once told Hayes, "I devote one hundred percent of my time and effort into trying to help you make money." This was trader-speak for flattering the client.

Goodman's daily email was sent out to all bank clients. Of course, Hayes knew that Goodman was in direct communication, and sharing predictions, with other LIBOR panel banks regarding yen LIBOR. Goodman's importance and influence was reflected in his nickname: Read and Wilkinson often referred to Goodman as "Lord LIBOR," or sometimes "Lord Bailiff." Goodman sometimes signed himself "Mlord LIBOR."

Hayes was not above using his influence inside ICAP directly on Goodman, as his emails revealed. On March 23, 2007, for example, Hayes explained to Goodman in an email message, "This may seem strange given my recent requests but really need a high/unchanged lm LIBOR today, low for everything else, thanks as always."

That wasn't a one-off request. Read was informed by Hayes on August 12, 2007: "i need lm to plummet! . . . i have loads of fixings coming up that way." Hayes added: "need 3m off and 6m to hold." On September 28, 2007, in another email exchange, Hayes wrote to Wilkinson that he "really need[ed] high 3m and 6m LIBOR pls."

These communications went both ways, as Wilkinson replied, "understood mate."

On April 28, 2009, Hayes told Read, "have big 6m . . . position fixing at start of july . . . need 6m up big time when 6m goes over the turn." Read assured Hayes that he would "get to work on Colin" and, in turn, was informed by Hayes that Hayes stood to gain or lose "about 3m usd a bp."

Translation? "3m usd a bp" means that Hayes had wagered a trading position that would gain or lose $3 million for each single basis point movement in the six-month published yen LIBOR fix. That is, $3 million per 0.01 percent. Even tiny increments translated into millions.

Primarily, Read was the person to request directly that Goodman change his "SUGGESTED LIBORS" email in order to influence the rest of the market.

For example, on October 24, 2006, Read told Goodman in an email exchange, "Realize it might be getting harder but need 6m kept as high as possible . . . tomorrow I have a massive fix, today just large!! Ta mate Get your curry order ready will send [someone] round tomorrow."

Ready to please, Goodman asked in response, "How high above 552?"

Read replied, "If you can get them up there and keep them there tomorrow reckon the trader from UBS Tokyo will come over and buy you a curry himself!"

This wasn't all about professional courtesy or the odd dinner. When it became apparent that Goodman was influencing LIBOR in Hayes's favor, Goodman's boss arranged for a kickback from Hayes's employer, UBS.

On February 22, 2007, Goodman sent his daily "run thru" email to Read. Later that morning, Read responded, "Can you get lmos and 3mos lower please. . . . UBS said he will try and do a deal with me to pay you!"

Although lots of people were making lots of money, by April 2007 Goodman was getting frustrated with how little he was being paid compared with how much his patron at UBS was raking in.

On April 18, 2007, Goodman sent an email message to Wilkinson asking, "With ubs how much does [Hayes] appreciate the yen LIBOR scoop?" He then added, "It seems to me that he has all his glory etc and u guys get his support in other things."

As the low man on the totem pole, Goodman complained, "I get the dribs and drabs. Life is tough enough over here without having to double guess the LIBORs every morning. and get zipper-de-do-da." His discontent prompted him to inquire, "How about some form of performance bonus per quarter from your bonus pool to me for the LIBOR service."

Minutes later, Wilkinson responded, telling Goodman, "As for kick backs etc we can discuss that at lunch and I will speak to Tom about it next time he comes up for a chat." But just a day later, bonuses landed and Goodman did not share in them.

Goodman turned petulant. The LIBOR riches rained down on everyone but him, and he threatened to end the rigging game.

In an email with the subject line "LIBORS NO MORE," Goodman threatened to discontinue sending out misleading "SUGGESTED LIBORS" after his boss, Wilkinson, informed him that a brokerage fee paid by Hayes was intended for a different yen trading desk and not for Goodman.

"As far as I was concerned tom was paying for the LIBOR assist for my assistance. You have as far as I am concerned have charged him bro on the deal. Happy days for u. fyak all for me again!!"

Goodman signed the email, "Mlord no more mr LIBOR."

Wilkinson responded to Goodman, "I have been thinking of ways of sorting you out. If the needs be I will look into it on a bigger scale eg your salary package."

On June 7, Wilkinson and Read discussed UBS's Hayes fee arrangement with the other yen desk at ICAP, along with a bonus for Goodman to ensure his ongoing assistance in influencing yen LIBOR submissions and fixes.

Wilkinson wrote to Read, "if you could speak to Tom out of hours and hint that Colin had said he would stop giving the LIBOR 'flows' then maybe Tom could push [Hayes's UBS manager in Tokyo] to make the payment, Tom said if it were down to him it would be paid as Colin makes him loads of money and i had to commit to paying lord baliff a regular bonus because basically while you were off he said it was all over and he would not help anymore if there was not enough money in it for him, ubs can look at is a back payment for the money Colin has made Tom the last 6 months."

In the end, UBS agreed to increase its monthly fixed-fee payment to the desk at ICAP by approximately £5,000. Every three months, approximately £5,000 would be paid to Goodman at the direction of Wilkinson.

On September 11, 2007, Goodman sent an email message to Read. "Hi Darrell. Will be Looking to move these LIBORs up tomorrow. 3m9 8 and 6m 1.07. Mlord LIBOR."

Read replied: "Much appreciated Colin . . . he still seems to have sold everything so far but I have warned him and high LIBORs 3m and 6m suit nicely. Make sure you cane the wine bill when out with the UBS boys!!"

Things didn't always go smoothly among the LIBOR schemers. At one point, Read too got frustrated.

On June 28, 2007, Read told Wilkinson in an email:

"DAN THIS IS GETTING SERIOUS TOM IS NOT HAPPY WITH THE WAY THINGS ARE PROGRESSING. . . . CAN YOU PLEASE GET HOLD OF COLIN AND GET HIM TO SEND OUT 6 MOS LIBOR AT 0.865 AND TO GET HIS BANKS SETTING IT HIGH. THIS IS VERY IMPORTANT BECAUSE [HAYES] IS QUESTIONING MY (AND OUR) WORTH."

On August 15, 2007, in an electronic chat, Read wrote, "Tom needs 6m as high as Colin can get away with." During the same chat, Read said, "when you speak to Colin can you ask him what he thinks they will come in at (his run he sends out is often skewed to help Tom)."

On September 20, 2007, Read again wrote to Wilkinson:

"TOM HAS AN ENORMOUS FIX IN 6MOS AND WILL BE ON YOUR CASE TO BADGER -COLIN. HE WILL BE AFTER LOW 6M AND HIGH 3M."

ICAP sometimes helped its best LIBOR customers by acting as messenger and go-between for rigging the rates.

On November 1, 2007, in an email exchange, Read told Wilkinson, "TOM WOULD LIKE YOU TO ASK [RBS trader] IF HE'S NOT FUSSED TO TRY AND KNOCK HIS LIBOR A BIT LOWER. HE HAS SOLD A LOAD OF 1-Y WITH ME TODAY AND HE HAS A LOT OF FIXES COMING UP. THANKS DAN."

Wilkinson responded, "ok mate, will do my best."

By the fall of that year, as the credit crisis was beginning, Hayes, the men at ICAP, and friends at other banks discussed the need to conceal, and use alternative methods to communicate.

On the same day he wrote Wilkinson the email above, Read also emailed Hayes:

"HI MATE, HAD A LOT OF COMPLIANCE PRESSURE RECENTLY DUE TO THE CREDIT PROBLEMS, WE BOTH

NEED TO BE A LITTLE MORE SUBTLE IN OUR 'VIEWS' . . .
IE I THINK THE FWDS ARE SUGGESTING THIS 6MOS
LIBOR SHOULD BE LOWER . . . ETC. MY EMAILS ETC.
NEED TO BE WORDED MORE CAREFULY."

On November 13, 2007, Read attempted more veiled language in requesting that Goodman keep his six-month "SUG-
GESTED LIBORS" low. "Hi Colin," he wrote, "in these days
of 'political correctness' is it true that there is a fair bit of pressure holding 6mos LIBOR down today? I think this will probably suit. Thanks for your opinions."

By the spring of 2008, when the press had got hold of the
LIBOR story, the traders in London, Singapore, and New York
began to worry. All of a sudden there was a new consciousness
that someone might be paying attention to the way their under-
handed business was being done. On April 10, 2008, an electronic
chat reflected the pressure from above. In that conversation, Read
told Hayes, "spoke to Danny last night to find out LIBORs and
got a bollocking for sending ib chats etc. regarding LIBORs . . .
compliance still coming down heavy in london. All my requests
will have to be phone calls or texts . . . don't send anything
yourself or call down any requirements over the line."

But the gaming continued. It was months later that Wilkinson, speaking over the telephone with a derivatives trader at
another London bank, revealed that Hayes was still "asking
about LIBOR" and that Hayes had requested help by talking to
submitters about moving LIBOR submissions because he "wants
LIBOR a certain place."

The miffed trader responded that he "had no intention of

doing" that and added that Hayes "shouldn't be phoning up another bank asking."

With false indignation, Wilkinson agreed: "Oh mate that's so illegal, it's ridiculous." The manipulations of LIBOR continued, even as a growing number of people recognized that, thanks in part to Tom Hayes, LIBOR was nowhere near reality.

CHAPTER 3

The World's Most
Important Number

Following publication of the *Journal* story, London's money brokers realized they had been found out. To their horror, this was a textbook example of the observer principle: Those observed change their behavior.

The LIBOR rate began to creep upward.

Alerts climbed the chain of command, reaching the highest levels at every bank around the City. Like a slow pulse after an injection of adrenaline, the world's most important number shot up overnight.

"The amazing thing?" Whitehouse recalled. "Over the next two days all the banks raised their LIBOR rates." It was the biggest jump since the previous autumn, when an increase had been precipitated by BNP Paribas, which had stopped redemptions in some mortgage-backed securities funds. That increase in the LIBOR had a clear cause, as the BNP Paribas moves had set the stage for the global crisis. But after the *Journal*'s LIBOR article ran on April 16, eleven of the sixteen panel banks increased their rates, producing a statistically significant change in the overall spread of the panel banks, at levels ranging from 1 percent to 5 percent, and the U.S. dollar LIBOR three-month borrowing rate climbed to 2.8175 percent, about 8 basis points more than the previous day's rate of 2.735 percent. This occurred entirely, it seemed, because of the *Journal* report on LIBOR's anomalous behavior. As there had been no systematic changes in LIBOR, the shift was clear evidence that the banks were, in fact, manipulating the rate.

As if to confirm suspicions, LIBOR rates that were reported for other currencies fell or remained relatively flat at the time the U.S. dollar LIBOR rose, more evidence that the latter was susceptible to manipulation.

Lobbyists for the banking industry scrambled to repair the damage. On April 17 the British Bankers' Association stated it would conduct an inquiry into LIBOR.

Whitehouse thought the timing of the rate rise tended to disprove that other risk factors could be the cause. This wasn't a coincidence; the numbers simply didn't lie. The next day too saw a rise, as on April 18 the LIBOR rate for three-month dollar loans climbed to nearly 2.9 percent, where Scott Peng had said LIBOR should be in order to be accurate.

"Suddenly, the banks changed their estimates of borrowing costs to the BBA—they were unmanipulating it, so to speak," Whitehouse said. "And that gave us an estimate of how much it was off."

A careful journalist, he acknowledged there could have been other, more legitimate reasons why LIBOR was too low. The collapse of Bear Stearns into the arms of J.P. Morgan Chase in March 2008 scared everyone. The question on everyone's lips was: Who will be the next Bear Stearns? But that had happened weeks earlier. Why the sudden adjustment now?

Another possible factor was that setting LIBOR involved mostly non-U.S. banks. Of the sixteen polled, only three were based in the United States (Citigroup, J.P. Morgan Chase, and Bank of America), and the dominance of European banks on the rate-setting panel could explain some of the fear: They didn't have a central bank to bail them out. The majority of the banks didn't have access to the liquidity programs offered by the U.S. Federal Reserve, which included direct access for broker-dealers to the discount window lending rate. But that wasn't new either.

For the rest of April, the interbank market corrected upward, with LIBOR soaring.

That was both good and bad. On the positive end, rates were now closer to fair value. LIBOR's rise also indicated that a recovery in interbank liquidity was under way.

The negative was that the benchmark's sudden volatility didn't look kosher. For those paying close attention, these changes only confirmed their suspicions. Suddenly, lots of investors were wondering: If LIBOR was rigged, for how long had it been rigged, and by whom?

One answer, though not apparent to outsiders at the time, was, of course, Tom Hayes. Even as his colleagues were worrying about the press revelations in London, Hayes carried on. In an electronic chat on or about April 28, he asked Roger Darin, one of the men who would later share the dock with him in

Southwark Crown Court, whether "we can try to keep [the six-month LIBOR] on the low side plse?"

"I'll submit something low" was the response.

That elicited "appreciate the help" from Hayes. The focus hadn't changed in Toyko; there it was business as usual among Yen LIBOR traders.

In 2008, the LIBOR rate was polled for ten currencies and in fifteen maturities, ranging from overnight to twelve-month loans. In response to the realities of the financial crisis, the BBA had by then changed the question asked of the banks to "At what rate could you borrow funds, were you to do so by asking for and then accepting interbank offers in a reasonable market size just prior to eleven a.m. London time?" The BBA claimed it had changed the question to be more realistic and because it expected more useful results if it asked banks what they could actually do, rather than a hypothetical question.

One man who got to sit in the room where the LIBOR was compiled, sociology professor Donald MacKenzie, described what he saw.

"The calculation of LIBOR is co-coordinated by just two people, who work in an unremarkable open-plan office in London's Docklands. I watched the process, which seemed utterly routine," MacKenzie recalled.

At seven a.m., traders at each of the sixteen major banks sat glued to their screens, monitoring the money markets and working out how much working capital their institutions would need to meet the billions of pounds of liabilities on their balance sheets. The contributing banks were chosen based upon their reputation, level of activity in the London market, and perceived expertise in the currency. Using the financial assessments, each compiled so-called ladder reports, setting out how much each needed to borrow. In the past, the traders had called in their finding for the LIBOR setting process via a daily telephone call, but the process had advanced as technology evolved.

If it wasn't a bank holiday, the designated trader (again, usually a junior boy) would submit his bank's estimate electronically. Sometimes he might make a quick phone call to confirm. Thomson Reuters then fed the data into a computer program, which discarded the lowest quarter and highest quarter of the estimates and calculated the average of the remainder.

The result was that day's LIBOR, or, more accurately, the day's 150 LIBORs, such as for sterling, the one-week euro, one-month yen, three-month U.S. dollar, and so on.

While the actual process was unremarkable to Professor MacKenzie, a specialist in the sociology of finance at the University of Edinburgh, he was struck by how seriously the BBA took this deliberation. The LIBOR submissions were so important, he noted, that there was a multilayered emergency plan in place in case of a terrorist attack.

"It's the back-up arrangements that tell you something about how much the calculation matters. The co-coordinators have dedicated phone lines laid into their homes so they can still work if a terrorist attack or other incident stops them reaching the office. A similarly equipped building, near the office, is kept in constant readiness, and there's a permanently staffed back-up site in a small town around 150 miles from London. Its employees periodically work in the London office, so that they're ready to take over if need be."

The precautions were necessary, MacKenzie understood, because if LIBOR suddenly became unavailable, large parts of the global financial system would be paralyzed. Yet, in spite of formalities and precautions taken, the bankers knew one another and, from the previous day, were aware of what their compatriots had submitted (the data and its sources were no secret). They had a decent idea who was in charge of submitting. It was all pretty cozy, even if very few outsiders actually knew how the BBA system worked to create the world's most important number.

The BBA's survey also remained just that—a *survey*—rather than a series of hard calculations based on actual trades. And more and more people were coming to an important realization about how accurately the LIBOR reflected the banking facts of the day. Ray Stone, founder of the Stone & McCarthy research firm in Princeton, New Jersey, would put it bluntly. "It forced people to lie," said Stone. "At the time, it was a forgivable sin."

Halfway around the world, Goldman Sachs' former chief economist William Dudley did his best not to call the LIBOR an outright lie. He had become the executive vice president of the influential Federal Reserve Bank of New York, and therefore everything he uttered had to be expressed in code.

"After a *Wall Street Journal* article on April 16 questioned the veracity of some of the LIBOR respondents and the British Bankers' Association threatened to expel any banks that they discovered had been less than fully honest, LIBOR spreads increased further," he told a crowd at the Chicago Fed's Forty-Fourth Annual Conference on Bank Structure and Competition. He was among friendly colleagues, but still, given his role at the New York Fed—considered the most powerful of the member banks in the Federal Reserve monetary system—he had to watch what he said.

It was clear the British banks didn't have the Federal Reserve or the U.S. government as a backstop in this global financial crisis, and that was undoubtedly one reason why they would distort what it would cost to borrow money. But if LIBOR could be rigged during a crisis, what else were the banks up to?

Dudley deep down must have known that, sighing: "This pressure on . . . funding rates has occurred in the United States, Euroland, and the United Kingdom. It is a global phenomenon. . . .

"During the past eight months, the financial sector as a whole has been trying to shed risk and to hold more liquid collateral. This is a very difficult task for the system to accomplish easily or quickly," Dudley added. That March, the "storm was at its fiercest," culminating with the crisis of confidence and the liquidity run at Bear Stearns.

But the full reality might be even more troubling, Dudley intimated.

"The foreign exchange swap market indicates that the funding costs for many institutions may be even higher than suggested by the dollar LIBOR fixing," Dudley said. "The funding cost of borrowing dollars by swapping into dollars out of euros over a three-month term is about 30 basis points higher than the three-month LIBOR fixing."

Behind the scenes, in late April 2008, the U.S. Federal Reserve's Open Market Committee met for two days, and Dudley brought up the *Wall Street Journal* story about false readings in LIBOR.

He told the committee, "The LIBOR indexes took a jump upward following a *Wall Street Journal* article that alleged that some of the sixteen LIBOR panelists were understating the rates at which they could obtain funding. The British Bankers' Association reacted by threatening to throw out any panelist that was not wholly honest in its daily posting of its costs of obtaining funds at different maturity horizons. The BBA announcement appears to have provoked an outbreak of veracity among at least some of the panelists."

He pointed to a chart in his presentation showing how the LIBOR fixing rose nearly 0.20 percent in the few days immediately after the article. "There is considerable evidence that the official LIBOR fixing understates the rates paid by many banks for funding," he concluded. In banker-speak, the banks weren't submitting true numbers, making their credit scores look better to the public than they were in reality.

Dudley may have put it differently behind closed doors, but his words confirmed what the *Journal* story had implied: LIBOR, the world's most important number, was a fiction.

In the weeks that followed the LIBOR article in the April 16, 2008, *Wall Street Journal*, Whitehouse, who continued his late nights at the London bureau, realized the paper had to write a follow-up story.

Questions needed answering. By how much were the data off? How long had the LIBOR fibbing been going on? Was there a way to measure the rigging, and if so, which banks were the worst offenders?

The financial world wanted to know whether the bankers were changing their LIBOR survey submissions in a vacuum. Or were they conspiring with one another to set the worldwide price of LIBOR? Were the worst-case worries accurate? Were the banks acting like bookies, and moving the line to benefit their own bets?

Whitehouse's MBA background from Columbia University came in handy. Moreover, he had context, having covered other financial crises in the past; he knew how they could ripple across international markets, what with the advent of instantaneous Internet news opening floodgates for heart-stopping capital flows of billions of dollars that zipped from one market to the next in seconds. This 2008 go-round wasn't that much different from Russia's debt crisis a decade before, except this time Whitehouse was in London and the debtors were Western governments and corporations.

Seeking to measure the magnitude of LIBOR's impact on the market, he decided to construct a comparison of lending capabilities of the major banks contributing to LIBOR surveys. He started by looking at credit default swaps, or CDSs.

The CDS was a relatively new instrument that allowed investors to bet on the default of a public company. If investors were feeling queasy about the fate of, say, General Motors, they could buy a CDS as protection against automaker GM's bonds defaulting. It's a contract that pays you if and when an institution doesn't make good on its debts. A CDS isn't so different from buying flood insurance for the first floor of your house, as Michael Lewis explained in *The Big Short*. The buyer understands the whole structure might not survive, but at least he'd get paid on part of it.

What did Whitehouse's examination of the CDS market reveal about the panel banks contributing to LIBOR?

"We decided that this CDS market was a place where people trade credit risk"—or the creditworthiness of an individual bank. "That gave us a sense of what the borrowing rates for each bank should be."

Whitehouse talked it over with one of his professors from Columbia, thinking he could reverse engineer the comparison and construct a truer risk measure. The risk-free rate was inflation, and the credit default swap "was supposed to represent that other piece, that idiosyncratic risk of each bank—over the risk-free rate. It was imperfect, but it was the best possible objective view."

Whitehouse gained a few useful insights, the first of which was that there were big disparities between the banks.

Royal Bank of Scotland, known to be in financial trouble, was submitting one of the lowest LIBORs in the market. Yet the bank's credit default swap—in effect, its default insurance—was priced as one of the highest. Whitehouse realized that meant investors were willing to pay up huge for insurance against RBS defaulting, probably because they thought it might actually happen.

Another insight? While all the banks contributed in a tight range to LIBOR each day, the credit default swaps for individual banks were all over the map.

How could that be? Darrell Duffie, a finance professor at Stanford, put it simply: "It doesn't make any sense. The [LIBOR] rates were far too close together."

It wasn't perfect, but the CDS analysis reinforced earlier hunches. "We could see from the statistics that they were lying," Whitehouse recalls. But he took the study one step further: The data suggested all the banks were lying in the first four months of 2008 through the day the initial story came out in April 2008, so Whitehouse turned the numbers around. Accepting that the LIBOR had been artificially suppressed—by 0.25 percent to 0.30 percent over a period of four months—you might think that meant a few pennies. In fact, Whitehouse found, a few basis points translated into billions of dollars.

"That's a lot. That's meaningful," he added.

Whitehouse also identified which banks were lowering their LIBOR submissions the most. He came up with names like RBS, UBS, Citigroup, and J.P. Morgan.

"They were way up there."

On April 28, 2008, Timothy E. Geithner's staff briefed him on what he didn't want to know. The meeting was the only one on

Geithner's calendar during that 2007–2008 stretch that was listed as focusing on LIBOR specifically. It had the ominous name "Fixing LIBOR."

That morning, the New York Fed sent a car around, as it always did, to pick up Geithner, the head of the Federal Reserve Bank of New York, at his stately home in Larchmont, New York. He bade his wife, Carole, and their two children good-bye when the car came promptly at seven thirty a.m. so that he'd get to the financial district in Manhattan's southern end by eight fifteen. He entered the fortresslike Fed building between Maiden Lane and Liberty Street, well aware that, as the financial crisis escalated, he was compelled to arrive ever earlier in the morning.

As usual, Geithner's day was packed. He met first with the Central Bank and International Account Services folks; then, at eleven a.m. he had a meeting to go over the BlackRock contract awarded to the investment firm at no bid. It was a sensitive subject for Geithner, as he had recently had to testify to Congress, alongside Treasury undersecretary Robert Steel, explaining exactly how and why the New York Fed had hired BlackRock to manage some toxic assets without opening up the bidding process to other banks.

Geithner lunched with a *New York Times* columnist in the Washington Room at the bank. At two thirty p.m. he went to the boardroom.

The usual New York Fed crew was in attendance: Brian Peters, Debby Perelmuter, Meg McConnell, Patricia Mosser, Sandy Krieger, Simon Potter, and William Dudley. The last was head of the Markets Group at the New York Fed and would go on to succeed Geithner as bank president the following year. Also invited was James McAndrews, a Fed economist who would put out his own report three months later questioning whether LIBOR was rigged.

The "Fixing LIBOR" presentation made the case that the chatter they'd been hearing appeared to be true, that the British-set interest rate on which so many transactions were dependent was evidently askew.

What Geithner's staff reported about LIBOR wasn't pretty. The mechanism for setting it was based on little more than a judgment call—namely, at what rate the banks *guessed* they could borrow in London each day.

In good times, the mechanism appeared to work fairly well. The daily LIBORs set the wholesale price of money between bankers, and from there the rates trickled out to smaller community banks, which turned around and lent to the masses at LIBOR plus some profit margin. To make a profit, banks typically set their lending rates at a certain "spread" above LIBOR: A company with decent credit, for example, might pay an interest rate of LIBOR plus 0.50 percent, one-half percentage point. A risky subprime mortgage loan might carry an interest rate of LIBOR plus 6.0 percent.

But bad times had arrived and, in crisis mode, banks had ceased lending. Banks didn't know who would survive until the following morning. That transformed a reasonably reliable system into a nightmare: How were the young bankers reporting the numbers on which LIBOR was based supposed to guess-timate the rates if there weren't any loans being made?

To make matters worse, Geithner was told, the London crowd was pretending there was no crisis. Every morning when, for example, the Royal Bank of Scotland or UBS submitted the borrowing rate to the daily survey, they made the numbers up. Three months later, questioning whether LIBOR was rigged, McAndrews would write in his report, "The banks in the LIBOR panel are suspected to under-report the borrowing costs . . . during the recent credit crunch."

Some of those in the room with Geithner might have recognized the truth in the later words of John Coffee Jr., Columbia Law School professor and director of its center on corporate governance. "Figuring out LIBOR was like asking how many unicorns were trading."

Questions about LIBOR had been circulating at the Fed and elsewhere for years prior to 2008. The compilation of LIBOR "made me uneasy" said longtime Wharton School professor Jack Guttentag, who'd worked down the hall from Paul Volcker and Henry Kaufman at the Fed doing economic research decades earlier. "I always had a question about the way the [LIBOR] data were compiled. The data were reported by one person to another in a ledger . . . a dysfunctional way of compiling a statistic that a lot of people were hanging their hats on."

Other voices in Washington and abroad echoed his senti-
ments. "There's always been a fudge factor with LIBOR," said
Sheila Bair, the former chair of the FDIC. LIBOR operated "in
a regulatory vacuum," said Rhodri Preece of the CFA Institute
in London. But no LIBOR alarm bells were rung in the Fed
offices until 2007.

Then, on August 28, an infamous email from a Barclays
employee with many recipients, including New York Fed officials, alleged that LIBOR submissions were artificially low and
probably not based on rates at which banks could actually borrow. Several other mass emails that autumn also noted low
LIBORs, and, suddenly, all banks started to submit U.S. dollar
LIBOR rates well below Eurodollar rates. This was unprecedented: Before August 2007 the two rates had moved in tandem,
even during major financial crises such as the dot-com bust and
September 11 terrorist attacks.

Within a matter of weeks, the difference between LIBOR
and three-month Treasury bill rates, a measure called the TED
spread, jumped to 2.40 percent from less than 0.50 percent as
banks became wary of lending to one another. In the prior
twelve months the gap had averaged about 0.38 percent.

The divergence made the rounds. In September, ICAP's research arm, Wrightson, also reported the one-month LIBOR
was lower than actual borrowing rates. "LIBOR is a different
animal right now," said Mary Beth Fisher, rates strategist at
UBS Securities in New York. The minutes from one of the Bank
of England's own meetings, on November 15, 2007, revealed

that several bank executives had expressed concern that LIBOR came in bizarrely low, signaling banks were masking their financial problems.

Meanwhile, over at the British Bankers' Association, a young, fresh-faced marketer named John Ewan crowed about how much revenue he had raised by licensing the LIBOR around the world. He did it publicly, on his LinkedIn profile, though in-house meeting minutes record that he offered assurances to his BBA colleagues that rigorous quality control measures were in place to prevent any problems.

Paul Tucker at the Bank of England was asked about the November 2007 meeting of the bank's Sterling Money Market Liaison Group. He offered the bank's take on why LIBOR fixings had been lower than actual traded interbank rates. Tucker reported he hadn't taken this to mean that some of the LIBOR banks were lowballing their submissions. "We thought it was a malfunctioning market, not a dishonest market," he told Parliament.

But a great many knew better. Gaming the LIBOR—that is, fixing the price of money—had become just that: a game. Playing it was the price of admission to a club of men who socialized together, skied in Europe courtesy of brokers and expense accounts, and reaped million-dollar bonuses.

"The deal was this," one portfolio manager in London would later say. "The interbank brokers were a huge part of it. They act as go-betweens, and in exchange they get, like, $50,000 commissions" for delivering the message between bankers.

"You have to understand. These brokers were entertaining bankers to the tune of millions." He went on, "Some of them would charter a private jet for the guys from, say, Goldman Sachs who wanted to follow Italy football—just the Italian team—and get them tickets to the Italian matches for every World Cup game, no matter where in the world it was."

The amount of money at stake was staggering. In its annual report for the year ending December 31, 2007, Citibank calculated that it would profit between $540 million and $837 million from a 100 basis point (i.e., 1 percent) decrease in LIBOR. Similarly, in its 2007 Form 10-K filing to the SEC, Bank of America estimated that a 100 basis point drop would yield a profit on its net interest rate exposure of more than $800 million.

The following year, however, an academic study by economists Connan Snider of UCLA and Thomas Youle of the University of Minnesota took a somewhat darker view than the Bank of England's Tucker, concluding in still guarded terms that bank portfolio exposure to LIBOR could be a "source of misreporting incentive."

The banks, in short, had a powerful financial motive, in addition to a reputational motive, to manipulate LIBOR.

No longer were governments the biggest borrowers; banks had now become large borrowers as well as lenders, fueling ever more of their own growth with funding from credit markets— so they now had a tempting incentive to push LIBOR around.

David Clark insisted there was no hint of rigging in the early days. "It worked for many, many years, with no problems," Clark recalls. Stanislas Yassukovich blames the modern bonus culture and emergence of "all singing, all dancing" megabanks for destroying loyalty to corporate customers.

After all, who would want to risk upsetting Exxon or the Shah of Iran? The answer: someone who would make a bigger bonus at the bank by manipulating interest rates. By the time the 2008 financial crisis crescendoed, traders in interest rates could make more money gaming the system than they could servicing borrowers—so why wouldn't they?

Confirmation arrived on April 11, 2008, when an unnamed Barclays employee spoke by phone with an employee of the New York Fed about the LIBOR manipulation, asserting that Barclays was underreporting the rate at which it could borrow funds from other banks in order to "avoid the stigma" of appearing weaker than its peers. The Barclays employee also revealed that other banks had been underreporting their LIBOR submissions.

In a transcript of that telephone conversation, which New York Fed official Fabiola Ravazzolo reported to her bosses in senior management, the unidentified Barclays employee told Ravazzolo, "We know that we're not posting, um, an honest LIBOR."

The Barclays employee went on to tell her that the bank was reporting low rates to "fit in with the rest of the crowd." When Barclays posted more honest rates, the employee said, the bank got negative press inferring it was in worse shape than other banks.

Fabiola Ravazzolo [FR]:

And—and why do you think that there is this—this discrepancy? Is it because banks maybe they are not reporting what they should or is it, um—

Barclays Employee [BE]:

Well, let's—let's put it like this, and I'm gonna be really frank and honest with you.

FR: No, that's why I am asking you. [*Laughter*] You know, yeah.

BE: You know—you know, we—we went through a period where we were putting in where we really thought we would be able to borrow cash in the interbank market and it was above where everyone else was publishing rates.

FR: Mm-hmm.

BE: And the next thing we knew, there was, um, an article in the *Financial Times* charting our LIBOR contributions . . . and inferring that this meant that we had a problem . . . and, um, our share price went down. . . . So it's never supposed to be the prerogative of a—a money market dealer to affect their company share value.

FR: Okay.

BE: And so we just fit in with the rest of the crowd, if you like. . . . So, we know that we're not posting, um, an honest LIBOR. And yet—and yet we are doing it, because, um, if we didn't do it, it draws, um, unwanted attention on ourselves.

FR: Okay, I got you then.

BE: And at a time when the market is so, um, gossipy . . . it was not a useful thing for us as an organization.

The same day that conversation took place, the New York Federal Reserve's weekly briefing questioned LIBOR's accuracy and the banks' "tendency to under-report actual borrowing costs." The weekly briefing circulated to officials at other Federal Reserve banks and the U.S. Treasury.

In Washington D.C., the head of America's central bank, Benjamin Bernanke, had slashed interest rates in a desperate bid to flood the financial system with fresh money. His subordinates at the Federal Reserve also briefed him on the LIBOR situation. "The LIBOR system is structurally flawed," Bernanke later told U.S. senators, suggesting it might be better to replace it with something else.

Years later, Bernanke testified that he'd first learned of the interest rate fixing around the time of that revelatory phone call in April 2008. "I'm not defending it," he would say in 2012 in response to tough questioning from Senator Robert Menendez, a New Jersey Democrat. "It is a major problem for our financial system, and the confidence in our financial system, and we need to address it."

Was it strange that the Federal Reserve Bank of New York initially received information from an employee of Barclays? Not really. Barclays had clearly decided it would be the first to rat out the circle of manipulators. The first bank to tattle would likely get the lightest punishment—or, at least, that was the hope. But the Barclays tipster wasn't among the top brass.

On April 17, 2008, when the British regulators finally awakened out of a paralysis in the wake of Mollenkamp's story the day before, the Financial Services Authority in the UK rang up Barclays. The BBA was furious, phoning around to various banks to find out the source of the rigging. At the same time, however, it was also clear they were trying to keep it under wraps.

"So, to the extent that, um, the LIBORs have been understated, are we guilty of being part of the pack? You could say we are," a Barclays manager said in a telephone call with the British regulator.

"We're clean, but we're dirty-clean, rather than clean-clean," another Barclays employee told the BBA.

The BBA representative responded, "No one's clean-clean."

Clean-clean?

The academic community came up with several explanations for the BBA lingo. "It is far easier to manipulate LIBOR than it may appear," law professor Andrew Verstein would later write in the *Yale Journal on Regulation.* "No conspiracy is required."

"It is false to say, as many do, that it would have required co-ordination," Verstein went on. "At least 75 percent of the panel banks may unilaterally affect the average by moving the quote in their preferred direction." According to his calculations, only one crooked trader, perhaps two, would have needed to lean on the rate fixing each day in order to move it up or down.

As the story unfolded in 2008, some at the BBA sensed legal exposure. According to the minutes and one person who was there, at an April 25 meeting with officials from the Bank of England, BBA chief Angela Knight argued that LIBOR had become too big for her organization to manage.

Her suggestion went nowhere.

Three days after the "Fixing LIBOR" briefing, on May 1, 2008, Deborah Leonard, a senior New York Fed official, speculated in an email to colleagues about what she referred to as the "lying premium" theory about LIBOR submissions. She said banks could have an "incentive to lie" if a large amount of derivatives used a particular LIBOR rate as a reference.

With the recognition that a potentially giant problem was simmering before their eyes, Geithner and his team put their heads together to try to devise a strategy. One logical step was to reach out to Mervyn King, who, as head of the Bank of England, was the UK's top banker.

Geithner and King were on a first-name basis. They met in Basel, Switzerland, roughly every other month, at a gathering sponsored by the Bank for International Settlements (BIS), a sort of central bank for central bankers. Switzerland's third largest city and long an international meeting place, Basel hosted the world's key bankers amid a flurry of dinners, meetings, and press attention. Geithner had other connections in the UK banking world too, having recently hosted the Financial Services Authority regulators Sir Callum McCarthy and Hector Sants in his New York headquarters.

Another BIS meeting was on the horizon, with both Geithner and King due to arrive in Basel on May 4, 2008.

Sir Mervyn and the American made an unlikely pair. Timothy Geithner stood tall like his father, Peter Geithner; both were Dartmouth alums. During the younger Geithner's childhood, the elder Geithner worked for the RAND Corporation and for Henry Kissinger, and the son grew up in privileged circumstances, both at home and abroad. Like his contemporary Barack Obama, Tim lived outside the United States for a sizable chunk of his childhood, gaining language skills during his father's Ford Foundation postings in India, Nepal, and Sri Lanka as well as USAID postings in New Delhi, Zimbabwe, and Zambia. (By coincidence, Geithner's father worked for a while with Obama's mother, Stanley Ann Dunham, during his years with the Ford Foundation. Dunham worked on microcredit programs in Indonesia for the organization, and President Obama spent four years at two local schools in Jakarta between 1967 and 1971.)

Slender, with a ski-slope nose and narrow face topped by light brown hair, the younger Geithner had a passion for tennis and played whenever he could with the likes of Fed head Alan Greenspan or Bob Steel from the Treasury. He had moved quickly up the ranks in public service. In a television interview, he would later complain that many Americans believed that he had arrived at the Treasury via Goldman Sachs, the Wall Street firm once headed by Robert Rubin, his mentor and predecessor at Treasury. In fact, Geithner had spent almost his entire career in public service and had never worked for a private bank. (Geithner's critics would seize on this as proof of his inexperience. "He never worked a day at a Wall Street firm, and was completely captured by his industry," snapped William Cohan, onetime mergers and acquisitions banker at Lazard Frères.)

The son of a railway worker, Mervyn King could not have come from a more different world. He wore owlish glasses, starched white shirts, and cuff links; King was a man who, in contrast with his counterparts in Frankfurt and Washington, struck a public posture that "bordered on demure," according to the *New York Times*. He taught economics at Harvard, MIT, Cambridge, and Birmingham before becoming professor of economics at the London School of Economics in 1984. He and Federal Reserve Chair Ben Bernanke had even once had adjoining offices at MIT.

King recalled, "We never imagined that thirty years later we would be colleagues as central bank governors, and even if we had, we would never have believed that the industrialized world would have faced an economic and financial crisis on a par with the problems seen in the 1930s. As young men we believed that economics, whether it was Keynesian economics or Monetarist economics, meant that those problems were in the past. Well, we were wrong."

King had left academia to join the Bank of England in 1991, becoming deputy governor in 1998. When he first joined, he was put in charge of the new quarterly inflation reports, which he worked on with Danny Gabay, who said King adopted "a very intellectual approach—and always did—to the Bank of England's work."

One person he'd taught at Cambridge was Bob Parker, who went on to become deputy chair of Credit Suisse Asset Management. "If you'd asked me the question over thirty years ago 'Did I think that he would eventually end up as governor of the Bank of England,' I think the answer was no," Parker once observed. "He was very likeable, very personable, very friendly, very approachable; taught economics in a very clear, easy to understand way."

King was a fitting figurehead for the Bank of England, an institution known as the Old Lady of Threadneedle Street. King remained a bachelor until his late fifties. He had finally married only the year before, in 2007, to Barbara Melander, his former Cambridge sweetheart, with whom he reconnected decades later. King later confessed that his personal life had suffered because of his determination to succeed. "I had relationships but never got married. I totally dedicated myself to my career. I traveled around the world for work and even in the summer I'd be off to the United States to teach. I never really had a domestic base. The career always came first and that was probably a mistake. It was a sacrifice."

For the British public, King personified the incarnation of the starchy matron that was the Bank of England. The bank, originally known as the Governor and Company of the Bank of England, had its origins in naval warfare. In 1694, the French had the strongest navy in the world; England needed to rebuild its naval forces, but King William III lacked the resources and the credit to do so.

The king solved the problem by creating the Bank of England. In exchange for creating a limited liability corporation, which would act as a bank for the government and have the right to issue banknotes, shareholders in 1694 loaned the bank £1.2 million at 8 percent interest. Over time, the Bank of England took on the responsibilities of managing the government's debt and becoming a bankers' bank, controlling interest rates through discounting and establishing a base interest rate. The bank was ultimately nationalized in 1945.

Bank of England contemporary David Blanchflower, whose term on the bank's Monetary Policy Committee began in 2006, took a dim view of King. "Mervyn King ruled [the Bank of England] with a rod and iron. And it's not clear he's a great manager."

Blanchflower clashed with King many times. He asserted that King had been "unprepared for the bank run on Northern Rock in August 2007, even though there were obvious signs that banks that depended on wholesale money markets were in trouble. All the academic talk of 'moral hazard' seriously damaged King."

In 2007, as central banks in the United States and Europe aggressively cut interest rates, the *New York Times* noted that King stubbornly kept British rates high in the face of mounting evidence that the economy was slowing down. King argued that any such loosening would unfairly reward bad banking behavior, but he was criticized for being "Victorian in his outlook and a slave to the concept of moral hazard."

By the time Geithner arrived at the convention in Basel for the meeting on May 5, 2008, he clearly wanted King to do something about the British bankers and the fact that the world's most important interest rate was being rigged in London.

Usually guests arrived in Switzerland via Zurich, where a car sent by BIS picked them up at the airport. The central bankers all stayed at the Basel Hilton. In the morning Geithner had meetings with other bankers, such as Stephen Green, chair of HSBC; Peter Wuffli, CEO of UBS; and Baudouin Prot, CEO of BNP Paribas.

A buffet lunch and the annual roundtable of central bank governors and CEOs of major financial institutions followed. At six thirty p.m., the heads of the G-10 country central banks met for an hour and a half, and then dined together, usually with a representative from the IMF.

We know that Geithner and King greeted each other because the cameras clicked and the press hovered. But precisely what they said about LIBOR isn't known.

"Geithner definitely said something to King," recalls one Bank for International Settlements employee. It was apparent, the BIS source went on, that "there was a frustration that there was a lack of control" over LIBOR and its method of setting interest rates coming out of London, particularly those concerning dollars.

How hard did Geithner push King?

"Central bankers are polite human beings. There is a sense of unease, a lack of law and order if you speak too loudly," said the BIS banker. "Nobody will pick a fight."

After he returned from Basel, Geithner and his team once again put their heads together, searching for a solution. On May 19, 2008, Geithner's deputy, Bill Dudley, telephoned Paul Tucker at the Bank of England and said that Geithner wanted some advice on feeding views to the BBA.

The New York Fed regulators were growing increasingly concerned about British inaction. A Fed report titled "Recent Concerns Regarding LIBOR's Credibility" had circulated among senior officials, highlighting "ambiguity in the reporting process."

The report provided an update on the developments regarding LIBOR and addressed the questions on everyone's mind: What was LIBOR, how was it determined, and why did it matter? What were the current shortcomings of LIBOR? What evidence existed that banks were misquoting to the LIBOR panel? What changes designed to enhance LIBOR's credibility had been proposed by market participants?

Interestingly, several weeks after Mollenkamp began to focus media attention on LIBOR's shortcomings, there remained widespread confusion over its definition, even among BBA panel banks and Eurodollar brokers.

Finally, in London, there began to be signs that the Brits might be coming around to the reality, albeit slowly. On May 22, 2008, a confidential memo circulated between the higher-ups at the Bank of England, including Paul Tucker, Michael Cross, and Paul Fisher.

"There is a long standing perception that LIBOR by virtue of the manner in which it is set is open to distortion: panel banks have no obligation to trade or to have traded at the rates that they submit, so it is at least plausible that these are influenced by commercial incentives. In normal times these might only have had a marginal effect, and could bias LIBOR different ways at different times. But this perception does mean that confidence in LIBOR is fragile."

But recognition didn't guarantee action: "However," the report continued, "anything that represented a material change to the definition of LIBOR would run into large, if not necessarily insuperable legal problems around the status of existing contracts." The BBA feared lawsuits—and lots of them.

In the States, LIBOR awareness continued to grow. On May 23, 2008, Hayley Boesky, a senior colleague of Geithner's, told him of her concerns about banks' deliberate misreporting. Boesky's credentials were impressive: In addition to serving as a senior officer and director of market analysis at the New York Fed since 2007, she had also held additional senior roles, including as director of derivatives at a top-tier hedge fund and as chief U.S. interest rate strategist at Goldman Sachs.

Boesky was, quite literally, a rocket scientist. One of her parents was an air force scientist who worked in satellite recognizance, so Boesky was exposed to space technology at an early age. She always had a telescope around the house and even witnessed a rocket liftoff from Cape Canaveral when she was a young girl. After earning a BA from the University of Pennsylvania and a PhD in astrophysics from Columbia University, she left academia for Goldman Sachs.

At the New York Fed, Boesky trained her scientific mind on LIBOR. She concluded that the banks weren't just trying to rig LIBOR to make themselves look better amid the crisis, but that the derivatives desks within each bank were profiting mightily from faking the rate.

She sent her email to Geithner, copying three other senior colleagues—Meg McConnell, Matthew Raskin, and William Dudley—and linked the incentive for banks to manipulate LIBOR borrowing rates to each bank's derivatives position.

"These individuals report to the head of [the] money market desk, who often reports to the same person who oversees the derivatives book. They verify the posting with the boss to make sure it suits their derivatives position," she wrote.

She laid bare for all to see a key motive for LIBOR manipulation. The banks were making big money off rigging the rate to suit whatever bets they had made for the bank and for their bonuses. The implied prophecy: The LIBOR rigging could, potentially, explode into a legal minefield.

CHAPTER 4

What Was *Really* Happening?

After Mark Whitehouse and Carrick Mollenkamp's first report appeared in the *Wall Street Journal*, Geithner and company had responded quietly. Publicly, the British Bankers' Association launched a media offensive, trying to defuse concerns about LIBOR. But the BBA had another motivation: to further conceal its own role.

Banks began circling the wagons. On April 21, not long after Mollenkamp's first story, Dominic Konstam of Credit Suisse blamed low LIBOR rates on the fact that U.S. banks, such as Citibank and J.P. Morgan, had access to large customer deposits and borrowing from the Federal Reserve and did not need more expensive loans from other banks. "Banks are hoarding cash because funding from the asset-backed commercial paper market has fallen sharply while money market funds are lending on a short-term basis and are restricting their supply." Credit Suisse, of course, was one of the BBA's member banks.

On May 16, J.P. Morgan said the LIBOR interbank rate-setting process "is not broken, and recent rate volatility can be blamed largely on reluctance among banks to lend to each other amid the current credit crunch."

The same day, Colin Withers of Citigroup assured the public that LIBOR remained reliable, emphasizing that "the measures we are using are historic—up to thirty to forty years old."

Then the *Journal's* follow-up story ran on May 29, 2008. Headlined "Study Casts Doubt on Key Rate" and bylined again by Mollenkamp and Whitehouse, the paper's second LIBOR report suggested that five of the sixteen banks whose rates were used to calculate LIBOR had underreported their cost of funds significantly from January 2008 until the publication of their initial article. The banks named were Citigroup, J.P. Morgan Chase, UBS, as well as Halifax Bank of Scotland (HBOS) and WestLB of Germany.

This time, the paper flushed out the British Bankers' Association. "The BBA says LIBOR is reliable, and notes that the financial crisis has caused many indicators to act in unusual ways. 'The current situation is extraordinary,'" BBA chief executive Angela Knight had told the paper.

Whitehouse held his breath that morning. "We were waiting for something to happen." Sure enough, the backlash began.

Influential financial blogger Felix Salmon defended LIBOR, dismissing the methodology of the *Journal* study as flawed. "There are lots of places where banks actually borrow real cash, like the commercial paper market. Why would the *Journal* try to use credit default swaps to gauge what cash borrowing rates should be, when they can look to something like the CP market instead? Clearly, I think, the answer is that the CP market wouldn't give them the answer that they're looking for."

In short, Salmon concluded in his May 29 post, "The way that the *WSJ* is reporting its findings they seem to think they're uncovering a major scandal. They're not."

That same day Citigroup claimed innocence as to LIBOR's malfunction, saying banks "submit LIBOR rates at levels that accurately reflect its perception of the market." HBOS similarly asserted that its LIBOR quotes constituted a "genuine and realistic" indication of the bank's borrowing costs.

Behind the scenes, on Friday, May 30, BBA's Knight sent a draft response on LIBOR to Bank of England Governor King. He didn't think it offered any serious changes.

He scrawled across the memo: "*Wholly inadequate. What should we do?*" But King would later testify that he had done enough. "I wrote a note to that effect and asked Paul Tucker and Mr. Cross at the Bank what we would do about it. They formed a team of people that liaised right through that summer with the BBA, the FSA, and the New York Fed."

The BBA promised to strengthen oversight of LIBOR. Yet in his internal bank email, King had said that the BBA response "seems wholly inadequate."

The initial response was generally dismissive of the Mollenkamp and Whitehouse article. But the critics were wrong. LIBOR was, to be kind, a fiction. More accurately, it was the average of a mix of guesses and outright lies told by London's banks to convince the public to think they were in better financial shape than they really were.

On June 1, Timothy Geithner dispatched an urgent message to Mervyn King. Geithner understood at least some of the potential ramifications of the LIBOR revelations. Among other concerns, he knew that untold billions of dollars of adjustable-rate mortgage loans were potentially wrongly priced, that many borrowers who shouldn't have been approved were approved, and that the chance of large-scale defaults was even greater than already feared. All in all, the horizon held worrisome possibilities.

"Mervyn: We spoke briefly in Basel about the BBA's LIBOR regime, and you said you would welcome some suggestions," Geithner wrote.

Geithner sent along a list of six points on how to improve the governance of the LIBOR rate. Among them were suggestions for eliminating incentives for bad behavior and establishing a "credible reporting procedure."

In the polite world of central bankers, this would appear to have been a call to arms. But as Ray Stone, a former Federal Reserve economist, observed, "That's the most that he could do. They didn't have the authority to change it."

Still, as president of the New York Fed, Geithner wielded immense, if indirect, power. "Whatever the limits of his formal authority over financial market practices, the New York Fed president is someone whose recommendations and advice to market participants are not to be ignored," explained Norman Carleton, formerly with the U.S. Treasury.

King, for his part, took Geithner's suggestions under advisement but, as in response to the *Journal* pieces, did little. "If King was unaware, he was ignoring what the president of the Federal Reserve Bank of New York was asking about," said longtime Wall Street analyst Richard Bove.

Stone went further. "The Bank of England had been very laissez-faire when it came to regulating the City. They couldn't do anything in public. At that time, if you had lending collapsing in the market, they weren't going to issue a statement" saying that interest rates were also phony. King was hardly unaware that the banking business faced rough weather since, in February 2008, he had helped engineer the nationalization of the failing bank Northern Rock. But when it came to LIBOR, King did not take the hint from Geithner.

"We discuss rules, not regulations. A lot of soft law is produced out of here," said another BIS employee of the Basel conversations between King and Geithner. "But with LIBOR, it was a self-regulation paradise, a large-scale gentleman's agreement. There were a lot of self-interested parties at play."

Much later, Geithner's email would resurface and Tory MP David Ruffley, a member of the Treasury Select Committee, would attack: "Sir Mervyn King now has serious questions to answer about what the top of the Bank of England knew and when it knew it." Ruffley went on to observe, "This email appears to show that the U.S. authorities were warning the Bank before the financial crisis unfolded that there was an incentive to deliberately misrepresent this rate—or as most people would call it, fiddle it. . . . [It] appears the U.S. was ringing alarm bells loud and clear in mid-2008."

David Blanchflower, who served on the Monetary Policy Committee with King, remembered King's failure to engage. "People told him about the LIBOR issue and he just wasn't interested," Blanchflower recalled. "He didn't share any of the information with the rest of us on the . . . committee."

In short, in the spring of 2008, King chose to ignore Geithner's striking of the gong.

King was hardly alone in knowing of, but doing nothing about, the problems in a public way.

In mid-May, the BBA held a private meeting of its Foreign Exchange and Money Markets Committee, a long-standing panel whose primary role was to make decisions about LIBOR. The committee was made up of banking industry officials whose names and affiliations the BBA won't disclose. The meeting's agenda was how to dress up LIBOR, rather than to stop the lies surrounding it.

"We need to adopt a minimal approach," said one bank executive. "Too big a change would cause an explosive reaction." IMF head Christine Lagarde blamed the messenger. "Tim's natural approach to things is very smart, but a little bit irritating at points," she said. "He's very quick, and he does things very promptly. He doesn't take no for an answer. The result of that is for people who do not operate as quickly as he does, he can be a little bit irritating."

The very banks that were rigging LIBOR had decided how to cover up its flaws, so nothing happened.

The subject of LIBOR had been raised in Washington D.C. when, on May 6, the New York Fed briefed U.S. Treasury officials on concerns about the LIBOR. The Fed had also discussed it with the heads of the regulatory agencies that made up the President's Working Group on Financial Markets. In the presentation made to officials at the Treasury, the New York Fed again acknowledged that contributing panel banks were "actually misquoting LIBOR" and that the misquoting may have been spurred by those banks' economic "incentive to avoid signaling funding challenges." In short, banks were lying to keep the secret about which might fail next.

Similarly, in a confidential presentation that the New York Fed made to the President's Working Group on Financial Markets composed of eighteen federal and state financial regulatory agencies, the New York Fed cited additional evidence of malfeasance, which included reports from brokers that contributing panel banks were bidding in the swaps market above U.S. dollar LIBOR quotes.

But no one took action.

In the months prior to Geithner and King's May meeting in Basel, two BIS economists, Jacob Gyntelberg and Philip Wooldridge, had presented a paper challenging everything central bankers knew about the cost of money. It signaled that the BIS was already aware that something was wrong at the time.

"Who else could write something like this?" said a BIS employee. "Let's say the central banks want to look at this. The instructions were that if we write about it, all the other players would have to pay attention. It was a hot potato, however, and no one wanted to take responsibility for it." The March 2008 issue of the *BIS Quarterly Review* included the report titled "Interbank Rate Fixings During the Recent Turmoil." Though it got some notice in the City of London, the economists said in interviews at the time that there was concern banks were manipulating the fixing process to prevent their borrowing costs from escalating.

Thus, many at the Bank for International Settlements knew what was going on. "The global banks have interest rate derivatives books of about $300 trillion. And one leg of this payment is linked to the variable LIBOR rate. The mechanism was quite smart, unless at least half wanted to push the rates in the same direction."

In May 2008, one of Barclays' own on the buy side finally outed the LIBOR shenanigans on Bloomberg TV. Tim Bond, head of asset allocation research at Barclays Capital, a Barclays subsidiary, observed that banks routinely misstated borrowing costs to avoid the perception that they faced difficulty raising funds as credit markets seized up.

"Our treasurer, who takes his responsibilities pretty seriously, said: 'Right, I've had enough of this, I'm going to quote the right rates.' All we got for our pains was a series of media articles saying that we were having difficulty financing."

Barclays, for a time, seemed to have donned the white hat of a good guy, at least when it came to submissions made during the financial crisis. Bond believed it. "The prior behavior of manipulating fixings for profit is inexcusable and tarnishes the good behavior during the crisis, when Barclays was more or less risking their reputation to deliver a public good," he said.

So Barclays knew too. As did the general public—or, at least, that portion of the financially aware who watched Bloomberg News and read the *Wall Street Journal.*

Mervyn King finally replied to Geithner on June 3. "The recommendations so proposed by the New York Fed seem sensible to us," King wrote. "We will ask the BBA to include in their consultation document the ideas contained in your note."

BBA chief Angela Knight responded to Bank of England deputy Paul Tucker, but also failed to acknowledge the seriousness of the accusations. "Changes are being made to incorporate the views of the Fed. There is no showstopper as far as we can see. I have spoken to the CEOs and made people sign confidentiality agreements, but as you know there are a lot of vested interests."

Knight was known as an industry flack, defending bankers at every turn, but defense of the BBA was her worst assignment to date. She had arrived on the job on April 1, 2007, at the start of what would prove to be an extraordinary period of crisis after crisis. "It was possibly the most difficult time for the industry for 150 years," she later said. Still, her training as an economic adviser to Home Secretary Kenneth Clarke in 1992 and then as spokesperson for the Association of Private Client Investment Managers and Stockbrokers prepared her for the shitstorm ahead.

Her first major test at the BBA had come in September 2007 when customers started to form waiting lines outside Northern Rock branches in the first run on a British bank since the nineteenth century. It was a memorable public debut that Knight was unlikely to forget, but that was just the beginning of the credit crunch, with the collapse of Lehman Brothers and the start of an unparalleled period of public exposure to follow. She later calculated that, in her five years at the BBA, she gave more than eight hundred broadcast interviews, gave a thousand speeches, and made nine appearances before the House of Commons Treasury Select Committee.

"I think it is safe to say that I appeared more times before the committee than all my predecessors together," she said.

She faced flack for more than the economic and banking crisis, as hard questions were being asked about bread-and-butter issues such as bankers' pay and bonuses and some £10 billion of missold payment protection policies. When there was a problem, Knight's job was to explain it away.

"It was an extraordinarily difficult period," she told one British newspaper. "I can't pretend it was easy. I had sleepless nights like everyone else. But I tried my best to explain. That is not to excuse these problems. Practices were being shown up that were unacceptable."

Knight's supporters would argue that for years she'd wanted an inquiry into the BBA's operation, but she'd been thwarted and her arguments for passing on the process to another organization were rejected.

Given that the chair of Barclays, Marcus Agius, was also the chair of the BBA, there were huge conflicts of interest built into the organization from the start.

No one wanted to take responsibility, as a June 5, 2008, email suggests. Writing to Knight and John Ewan of the BBA, the Bank of England's Michael Cross (with his colleague Paul Tucker included on the message) insisted that the British central bank's name not enter the new LIBOR recommendation at all. "On the Bank's name, we have a clear line that it should not be used. I understand that the FSA and the Federal Reserve have the same position. Neither can we accept 'relevant central banks . . . etc.'

"That will obviously be taken as implying our endorsement of the proposals you make. Hence our suggestion that you refer to 'all interested parties.'"

In short: Let us do nothing—and keep our names out of it.

A June 10 Bank of England memo on the BBA proposal reiterated that officials there didn't feel it was appropriate for the central bank to get involved in an industry rate. Otherwise, bank officials said they found the proposal satisfactory, and thought the Fed did too.

On the other hand, the British maintained a silent nationalistic mandate: *Don't let the LIBOR leave London.* By any means necessary, they wanted the business to stay on their side of the Atlantic.

"For the dollar LIBOR fixing in particular, wider participation by US banks is the BBA's best chance of ensuring that it retains the initiative rather than seeing it pass to New York," a BBA internal proposal stated.

In the face of new awareness in spring 2008 in London, New York, and Washington, no meaningful moves were made to address the LIBOR scandal. One word for it? Collusion. On a worldwide scale, the bankers and regulators sat idly by and watched as the price of money began to disintegrate.

By July 2008, when the Federal Reserve Board granted the Federal Reserve Bank of New York authority to rescue the Federal National Mortgage Association (Fannie Mae) and the Federal Home Loan Mortgage Corporation (Freddie Mac), the knowledge that LIBOR was rigged was widespread, despite the refusal of anyone in the BBA or the British banking industry to take the heat.

LIBOR-based derivative trades during this time were taking place all over American jurisdictions. But there was still denial on Wall Street that the supposed firewall between traders and those who submitted the bank's LIBOR rates was a fiction. While the housing bust raged, the stock market crashed, and global credit markets froze, no one wanted any more painful truths to emerge.

As one economist told the *Telegraph*, "They don't want to admit the problems that there are out there with funding. It's like a mutual thing: I'll pretend you're thin if you pretend I'm six feet tall."

Panic and inertia set in after Lehman Brothers collapsed in September 2008 and the New York Fed extended to AIG an

$85 billion line of credit. The bailout deal's interest rate? It was based on the LIBOR.

On October 24, 2008, a Barclays trader again told an official at the New York Fed that the bank's LIBOR submission is "a touch lower than yesterday's but please don't believe it. It's absolute rubbish." He described how money brokers Tullett Prebon, ICAP, and Tradition were finding it difficult to even provide quotes about the price at which banks could borrow.

Of course, Barclays wasn't the only one manipulating LIBOR. Earlier in the summer, during the week of June 16, a Zurich-based UBS senior manager had instructed his U.S. dollar LIBOR submitters to lower their submissions over the next three days "to get in line with the competition" and avoid being noticed as an outlier when compared with other contributor panel banks.

UBS's three-month U.S. dollar LIBOR submissions immediately dropped 0.05 percent to the "middle of the pack" of the submissions from other contributor panel banks. Like other banks, UBS hoped the false LIBOR submissions would help portray it as financially healthy and avoid negative publicity during the financial crisis. In reaction to increased media scrutiny of the financial standing of banks and banks' LIBOR submissions during the financial crisis, UBS issued directives to its LIBOR submitters intended to "protect our franchise in these sensitive markets."

These orders varied over time, but for a significant part of the period—from at least June to December 2008—the idea was to ensure UBS's LIBOR submissions did not attract negative media comments about UBS's creditworthiness.

Internally at UBS, some employees questioned the false LIBOR submissions in order to be below or within the pack of other panel contributors. In an internal exchange via electronic chat on September 22, 2008, two UBS employees traded information on LIBOR:

FIRST UBS EMPLOYEE [UBS 1]:

Why is the [investment bank] cash curve for USD so much higher than LIBOR? Offered 35bps above LIBOR currently

SECOND UBS EMPLOYEE [UBS 2]:

Because the real cash market isn't trading anywhere near LIBOR . . . LIBORs currently are even more fictitious than usual

UBS 1: Isn't LIBOR meant to represent the rates at which banks lend to each other?

UBS 2: That's the theory . . . in practice, it's a made up number . . . hence all criticism it was getting a few months ago

UBS 1: Why do banks undervalue in times like this?

UBS 2: So as not to show where they really pay in case it creates headlines about the bank being desperate for cash . . . I suspect

USB 1: It's a made up number [so as] to not show where

they really pay in case it creates headlines about . . .
being desperate for cash.

One UBS senior manager would explain it away. "The answer would be because the whole street was doing the same and because [UBS] did not want to be an outlier in the LIBOR fixings, just like everybody else."

Denial didn't make the problems go away. On September 12, 2008, the three heads of the U.S. economic agencies—Treasury Secretary Henry Paulson, SEC Chair Christopher Cox, and New York Fed President Timothy Geithner—called a half dozen masters of the universe to a weekend meeting at the downtown offices of the New York Fed, the fortress with its own police force and vault full of gold.

Within two months of that meeting, immense changes roiled the world of finance. Fannie Mae and Freddie Mac had been put into conservatorship; Merrill Lynch sold itself to Bank of America; then Lehman Brothers filed for bankruptcy after the company was told that the government would not put any money on the line as the Fed had done with Bear Stearns in March. Yet AIG became the beneficiary of a government rescue two days after Lehman's bankruptcy, and the FDIC put Washington Mutual into receivership.

In addition, the Bush administration asked Congress for $700 billion to stem the financial crisis, an amount that, amid enormous controversy, was finally provided in early October. The Treasury, in a novel and aggressive use of the Exchange

Stabilization Fund, established a temporary guarantee program for money market mutual funds.

On the other side of the Atlantic, in October 2008 the British government injected billions in state capital into three leading banks, including RBS and HBOS. RBS required a £47 billion cash injection and HBOS a £17 billion cash injection, while insiders who had warned of risks there were silenced, pushed out, or fired, according to Paul Moore, onetime head of risk at HBOS.

Without near nationalization, RBS and HBOS would almost certainly have suffered a run on their remaining reserves and been plunged into insolvency. Their share prices took a hammering.

Yet, with the banks teetering, their LIBOR submissions still didn't reflect the crisis. The world's most important number continued to signal that nothing was wrong. After Lehman Brothers collapsed in September—when the panic in the markets should have forced the banks in London to submit higher lending rates between one another—the LIBOR rate barely budged, particularly the U.S. dollar LIBOR rate.

Neither the Fed nor the Bank of England admitted there was fraud taking place. In fact, just the opposite. The Fed continued to recite the dodgy LIBOR benchmark even after Fed Chair Ben Bernanke summoned the head bankers of all the Federal Reserve members around the United States onto an emergency conference call on October 7.

The LIBOR rate was so out of whack that Bernanke wanted to have a discussion about why his emergency interest rate cuts didn't seem to be bringing LIBOR down.

Jeffrey Lacker, president of the Federal Reserve Bank of Richmond, piped up first with questions to William Dudley of the New York Fed.

"I want to ask you about the LIBOR spread. It's pretty striking, but I'm wondering, do you have data on the quantity of borrowing that's going on in that market and what that LIBOR figure really represents? We have a bank in our district that reports on the LIBOR panel but reports borrowing at 1.00 to 1.50 percent below it."

Dudley didn't say it in so many words, but he drove home what the market knew: LIBOR was phony. "The LIBOR panel may understate the pressure on funding costs for some banks," he explained.

"I think the reality right now is that LIBOR does not mean very much," Dudley added. "So I think that there are rates that are posted in LIBOR, and they pull them off. But you could argue that in some ways it's even worse than the rate that is posted because, according to the reports that we've gotten, there's just very little activity at term not just in the interbank market but in the broad array of markets."

In short, the LIBOR manipulation worked counter to what the Federal Reserve—the world's most powerful central bank— needed to do to help the global financial system out of crisis. And yet the Fed didn't walk away from the LIBOR.

On November 10, 2008, the federal government and the U.S. Treasury announced a restructuring of the government's financial support of AIG. The Treasury purchased $40 billion of AIG preferred shares under the TARP, a portion of which was to be used to reduce the Federal Reserve's loan to AIG from

$85 billion to $60 billion. The terms of the loan were modified to reduce the interest rate to the three-month LIBOR plus 300 basis points.

That same month, when the Fed established the Term Asset-Backed Securities Loan Facility (TALF), it again used the LIBOR to set the interest rate.

Though New York Fed President Geithner had done little about LIBOR, he would soon be rewarded with a new job. On November 24, President-elect Barack Obama announced that Geithner was his choice for Treasury secretary.

Years later, in 2012, Geithner defended his action—or inaction—on LIBOR.

"We brought it to the British attention, pushed them to move on it. . . . They gave us every indication they would be on it," Geithner said. "We brought it to the attention of the British and took the exceptional step of putting into writing to them a detailed set of recommendations that revealed the extent of the concerns in that context."

Mervyn King, however, refuted that. "At no stage had the New York Fed raised concerns with the Bank that they had seen wrong-doing."

King's deputy, Paul Tucker, admitted that "with hindsight" he should have heard alarm bells ringing in 2008 when the U.S. Federal Reserve warned of "deliberate misreporting" of LIBOR fixes by banks.

"Looking at those emails, it looks like they had pretty explicit notification of some very bad behavior, and I don't understand why they didn't investigate," former FDIC head Sheila Bair said of Geithner's New York Fed. "They did have authority to do that." Yet she added that Geithner and the New York Fed "deserve credit for trying to suggest some reforms, but again, even then those reforms did not tackle the core problem, which was that it wasn't a transaction-based survey; it was a judgment survey."

In a time when everything seemed in flux, the dirty little secrets of LIBOR had become widely known. But a mix of fear, denial, and self-interest on both sides of the Atlantic left LIBOR in place.

CHAPTER 5

Hedging the LIBOR

More than banks had played—and would continue to play—a role in manipulating LIBOR, EURIBOR, and other key market indicators. Some of the hedge funds exerted their influence too.

Brevan Howard was Europe's largest hedge fund, founded in 2002. The first part of its name, Brevan, had been derived from the initials of its founding partners. The *B* was Jean-Philippe Blochet, who left the firm in late 2009; *R* stood for Chris Rokos, who departed August 2012. The *V*, *A*, and *N* were James Vernon, the former chief operating officer who left in 2011, and cofounders Alan Howard, ex-head of proprietary trading at Credit Suisse First Boston, and Trifon Natsis.

The central figure, Alan Howard, was something of a mystery. He donated heavily to conservative American and British politicians and was usually ranked among the top one hundred wealthiest people in Britain. He donated £19,500 to Liam Fox, former UK defense secretary, and £5,000 to William Hague, the foreign secretary. Collectively, Brevan Howard had lots of powerful friends too, as in June 2008 the firm would fly George Osborne, then Britain's shadow chancellor, from New York to Vail, Colorado, to attend the American Enterprise Institute World Forum.

Brevan Howard grew so large that it had to register with U.S. regulators. Partners shared $436 million in pay in the year ended March 2012, and its performance beat out rivals such as BlueCrest Capital Management, the third largest European hedge fund.

Brevan Howard employed a strategy that focused on what it called "asymmetrical outcomes." It applied this philosophy to all of its investments, from interest rates to currency, equities to commodity price movements. Although the fund focused on making risk-averse investments based on macro events, there were always risks you just couldn't prepare for—and some over which you could exercise some control, such as the LIBOR.

A well-informed Barclays trader explained to the New York Fed how hedge funds like Brevan Howard and BlueCrest communicated how they wanted the LIBOR moved up or down. In a 2008 phone call, the trader confided: "Talking to a lot of our salespeople here, the ones that speak to hedge, um, funds, it's quite obvious that a lot of the bigger, more active sort of trading derivatives guys in London like Brevan Howard and Blue, uh, Crest that they've been, um, um, on the bandwagon if you like of looking for higher LIBOR OIS spreads and they're still trading that—that way round of it and they're—they're quite aggressive in the market."

In plain English, being "on the bandwagon" meant hedge fund managers would call each bank's salesperson and encourage the trading desk there to submit a rate quote higher or lower, depending on what was good for the hedge fund manager's bottom line. Customers, in short, were dictating the LIBOR and other interest rate settings, and the brokers were complying with their requests.

In one particular 2007 case, according to court documents filed as part of a wrongful dismissal suit in Singapore High Court, a Royal Bank of Scotland trader alleged that Brevan Howard called on RBS directly to change the LIBOR rate. Tan Chi Min, who was RBS's Singapore-based head of short-term interest rate trading for the Japanese yen, said Brevan Howard telephoned him at the bank and asked if they could change the bank's submission.

"Brevan Howard telephoned on 20 Aug. 2007 to ask the defendant to change the LIBOR rate," Tan Chi Min said in court papers. The bank "received this request without objection." (The hedge fund isn't a party in the suit and isn't being sued for wrongdoing.)

Scott Nygaard, listed as head of short-term markets finance at Edinburgh-based RBS, knew about the call from Brevan Howard, Tan said in his filing. Tan reported it was "common practice" among the bank's senior employees to make requests on LIBOR to its rate setters, and that RBS's senior management knew what was going on.

On another occasion, the morning of March 27, 2008, Tan Chi Min told Neil Danziger, an RBS trader who reported to him, to make sure the next day's submission in yen would increase.

"We need to bump it way up high, highest among all if possible," Tan, known by colleagues as "Jimmy," wrote in an instant message to Danziger.

The next morning RBS reported that it paid 0.97 percent to borrow in yen for three months, up from 0.94 percent the previous day.

If RBS's submission had remained in the same range with the others, the cost of borrowing in yen would have fallen one-fifth of a basis point, or 0.002 percent, according to data compiled by Bloomberg. Instead the bank gained $250,000 on a position of $50 billion.

On other occasions, it was the U.S. dollar LIBOR that was manipulated.

Barclays traders Jonathan Mathew, Peter Johnson, and Stylianos Contogoulas were all busy between June 2005 and August 2007.

"They entered into a dishonest agreement with Barclays derivative traders in New York, submitting false and misleading LIBOR rates," according to James Hines of the UK's Serious Fraud Office. "Their hope was that the US dollar LIBOR rate would be affected and they would thereby create an advantage for themselves."

Johnson, based in London, was a submitter of rates to LIBOR; he had worked for Barclays for thirty years. Mathew reported to

Johnson, while Contogoulas was a trader of U.S. dollar fixed-income swaps.

As Tan Chi Min's lawsuit alleged, traders weren't the only ones caught up in the rate rigging. Their clients were egging them on.

The traders and brokers at the center of the rigging were spread out across different banks, in different countries, and communicated by phone, email, or instant message. The open secret was that many of their bosses higher up in management either condoned what they were doing, expecting them to rig rates for the benefit of the bank, or turned a blind eye.

RBS traders such as Tan also were heavily involved in the day-to-day wrangling of the interest rate. On August 19, 2007, Tan sent an instant message to a trader at rival Deutsche Bank, remarking that it was "just amazing how LIBOR-fixing can make you that much money or lose it if opposite."

Tan added: "It is a cartel now in London."

The biggest temptation for traders to game rates came in the days before International Money Market (IMM) dates, when three-month Eurodollar futures settle. Why? Because that's when the banks set rates they would pay to money market funds.

The IMM dates were key because the value of traders' positions—often billions of dollars—was affected by where the dollar LIBOR rate was set the third Wednesday of March, June, September, and December, namely the last month in each quarter, the maturity dates of money market futures and options.

Charles Schwab, for instance, might offer its investors a money market fund returning 1 percent on deposits, but if the banks setting the interest rates could keep the rates artificially low, then they paid Schwab and its investors less, cheating them out of interest payments.

This particular manipulation of LIBOR—in dollars, in euros, and in yen—was discussed openly at banks.

"We have an unbelievably large set on Monday," one Barclays swaps trader in New York emailed the firm's rate setter in London on March 10, 2006. "We need a really low three-month fix, it could potentially cost a fortune."

Later that year, on October 26, a trader at another bank requested a low LIBOR setting from Barclays. When Barclays agreed, the trader responded: "Dude I owe you big time! Come over one day after work and I'm opening a bottle of Bollinger! Thanks for the LIBOR."

In March 2007, five months before the onset of the credit crisis, a dozen traders from firms including Deutsche Bank, J.P. Morgan, and Lehman Brothers traveled to Chamonix in the French Alps. According to Bloomberg, these traders of yen-based derivatives went skiing before toasting glasses of wine at a local restaurant. They flew back late on Sunday, in time for the opening of the markets the next day.

The trip was organized by London-based ICAP, the world's biggest interdealer broker, which stood as a middleman between buyers and sellers of securities and was paid a tiny percentage from every trade. Brokers such as Tullett Prebon, Tradition, GFI, RP Martin Holdings, and ICAP were sounding boards for those trying to set rates on everything from interest rates to currencies to energy.

Of course, the rate rigging didn't happen only in London, even though the rates were technically set there. Traders emailed and instant-messaged their pals in Stamford and New York, in Tokyo and Singapore, even in New Zealand. They maintained a twenty-four-hour dialogue zipping around the globe based on whose market was open, whose interest rate setting was coming up next, and who had the most to gain financially.

In August 2007, for instance, Paul Walker, RBS's head of money market trading and the person responsible for U.S. dollar LIBOR submissions, discussed with Scott Nygaard, the American Tokyo-based head of short-term markets for Asia, how banks were using LIBOR to benefit their trading positions.

"People are setting to where it suits their book," Walker said in a phone call with Nygaard. "LIBOR is what you say it is."

"Yeah, yeah," agreed Nygaard.

It was in this context that traders such as Tan Chi Min were routinely taking calls from, or requests from, clients of the bank poking around about LIBOR. As Japan melted under its worst heat wave in a hundred years, on August 20, 2007, a sales manager at RBS in Tokyo received a call from a trader at hedge fund Brevan Howard in Hong Kong.

RBS's rate setter halfway around the world in London had increased the bank's submission for three-month yen LIBOR by 0.09 percent from the previous week, helping to push the benchmark to its highest level since 1995. Brevan Howard wanted to know why the rate had jumped, even after the U.S. Federal

Reserve had taken unprecedented steps to slash interest rates and flood the markets with liquidity, something that should have lowered the yen LIBOR rate as well.

RBS employees in London and Tokyo discussed the hedge fund's call in instant messages. Nygaard phoned Walker in London to warn that RBS should be "careful how we speak with them about . . . how the rate is set."

On a conference call later that day, Danziger, Walker, and RBS sales manager Darin Spilman told the Brevan Howard trader how the bank calculated its submissions in the absence of any cash trading. Walker gave his views on what he expected to happen to the Tokyo Interbank Offered Rate, or TIBOR. It's unclear whether they told the truth or lied about the submissions.

Hedge funds weren't the only winners. So were the brokers, the middlemen standing between the customer and the bank.

Neil Danziger's trades for RBS generated rich commissions for the brokers who handled them. Danziger and Tom Hayes—remember him?—paid £211,000 alone to two brokers, one from RP Martin Holdings.

In return, brokers at London's Tullett Prebon took Danziger to strip clubs and spent long weekends with him in Las Vegas. Brokers at RP Martin, another London firm, gave him early access to lucrative trades.

On one occasion, BGC Partners, a New York brokerage, ordered limousines sent to the homes of top traders at London banks.

The hired cars transported the traders' wives and girlfriends to a helicopter, which then flew the crew to the Royal Ascot, a marquee event on London's social calendar, for a day of horse racing and carousing.

Bank management not only knew about but sometimes encouraged rate rigging by employees, according to the revelations of Tan's wrongful dismissal suit in Singapore. Tan contended executives including Nygaard and Kevin Liddy, global head of short-term interest rate trading, were aware of the behavior.

Other RBS managers also tried to rig the benchmark by themselves. In an instant message conversation on December 3, 2007, Jezri Mohideen, then RBS's head of yen products in Tokyo, asked colleagues in the UK to lower the bank's six-month LIBOR submission that day, according to Bloomberg.

"We want lower LIBORs," Mohideen said in the chat. "Let the money markets guys know."

"Sure, I'm setting," said Will Hall, a trader in London who set the rate that day in the absence of the rate setter.

"Great, set it nice and low," Mohideen said.

Hall subsequently set the rate at 1.01 percent and followed through with the request, Bloomberg's data show.

How much money did Barclays and other banks actually make from rigging interest rates? One example illustrates it well.

In September 2006, a senior euro swaps trader wrote to the Barclays rate submitter for EURIBOR, the euro-based interbank lending rate set in Brussels by averaging forty-four banks' sub-missions.

SENIOR TRADER: I have a huge 1m [one-month EURIBOR] fix-ing today and would really help to have a low 1m tx a lot.

SUBMITTER: I'll do my best.

SENIOR TRADER: I am aware some other banks need a very high one . . . if you could push it very low it would help. I have 50bn fixing.

A €50 billion one-month fixing meant huge profits: Every basis point change was worth about €417,000, if they shaved 1 basis point (or 0.01 percent) off the one-month EURIBOR. If Barclays repeated this from mid-2005 to fall 2007 and there-after, in various tenors and currencies, it's quite possible that they made more money on the manipulation than they would ultimately pay in fines.

If the rigging affected $350 trillion in swaps, $10 trillion in loans, and $437 trillion in CME Eurodollar contracts indexed to LIBOR, Barclays alone caused roughly $5 billion worth of price distortion with its fake LIBOR submissions. The CME, Chicago Mercantile Exchange, had embraced the Eurodollar contracts as one of its most popular products.

In another EURIBOR interest rate rigging, a senior euro

swaps trader asked his rate submitter at Barclays, in an October 2006 exchange, "I have a huge fixing on Monday . . . something like 30bn 1m fixing . . . and I would like it to be very very very high. . . . Can you do something to help? I know a big clearer will be against us . . . and don't want to lose money on that one."

His submitter at Barclays complied, and even forwarded the request to another EURIBOR submitter outside the bank, adding, "We always try and do our best to help out."

Sometimes Barclays convinced other banks to go along with its plans, but sometimes it was shooting against other banks. One banker or hedge fund might want LIBOR nudged lower; some wanted it high. Bankers all knew this; the people on the street did not.

Who was that Barclays euro swaps trader? According to the *Financial Times*, he was Philippe Moryoussef, who came under investigation by the U.S. Commodity Futures Trading Commission (CFTC), the U.S. Department of Justice, and the UK Financial Services Authority for colluding with his counterparts at Deutsche Bank, Crédit Agricole, Société Générale, and HSBC to influence EURIBOR. Moryoussef, listed in the files of Britain's regulators as "Trader E," specialized in gaming EURIBOR. The CFTC didn't mention Moryoussef by name in its investigation, but instead described a senior euro swaps trader who "orchestrated an effort to align trading strategies among traders at multiple banks . . . in order to profit from their futures trading positions."

"The trick is that you can't do it alone," he bragged to his colleagues at the above-named banks who were in on the scheme.

Moryoussef, educated at the Lycée Descartes in the Moroccan capital of Rabat, traded interest rate derivatives for SocGen in Paris in the 1990s before moving to London. After leaving Barclays' euro swaps desk in 2007, he worked as a trader at Royal Bank of Scotland and Morgan Stanley in London and was later recruited to join Japanese bank Nomura's Singapore office. He was described by friends as a "cool, calm" highflier with an expensive apartment in St. John's Wood, London.

Each day he and his circle would talk about submitting false rates to the daily setting of the EURIBOR benchmark interest rate for the euro. His strategy was based on the fixing of three-month swaps pegged to EURIBOR. Moryoussef, the newspaper added, contacted a number of traders he knew at other banks, either through previous employment or via professional or personal networks. Regulators suspected communications with Michael Zrihen at Crédit Agricole, Didier Sander at HSBC, and Christian Bittar at Deutsche Bank.

In 2007, Moryoussef hatched a plan to fix the EURIBOR "cash" rate so a trade linked to it would make a bigger profit; he sent a message to a trader at another bank on the EURIBOR panel: "If you know how to keep a secret I'll bring you in on it . . . we're going to push the cash downwards . . . if you breathe a word of this I'm not telling you anything else. . . . I know my treasury's firepower . . . which will push the cash downwards . . . please keep it to yourself or it won't work."

The trick appeared to work, with Moryoussef delightedly telling another trader: "This is the way you pull off deals like this chicken, don't talk about it too much, 2 months of preparation . . . the trick is you must not do this alone . . . this is between you and me but really don't tell ANYBODY."

Another *Financial Times* article reported that Moryoussef had daily conversations with traders at the other banks that submitted rates to determine EURIBOR. In these phone calls, emails, or instant messages, the traders allegedly agreed to contact submitters at their respective banks to pressure them into submitting a rate that would benefit their derivatives positions.

One such trader was Christian Bittar, head of money market derivatives trading at Deutsche Bank and a top earner at the bank—in 2008, for example, he was apparently awarded a bonus of €50 million. Bittar joined Deutsche Bank in 1999, and for years he was apparently one of the bank's largest sources of revenue. He was a rising star under the bank's ambitious co–chief executive Anshu Jain and Jain's right-hand man, Alan Cloete.

Jain, a British citizen of Indian heritage, spoke fluent English but very little German when he took over as co-CEO of Deutsche Bank. He began his career selling interest rate swaps and other products to hedge funds at Merrill Lynch before following his mentor, Edson Mitchell, to Deutsche Bank in 1995. After Mitchell died in 2000, Jain took over as head of debt. In 2004, then CEO Josef Ackermann promoted Jain to lead the combined debt, equity sales, and trading unit and, ultimately, to serve as co-CEO.

Jain had loyalists, and among them was Cloete, who'd served as head of foreign exchange and global finance when Jain was head of the corporate and investment bank unit. Cloete was a potential candidate to succeed Jain as head of that unit when Jain became co-CEO with Juergen Fitschen in June 2012. Ultimately, Cloete was named to the group executive committee, the highest-ranking group after the management board, as Jain promoted bankers with whom he had worked closely.

While he was running Deutsche Bank's investment banking operation, Jain seated the team responsible for cash trading, where the LIBOR rates were calculated, close to their colleagues in derivatives trading.

"Combining cash and derivatives businesses has paid rich dividends in our credit, rates and foreign exchange franchises," Jain proudly reported in 2005. The idea also fostered collusion at Deutsche Bank, something that Jain asserted he only later realized.

It's unclear how well Jain knew Bittar, who reported to David Nicholls, who reported to Cloete. Within Deutsche Bank, Cloete reported directly to Jain, and Jain reportedly regularly saw Bittar on the trading floor.

According to a profile of Bittar in the German magazine *Der Spiegel*, it was during the crisis year of 2008 that, ironically, Bittar posted his greatest trade ever. Bittar reportedly earned over €500 million for the bank. Despite this big win, however, his employer overall suffered a pretax loss of €5.7 billion that year.

In 2008 Deutsche Bank's board decided it was politically unpalatable to pay out such a massive bonus. So the board spread Bittar's bonus payout over a number of years.

By 2011, Bittar had left the bank. He went to work for hedge fund BlueCrest. The Financial Conduct Authority in mid-2014 said it would seek to fine Christian Bittar 10 million pounds sterling ($17 million) for his role in the rate-rigging scandal.

Despite investigations launched by the likes of the CFTC, the rigging didn't stop. Instead, traders openly joked that they were "not allowed to have those conversations over Bloomberg."

CHAPTER 6

The Golden Banker

Just a few months after the two groundbreaking LIBOR stories ran in the *Wall Street Journal*, Robert E. Diamond, the head of Barclays Capital, was strolling the green at The Barclays, the PGA golf tournament that his bank sponsored.

The golf industry oozed money. It was August 24, 2008, and Vijay Singh had just beaten Sergio García with a birdie on the second hole. The purse was $1.26 million.

Diamond was a golf nut and had become close, personally and financially, with pro golfer Phil Mickelson. Barclays had signed him to sponsor the tour years earlier, and multimillionaire Mickelson appeared in Barclays commercials and wore the bank logo on his shirt. He was also a client of Barclays private banking. Mickelson was exactly the type Diamond wanted: American, with a *Forbes* ranking net worth ($47 million), and, most of all, a golfer.

Diamond was a member of the Westchester Country Club in New York, but was living in London as president of Barclays. In

2006, the former Greenwich, Connecticut, resident played in a group with defending tournament champ Padraig Harrington. And that day Diamond told a local paper the tournament meant more to him than being the title sponsor. "For us, the branding is first and most important," Diamond said. "But also to get a chance to spend a day with our clients in the pro-am, playing with the pros, having lunch together, sharing some laughs, getting to know each other, that's a big part of it as well."

Diamond was keen to link the game of golf with the Barclays brand, particularly in emerging markets like Asia, where the bank wanted to hook up with China's newly minted millionaires and billionaires. What better place to do that than on the golf course? Barclays had become a key player in the golf business and sponsored the first FedEx Cup play-off event on the PGA Tour, an event on the European Tour, as well as Mickelson himself, who had signed a multiyear deal with Barclays in March 2008.

Diamond may have contracted golf fever, but once he moved to London he had become a passionate fan of soccer as well, in particular the English football team Chelsea.

By 2005, Diamond and his teams had been winning on all fronts. Having worked for the bank since 1996, he ultimately joined the Barclays board, and because of that for the first time disclosed his £15 million pay package.

In public, Diamond demurred about whether the pay was too high. "I don't think it would be surprising and I don't think I'm alone in searching for privacy with my family," he famously told a British interviewer. "It's not pleasant for anyone" to have their pay deal being talked about. "I can't imagine anyone who'd enjoy it."

He also indicated that, ten years earlier, his American-style supersized pay deal might have created more of a backlash in England. "Ten years ago I don't think the UK was mature enough to accept a performance-based pay," he said. It is, in part, the "maturing reaction of shareholders and also, to be frank, the business has been outperforming. Some of the angst had been when paid ahead of performance or in spite of performance."

Anyway, he chimed: "It's done."

Diamond had been paid more handsomely than any banker in the City of London's history.

Diamond first went to London with Morgan Stanley in 1986, starting out as a bond trader. His brownish red hair, slight Boston accent, and rimless glasses gave him the look and sound of a parson or a news anchor more than a fat-cat banker.

He had done very well for a solidly middle-class Irish American kid, the oldest of a string of children born to two teachers in Concord, Massachusetts. His mother, Anne Diamond, left teaching to be a homemaker, and his father, Robert Edward Diamond Sr., rose from being middle school principal to superintendent. The elder Diamond had a huge influence on his son.

At Colby College, Diamond became a fraternity brother at Phi Delta Theta and graduated with a degree in economics in 1973. He married a Midwestern brunette who studied engineering. Fancying himself a future academic like his father, Diamond lectured at the University of Connecticut while studying for an MBA there. He took a low-paying job at U.S. Surgical in

Hartford, Connecticut, and then in 1977 followed his boss to Morgan Stanley.

He quickly rose to oversee the international fixed-income trading and interest rate trading, spending five years in London with Morgan Stanley. "At that time I covered most of the trading areas outside of the United States, primarily the UK, Europe, and Japan." With a sunny disposition, and a rabid fanatic of his native New England Patriots and Boston Red Sox, Diamond made friends easily, but along the way a few key enemies.

When he left Morgan Stanley for Credit Suisse First Boston (CSFB) in 1992, Diamond took with him almost an entire trading team, putting the firm's liquidity at risk. Not surprisingly, his relationship soured with some of Morgan Stanley's senior executives, including the future CEO John Mack. For a long time, Diamond was "considered public enemy number one around here," one Morgan Stanley exec recalled.

At the time, Allen Wheat, the head of the investment banking arm at CSFB, who would ultimately rise to become chief executive, was the king of the realm. Many traders looked up to him, as he was among the first to allow them to keep a piece of the profits they brought in, kind of like mini hedge funds. Under Wheat, CSFB rapidly expanded, buying large parts of rival investment banks Barclays de Zoete Wedd in Britain and DLJ in the United States, the latter through a $13.7 billion deal aimed at underlining CSFB's challenge in global capital markets.

The compensation model was one many banks would adopt later to keep prized employees. Wheat ran "almost an investment bank within the bank," according to one of his former subordinates. But Diamond, who moved his family to Tokyo so he could become chief of CSFB's global bond operations and foreign exchange, wasn't a part of that action. "Diamond would not have liked that, as he was Wheat's peer and in charge of fixed income, and that meant he couldn't control Allen Wheat."

In his own sphere, Diamond was beloved by some, and dismissed outright as simultaneously arrogant and awkward by others at CSFB. One equity salesman recalled bringing one of the bank's largest clients, who was paying $5 million a month in commissions, for a late-day meeting with Diamond in New York. Diamond began the brief meeting by saying, "I only have a few minutes. My wife and I and another couple are leaving to go see a play." Diamond then handed the client his personal business card, saying, "We'll see to it that you get proper sales coverage from now on." Having insulted both the salesman and the client, he abruptly left.

Wheat and Diamond inevitably clashed, and Diamond ended up leaving CSFB after just four years. Not surprisingly, he resigned amid turmoil over 1995 bonuses. First Boston boosted its 1995 bonus pool 30 percent to $455 million. But First Boston traders and bankers got upset after they discovered that top executives took home big paychecks, relative to what they considered "paltry" bonuses. Diamond reportedly felt his $8 million bonus just wasn't enough.

After leaving CSFB, Diamond had spent a few months in the wilderness before being tapped by chief executive Martin Taylor to join Barclays de Zoete Wedd (BZW), the group's investment bank. Diamond arrived as a "hotshot newcomer," recalled

Martin Vander Weyer, a former BZW director. "Everyone wanted to get near him, to touch his golden sleeve. There was a kind of expectation that we were all going to be Americanized, we were all expected to be more like Bob," the elder banker remembered.

Diamond, then forty-five, was the archetype of what every City of London banker wanted to be: a sports-crazy, salad-fueled trader of government bonds and foreign exchange, according to Vander Weyer. He oversaw all the global markets: BZW's fixed income, derivatives, foreign exchange, treasury, futures, and metals operations. He was the father of three, with a daughter, Nell, named after his grandmother, and two sons, Robert E. Diamond III and Charles. Diamond and his family settled permanently into life in London.

Inevitably, Brits were shocked that an American ended up running what was left of Barclays asset management and the rump of BZW, which he eventually renamed Barclays Capital. "[Barclays] is seen as one of the truest English institutions, just like English tea, public schools, and Burberry," said Lothar Mentel, formerly of Barclays, who became chief investment officer at Octopus Investments. But here was Diamond at the helm.

At one time a regional bank that brought ATM machines to the UK in the 1960s and introduced Barclaycards as one of the first credit cards, Barclays under Diamond spread its ubiquitous blue eagle mascot across bus stops and tube stations. It would eventually grow to be the fifth largest lender in the world.

Diamond did Americanize his new fiefdom, bringing in Thomas Kalaris, Rich Ricci, Jerry del Missier, and others. By 2000, the so-called "Friends of Bob" had coalesced into a remarkably tight-knit team but one that the catastrophic Russian debt losses of 1998 failed to tarnish.

"Team" was an important word in the Diamond lexicon. His nickname was "Coach," since he managed his children's baseball team on weekends. He also claimed to be a strong proponent of what John Mack, his former Morgan Stanley boss who would go on to replace Wheat at CSFB, coined "the one-firm firm," in reference to a united bank.

In 2001, Diamond poached twelve traders from Deutsche Bank in a deal worth £60 million; he aimed to add to his team by increasing the company's head count by 15 percent. The investment bank, with five thousand staff worldwide, awarded at least £1 million in bonuses to more than a hundred of its traders.

Four of his traders famously treated themselves to a £44,000 meal at Gordon Ramsay's Pétrus restaurant in London that summer. Mahish Chandra, Iftikhar Hyder, Dayananda Kumar, and Ruth Cove drank bottles of claret costing up to £12,000.

In 2002, Diamond was ecstatic when Barclays finally landed an American base, opening offices in the MetLife Building in midtown Manhattan. The next year, under Diamond's management, Barclays grew to be the fifth largest underwriter of syndicated loans in the world and the second largest underwriter of European bonds. Still, Diamond had his disappointment: He lost out on the top job to John Varley, an Oxford-educated Barclays veteran who was a distant relative to the original Quaker founders.

Diamond announced he wasn't going anywhere. "I'm not disappointed; I'm actually pumped up," he told an interviewer. He had been given responsibility for the corporate clients at Barclays that he did not already oversee as part of the shake-up of the top job, and claimed to be eager to grow Barclays' market share in the United States.

But would he still be there in six months? "I promise," Diamond replied.

Indeed, the following year was a good one for Diamond as chief executive of Barclays Capital. Not only did Barclays Capital post record earnings, but Diamond's favorite American baseball team, the Red Sox, won the World Series that year for the first time since 1918, breaking the team's long-held curse. It was a year of vindication for both Diamond and the Red Sox.

Diamond rightly believed that a single European currency would indeed materialize, allowing European banks the opportunity to compete head-on with U.S. bulge-bracket firms by raising capital for European companies in euros. By building on its UK and European home markets, Barclays Capital would be able to expand in the United States. He turned out to be right, partly, in his reckoning, because of the repeal of the Glass-Steagall Act.

Pressure on Congress had led to the elimination of barriers that separated commercial from investment banking. Glass-Steagall, a law dating back to the Depression era, had kept investment firms and banks separate; the idea was that the deposits of regular folks should not be used to gamble in the stock and bond markets. But following Citicorp's 1998 merger with the Travelers Group, producing Citigroup, in 1999 President Bill Clinton signed into law the Gramm-Leach-Bliley Act, permitting financial services conglomerates to consolidate commercial and investment banking, along with insurance underwriting and brokerage.

"The restraint of government and its agencies disappeared," Citigroup's cochair John Reed would admit years later with remorse. "We created a monster."

But Diamond foresaw that once Glass-Steagall was repealed, a more level playing field would give commercial banks like Barclays new opportunities.

By 2005, Diamond had been named president of Barclays and joined the board—and for the first time he would have to disclose his pay package. The *New York Times* dubbed him Britain's "$15 million man."

But his full compensation that year was actually more like $28 million, and the public talk of such sums prompted Barclays shareholders to bristle against the massive American-style pay. But Diamond's disposition grew even sunnier. "Bobtimistic" is how Rich Ricci, Barclays Capital's co–chief executive officer, described Diamond's eternally upbeat attitude.

Not long after Diamond was appointed president of Barclays, Prince Andrew, Duke of York, accepted an invitation to be the bank's guest of honor for the final two days of the Barclays Classic golf tournament. Prince Andrew was greeted by none other than the ultimate Yank: the well-compensated Diamond from Concord, Massachusetts, one of the original Revolutionary War battle towns in the former British colonies.

Diamond maintained a highly visible public persona. He was

the designated presenter when the Premiership Trophy was awarded to Chelsea's football captain John Terry in 2005. He and his wife, Jennifer, frequented the social scene in London and New York. As a trustee of his alma mater, he and his family foundation gave $6 million to Colby College for a new building. Diamond regularly appeared on financial television outlets like CNBC and Bloomberg, and he rang the opening bell at the New York Stock Exchange. As a generous backer of the mayor of London, Diamond gained a nickname, compliments of Mayor Boris Johnson himself: "the Mayor's Best Friend." Under Diamond's leadership, Barclays sponsored Johnson's idea of rental bikes—Barclays Cycle Hire—helping dot the city with bicycles the color of the bank's signature blue. The mayor of London joked that Diamond was "an extremely wealthy man. . . . I know how much money they make at Barclays because they rip me off with their charges the whole time." (In 2006, Barclays hiked the fees for a bounced check from five pounds to thirty-five pounds.)

If Diamond's name was often bandied about in London, more often it was his compensation that was the talk of the town.

In 2007 he was said to have made £21 million in cash and shares. In the difficult year of 2008 he had to make do with his £250,000 basic salary after executives at Barclays caved in to pressure and agreed to give up the chance of seven-figure bonuses, but in 2010 it was revealed he had landed a record five-year pay package of £63.3 million, including £384,000 a year in basic salary and perks (sixteen times the average British wage), plus a staggering performance-related package of shares and perks.

"Even housewives in Hendon have heard of him, or rather how much he earns. He's no longer just a City phenomenon. He's a brand. Nigella the sexy cook. Bob the golden banker," quipped Abigail Hofman of *Euromoney*.

That Diamond was unapologetic about his pay package rubbed the old boys in the City the wrong way. Couldn't he just keep his head down like the rest of the crowd and stop drawing attention to how much money was being made? "Bob Diamond, Diamond Bob—even his name seems to epitomize wealth," wrote the London *Times* in 2011. "The Barclays chief executive has big bonuses, high profits and swanky offices. His doorman is dressed in fur, and dozens of lavishly decorated Christmas trees are scattered around the foyer at his bank's headquarters in Canary Wharf, East London."

Now that he was, as the British papers wrote, a real, live "master of the universe," the sentiment was that he was rubbing the public's nose in his success. That was not a very English thing to do.

Diamond had continued to install American loyalists all around him. Known as "Bob" within the bank and thought of as "charming and ambitious," he spread his tentacles further throughout the Barclays empire by promoting key lieutenants to help with his expanded responsibilities.

Diamond replaced himself at the top of the funds management division, bringing over Ricci and Kalaris from the United States, and made Del Missier and Grant Kvalheim copresidents of Barclays Capital. The chief casualty was the well-respected Andrew Skirton, who left as joint chief of Barclays' funds management arm "to pursue other interests." Del Missier, who climbed mountains as a hobby, would eventually take over all of Kvalheim's duties too.

In earnings, Diamond was eager to boast about the bank's three areas of profitability.

Take the first half of 2005, a time of particularly heady earnings. As Diamond put it, "There were three asset classes for which we saw above-trend growth, not only for us but for the entire industry. Those were credit, particularly derivatives and structuring; structured equity product, particularly principal-protected products which can provide some upside and be particularly useful to the private bank and to the retail investors; and the whole area of commodities. Each of those has been a huge area of growth for us."

He went on. "Our client business in the U.S. was up 60 percent for the first half of this year. Our European business was up 70 percent. Commodities was double any six-month period we ever had. Equity derivatives was up 50 percent. There are opportunities for growth at a similar pace to the last few years. And it's not coming from piling up the risk in proprietary trading. It's sustainable. It's real."

But his optimism reached further. These are three growth areas out of how many, potentially? "Well, interest rates, currencies, traditional cash equity, as well as credit, structured equity, commodities . . . three of six or seven."

Clearly, Diamond had a good handle on what made the bank

tick—and which trades were most profitable. One of the areas—trading in interest rates—was coining it for Barclays.

By late 2006, Diamond was making the rounds of his alma maters, dispensing advice to new Colby and UConn graduates. He recalled his father's advice about trying out for the catcher position on his Little League team. The younger Diamond didn't want to be catcher—"No boy ever wants to be catcher," he laughed—but it helped him land on a team he otherwise wouldn't have made.

That lesson had stuck with him, he recalled. He never passed up the entry-level job in a great firm just because it didn't pay a lot of money or earn him a fancy title. That career strategy eventually helped land him at the top of Barclays.

"Find the place where you can succeed and make the most of what you have," Diamond told the UConn grads, claiming his first job with a tiny medical supply company was the lowest-paying job taken by anyone in his graduating class at the university's business school.

By 2007, the three-hundred-year-old British banking giant was slapping its name on a stadium in, of all places, Brooklyn, New York. To raise its profile in the United States, Diamond signed a marketing deal with the NBA's Nets team. The price tag was $300 million.

"This is a statement that we are serious about growing our business in the U.S.," said Diamond.

Having for years poached and hired outside for new talent, he claimed he would never agree to a merger that created overlapping jobs, known in corporate circles as redundancies. But in June 2007, Diamond changed his mind about growing Barclays "organically." He put together a $91 billion bid for ABN Amro. Diamond needed to find new ways to maintain the record growth.

The acquisition was a gamble. "This is his roll of the dice," said Justin Urquhart Stewart, a director at Seven Investment Management in London. "If he wins he gets a bigger footprint; if he doesn't, Barclays Capital will find it more and more difficult to sustain that growth rate."

In 2008, Diamond and his wife decided to spend more time in the United States. They would divide their time between a million-dollar house on Nantucket and a four-bedroom, fortieth-floor penthouse overlooking Central Park in New York. Diamond's older son, Rob, was in college at Princeton, from which Nell, his daughter, had already graduated. The move would coincide with the high school graduation of his youngest son, Charles, in London; he had plans to attend his father's alma mater in Maine.

The Diamonds would maintain a residence in London, but they were going to sell their massive home in West London, a seven-bedroom town house in Kensington, close to the home of Harry Potter author J. K. Rowling. The mansion boasted eight thousand square feet of space, an indoor swimming pool, a gym, and an underground garage for seven cars. (Diamond ultimately sold it for an estimated profit of at least £10 million.)

Even before his property windfall, the American-born banker had become a controversial figure because of the scale of that year's £36 million pay, bonus, and share package at a time when Barclays was being forced to write off £1.6 billion in bad debts. At the bank's annual meeting in 2008, one shareholder said

Barclays had gone "berserk" because it was paying Diamond twenty-four times as much as Bank of England Governor Mervyn King.

With the credit crisis in full swing by summer 2008, Diamond's ABN Amro bid failed spectacularly. Barclays withdrew in the face of determined competition from RBS. But other targets started to surface.

In April 2008, Diamond had quietly traded phone calls with Robert Steel at the U.S. Treasury. The subject was buying Lehman Brothers. Publicly, Diamond denied any interest.

Steel had phoned Diamond right after the collapse of Bear Stearns. The U.S. government had helped engineer a forced marriage of Bear Stearns and J.P. Morgan, and Steel was feeling out candidates for another such deal. "If there were another leg down, if Lehman were in trouble, is there a price at which an acquisition of Lehman makes sense to Barclays?" he asked Diamond.

Diamond waited for the second question: "And if so, what would you need from us?" Steel asked.

Diamond and Varley had discussed such a possibility as far back as 2007, when the credit markets first began to crack. "I discussed with John Varley and with the board that the crisis would create opportunities, it was a potential crisis in the financial markets which would impact us, but it would offer great opportunities" to build in the United States.

What most investors didn't know was that Barclays had already been in talks with UBS, the Swiss banking giant, to potentially buy some of its investment banking operations in Asia and the United States. "They were substantive, but at a very high level, and very private," Diamond recalled later. The conversations involved just the top two people at each bank. At that time, Marcel Ospel was group chair of UBS, and Marcel Rohner the CEO. Steel at U.S. Treasury may have known about the talks, but no one else did at a high level in government.

Without naming names, Diamond conceded publicly that Barclays might be tempted to bid for a large U.S. banking company forced to sell itself in distress. "That could certainly change the dynamic," he told *American Banker* magazine. "Because of dislocations, there may be opportunities that would never have been there before. We never say 'never,' but we are still focused on our higher-growth businesses."

The UBS talks had faded, but Lehman remained an itch that Diamond needed to scratch. Privately, Diamond had also taken one phone call from Lehman's chief, Dick Fuld, who wanted to get Barclays involved in the Robin Hood Foundation.

After exchanging pleasantries, Fuld wound up the call with an intriguing question.

"There isn't something else we should be talking about, is there?" Fuld queried Diamond.

Diamond didn't bite. But months later came the same question from the U.S. Treasury, and Diamond made clear that, if Barclays were to take over Lehman, he would have to be the man in charge. It wouldn't be Dick Fuld, the aggressive onetime wrestler and hockey player.

Barclays would buy Lehman only on the cheap. In his

conversations with Steel, Diamond insisted, "The only way that works was if the price was distress in price and management be distressed so we have clarity on who's running. It couldn't be a merger of equals. It was going to take one person in charge and making the decisions."

He and Varley relayed the conversations to the board of Barclays later in the spring of 2008. In the end, Diamond would get his way, although events unfolded in a way no one expected when, in September, Barclays bought Lehman's prize assets out of bankruptcy. Barclays lost no time in integrating the Lehman business.

Despite the precisely targeted and well-timed purchase, however, Barclays took flack for buying into the bankrupt Lehman without actually having the cash. Abigail Hofman at *Euromoney* observed, "Barclays acted like a feckless teenager, it saw a Prada handbag and pounced on it. But there was a small problem. When the credit card bill came, they didn't have the money to pay."

Barclays needed to raise substantial amounts of capital for other reasons. In October 2008, in the wake of the financial meltdown, Britain's banking regulator, the Financial Services Authority, put British banks through a so-called stress test. Each bank permitted regulators a look at its books to determine what would happen in an extreme case of financial stress. The ultimate question was: Would the bank survive or not?

By 2009, other British banks, like HBOS, RBS, and others, took government bailouts, but Barclays—in particular Diamond— refused. His reasoning was opaque, but James Eden, an analyst at Exane BNP Paribas, suggested that there was one obvious reason that Barclays management had avoided government help: Its executives wished to continue to pay themselves immense bonuses. Government owners wouldn't stomach Diamond's Barclays-level pay.

Diamond chose a different route to raise needed funds. Instead of the UK government, Diamond went to Asia and the Middle East, in particular the China Development Bank, Singapore's Temasek, and Japan's Sumitomo Bank. He also hit up Qatar's sovereign wealth fund and Abu Dhabi investors in search of billions in capital. Not long afterward, he sold the bank's crown jewels—the exchange-traded fund business with the trademark iShares and the rest of Barclays Global Investors (BGI)—for $13.5 billion to BlackRock.

The deal netted Diamond personally £20 million, thanks to the three hundred thousand shares and share options he acquired in BGI as part of a phantom stock plan. More than four hundred top executives at Barclays pocketed a total of £380 million from the BlackRock transaction.

"Diamond is either a modern-day banking great or the archetypal financial devil," quipped one British daily.

The day after the September 17, 2008, announcement of Barclays' acquisition of Lehman Brothers, a Barclays rate trader told his manager he would put in a submission to LIBOR of 4.75 percent. But after their conversation, the trader cut that to 4.50 percent. It was 0.50 percent over the next highest submission.

A lower LIBOR would certainly help Barclays. In retrospect,

the move also begged an obvious question, especially given the fact that Barclays later needed to find other sources of cash to pay the bill. Would Diamond have been able to go ahead with the purchase of Lehman if it had been further outside the LIBOR pack?

Diamond had cultivated ties in New York and Washington. A review of Timothy Geithner's calendar during his time at the New York Fed, originally obtained by the *New York Times*, shows that he repeatedly spoke with senior executives at Barclays between April 2007 and October 2008, including one morning meeting with Bob Diamond on October 10. The calendar indicates that Geithner also participated in conference calls with unnamed representatives of Barclays and Treasury Secretary Hank Paulson on the afternoon of September 13, three days before Barclays announced its takeover of parts of Lehman Brothers. That following weekend, RBS and Lloyds would be partly nationalized by the British government, but Barclays, desperate to avoid nationalization, remained independent as Diamond persuaded the government to let it raise capital privately.

Odd juxtapositions in the known record abound: Just days earlier, one of the Barclays submitters said over the phone that his manager had asked him to put in a lower rate than the day before "to send the message that we're not in the shit."

Then, weeks later, on October 29, Paul Tucker of the Bank of England telephoned Diamond, telling him the central bank had "received calls from a number of senior figures within Whitehall to question why Barclays was always toward the top end of the LIBOR pricing." Diamond and Tucker were friends; after it was announced that Tucker would become Bank of England deputy governor, Diamond had emailed to congratulate him. "Well done, man. I am really, really proud of you," Diamond wrote.

Tucker was equally friendly in his response. "Thanks so much Bob," Tucker emailed back. "You've been an absolute brick through this."

Diamond jotted down notes of these exchanges. The next day, October 31, 2008, Barclays announced it didn't need British government intervention. Diamond's Asian and Middle Eastern investors had come through with the needed cash.

Hugo Dixon, a columnist at Reuters, later posed the pregnant question: "Would the Middle Eastern investors have been so willing to invest in Barclays if the bank's LIBOR rates had been even more out of whack? And if so, would the UK government have had to step into the breach?"

Moreover, what had Bob Diamond known about LIBOR, and when? Although he operated at a level well above the likes of Tom Hayes, Diamond was on the receiving end of news of shenanigans of the sort Hayes was propagating at UBS. In August 2007, Diamond and Barclays' colleague Rich Ricci received an email from Jerry del Missier. Referring to "the whole Libor curve," Del Missier wrote, "the real story is that these are all fantasy rates." Clearly, Del Missier was familiar with how LIBOR was calculated, and now so was the rest of the top brass.

Much later still, Diamond would have to face many such questions as he confronted the wrath of shareholders and the public when the interest rate rigging scandal reared its head in public. In time, it would cost him his job.

CHAPTER 7

An Open Matter

In the 1980s and early 1990s, Wall Street had showered Gary Gensler with success and prizes, making him a multimillionaire. But in 2009, Gensler seemed poised to slap the hand that had fed him. Or so they felt on the Street.

Gensler's confirmation as head of the Commodity Futures Trading Commission after Barack Obama's election proved rocky. His personal history just didn't seem to align with what he was about to do. He felt the time had come to wrestle the trillion-dollar derivatives market from out of the shadows and onto exchanges, where derivatives could be cleared on a daily basis, via computer databases, and priced for all to see, much like stocks.

Ten years before, Gensler had passed on regulating derivatives. In an earlier stint as a regulator, he'd worked for his mentor, Robert Rubin, the former cochair of Goldman Sachs and Treasury secretary, and shared his bosses' laissez-fare approach. But by the time Obama was sworn in, the landscape looked different to Gary Gensler. After the arrival of the financial crisis and the AIG bailout the previous year, there were enough derivatives traded to represent three hundred dollars for every single American, while there remained next to no public information about them.

The banks didn't like what he was planning, especially since trading in over-the-counter derivatives was one of the last profitable bastions for financial firms and for Wall Street. Their lobbyists screamed, their lawyers wrote letters, they asked for exemptions. But Gensler vowed he wasn't going to let the opportunity to regulate derivatives slip away this time.

Gensler's father had installed and serviced cigarette machines and pinball machines in bars in Baltimore; son Gary used to tag along to take the nickels out of the machines and count them. That had been his first foray into business and the world of finance. Later, he ran for class treasurer at Pikesville High School in Baltimore, an early sign of what would emerge as his deep passion for politics and government.

Retaining his *Baw'lmor* accent, Gary graduated from Pikesville in 1975, having already studied advanced math in a program at Johns Hopkins University for gifted teenagers. At college, Gensler was impatient, graduating from the University of Pennsylvania and its Wharton MBA program in just four years after begging the dean to permit him to take more classes per semester than was allowed. In 1979, at age twenty-one, he began working at Goldman Sachs, going on to become one of Goldman's youngest partners ever. In 1988, he made partner along with future CEO Lloyd Blankfein; Blankfein was thirty-four, Gensler a mere thirty years old.

In 1990, while at Goldman, he advised the National Football League in television negotiations that led to a record contract, raising the price paid per team to $32 million a year (up from $17 million). By 1995, Gensler was cohead of finance for Goldman worldwide.

In 1997 Gensler made a major career move, accepting an appointment as assistant secretary of financial markets at the U.S. Treasury, rejoining his longtime Goldman colleague Robert Rubin, by then secretary of the Treasury in the Clinton administration. Government service (and, by extension, politics) became Gensler's new career. According to the Center for Responsive Politics, starting in 1994 he would contribute more than $260,000 to various Democratic candidates, including the campaigns of Hillary Clinton and Maryland's Ben Cardin, as well as Tom Daschle, John Kerry, and Kweisi Mfume.

Early in his public service career, in 1998, Gensler watched firsthand the spectacular implosion of the hedge fund Long-Term Capital Management. LTCM had made billion-dollar bets—the wrong ones, as it turned out—on the stock and bond markets.

James G. Rickards, a longtime Wall Street lawyer and hedge fund investor, remembers working with Gensler as derivatives nearly took down the financial system. Russia's 1998 devaluation and debt default were unfolding, and the events overseas had thrown the fixed-income bets Long-Term Capital had made completely out of whack. Though overseen by Nobel Prize winners and PhDs,

LTCM had been taken by surprise, and the fund was losing hundreds of millions of dollars each week.

As the crisis climaxed, Rickards, as the hedge fund's legal counsel, had worked long into a September weekend trying to make sense of LTCM's books. Secretary Rubin dispatched Gensler as a friendly government observer, the eyes-and-ears man for the Treasury. Peter Fisher, executive vice president at the New York Fed, joined them to take a look at the LTCM portfolio.

On Sunday, September 20, 1998, at LTCM's offices in Greenwich, Connecticut, the men, together with Fed colleagues and bankers from Goldman and J.P. Morgan, listened to what was happening. They were shocked by what they heard.

"We took them all through our 106 strategies," said Rickards.

When it was over, an ashen Fisher looked back at Rickards and said, "We knew you might take down the bond market, but we had no idea you might take down the stock market too."

"Gensler barely said a word, but it was clear he was taking it all in," remembered Rickards, who spent six hours in the same room with Gensler. Also in attendance was onetime ace trader Lawrence Hilibrand. An investor in LTCM, Hilibrand was reduced to tears, not by the havoc his hedge fund had caused but by the decision that it would be necessary to turn over the firm to a consortium of fourteen banks.

Gensler watched in shock as Long-Term Capital unwound huge derivatives contracts. LTCM alone had a billion-dollar credit default swap that Rickards personally had helped craft. Gensler picked up the telephone and called Washington to report back to his boss, consistently addressing Rubin by the formal title "Mr. Secretary," during this tense time of LTCM's demise.

Despite the disaster surrounding LTCM, Fed Chair Alan Greenspan, along with SEC Chair Arthur Levitt and New York Fed President Timothy Geithner, ultimately decided against regulating derivatives. Greenspan, a devotee of Ayn Rand and unfettered free markets, claimed next to nothing should be regulated in the financial markets, including derivatives. It was a stance he would come to regret publicly after the 2008 financial crisis.

But in 1998 it hadn't been a unanimous call. At that time, Brooksley Born was head of the Commodity Futures Trading Commission, the same position Gensler would occupy a decade later. She was widely recognized as a brilliant lawyer who wasn't afraid to face off with the men on the other side, including Rubin, Greenspan, and Levitt, with Gensler in a supporting role.

"We were afraid the CFTC was asserting jurisdiction over the market," said a former Treasury official; it was a turf battle with the CFTC, which was viewed back then as a provincial, backwater agency. Born's calls to regulate the explosive derivatives industry were drowned out by the collective voice of the others, and she left her post as chair not long afterward. She was remembered as being intransigent at times, unable to play politics to advance her agenda or that of the CFTC. Observed a former Treasury official: "If Born had been a better politician she could have gotten Rubin and Levitt away from Greenspan." But that wasn't what happened. After a particularly nasty exchange, Rubin went so far as to ignore Born's outstretched hand one day, instead walking right by her. "Rubin treated her very shabbily," said one person who was at the meeting. "She was right, but she was stubborn."

Ever loyal, Gensler had sided at the time with his boss Rubin, perhaps believing that the derivatives market did not pose the threat of "weapons of mass destruction," as billionaire investor Warren Buffett exclaimed. After President Clinton signed the repeal of Glass-Steagall in 1999 and Congress passed the Commodity Futures Modernization Act the following year, the derivatives markets remained unregulated. "We all thought these things were good," Rickards said.

Gensler's chance to rethink his position was coming.

In April 2008, Vincent A. McGonagle, a top enforcement official at the CFTC, perused the newspapers. Like many federal regulators, he scanned the press as a way to sift through the many small-time scams and focus on building potentially much larger cases.

McGonagle had just finished signing off on a case in which Dubai-based Aaristo Commodities had been ordered to pay a $100,000 penalty related to charges of illegal trades. Yes, the CFTC was in Washington, but everyone around the world traded futures on the futures contracts offered by the mercantile exchanges, such as New York's NYMEX or the Chicago Mercantile Exchange.

On this particular day, McGonagle read the *Wall Street Journal* story by reporters Mollenkamp and Whitehouse about how a key interest rate used worldwide may have been rigged over in London. He quickly scanned the story on the interest rate, opened a file folder, and wrote on it, "*LIBOR*."

Then he went to his boss, Stephen J. Obie, who had joined the commission in 1998 and worked as a senior trial attorney.

"I think we have something here," McGonagle said simply.

His few words spoke volumes, but the moment wasn't right.

In the early years of the George W. Bush administration, Gensler served as an adviser to Senator Paul Sarbanes, who, as chair of the Senate Banking Committee, cosponsored the Sarbanes-Oxley Act of 2002, which reformed accounting and securities laws. That same year Gensler published a book, *The Great Mutual Fund Trap*, in which he advocated that mom-and-pop investors stick to using low-cost index funds.

During this period, he was also a key Democratic fund-raiser, often raising money by hosting parties at his expansive Maryland home. Some estimates put his fortune at $15 million, but it would have been higher had he stayed for Goldman Sachs' initial public offering. Not bad for the son of a man who never went to college.

Gensler had a reputation as the type of guy who would ford rivers and climb mountains for the people he cared about. He was known to be immensely loyal. Like the time he donned a witch's hat and black wig for Halloween and posed for photographs with his three young daughters. Or the countless times he sat at his wife's hospital bed as she underwent treatment for breast cancer. "My husband Gary has always been there for me—beginning to end," Francesca wrote in a photo caption. An artist and filmmaker, she decided to document her illness and treatment. In one picture, Gensler wore an exhausted look, glasses, and a five o'clock shadow. Francesca wore a metal brace.

After she passed away in 2006, Gensler became a stay-at-home dad. He helped with the laundry, bought the groceries, and made sure the dogs were fed. When then senator Hillary Clinton was preparing to run for president, Gensler told her that he wanted to help her in any way he could, even joining her team full-time.

Hillary Clinton ended up losing the nomination to Barack Obama, but, good foot soldier that he was for the Democratic Party, Gensler supported the nominee. When Obama was elected, the phone call came, giving Gensler a shot at serving another president. And to revisit the matter of regulating derivatives.

With the 2008 financial crisis, the failure of Lehman Brothers, and the government bailout of AIG's huge derivatives position, a lot of people were rethinking the absence of regulation. Gensler was among them, as was his fellow veteran of the CFTC case, James Rickards.

"I can understand his change of views," Rickards explained. After waging a personal intellectual odyssey to figure out what had gone wrong, Rickards himself had concluded that complex derivatives, such as interest rate swaps, should be traded on an exchange, much like stocks. "I too am anti-swaps now," he said. "And I helped invent them."

Yet even though Gensler had officially changed his position on the subject, there were some in Congress who didn't believe him.

According to a profile in the *New Republic*, hours after President Obama named Gensler to head the CFTC, incoming White House chief of staff Rahm Emanuel informed Gensler that certain congressional reps would oppose his nomination. Gensler promptly called them at home, looking to persuade them otherwise.

"Washington Senator Maria Cantwell worried that Gensler would be soft on derivatives. Vermont's Bernie Sanders was skeptical of Gensler's tour under Treasury Secretary Robert Rubin. The two senators [wanted] . . . assurances that he and his Obama colleagues planned to rein in the financial markets," the magazine wrote in 2010.

Gensler dug in his heels in his testimony. "They wanted him to say he'd been wrong, and he wasn't going to," explained Michael Greenberger, professor of law at the University of Maryland and a former CFTC commissioner in charge of trading and markets.

On the other hand, Gensler did acknowledge that the Clintonites hadn't done enough to protect the public. "There's not a day that goes by that I don't think what we might have done differently," Gensler recalled.

The collapse of Long-Term Capital Management, he said, served as an example of a failed company that may not have had such a sweeping impact on the economy if it had been more heavily regulated. AIG had to be bailed out precisely because its derivatives investments had gone south. "They said they were hedging their business, their business was investing," Gensler said of LTCM. "That was a systemic issue to the American public."

Gensler's subordinates at the U.S. Treasury remember him as both charming and ruthless. So did the bankers with whom he lunched one day after he got the CFTC job. Now that he was head of the powerful commodities regulator, whom was he going after?

"You guys," he told them, smiling.

It became official on May 26, 2009, when Gensler was sworn in as chair of the CFTC.

Vincent McGonagle had been appointed the CFTC's senior deputy director in 2002. Having joined the agency in 1997, he'd served as senior trial attorney and special counsel to the director. He had not shrunk from the big cases.

In 2003 he'd grabbed hold of the Enron gas price manipulation case, arguing the CFTC was entitled to jurisdiction, due to the close link between the Henry Hub spot market price for gasoline and the NYMEX futures, which makes it possible to manipulate the exchange-traded contract through heavy spot trading; at the time, he remarked, "We take the cases as we get them." He had handled the agency's cases against Duke Energy, American Electric Power, and the hedge fund Amaranth in 2007. He'd been involved with allegations of playing around with gas prices, small-time hedge fund frauds, commodity pool operators in states all over the country, and investigations in places as far away as Dubai.

His boss, Stephen Obie, was no slouch either. He had joined the commission in 1998 as a senior trial attorney in its New York Division of Enforcement office. After receiving his law degree in 1991 from SUNY Buffalo Law School, he'd clerked for Judge Jerome F. Hanifin of the New York State Court of Claims and at the Office of the Staff Attorneys for the U.S. Court of Appeals for the Eighth Circuit. More recently, during his tenure at the CFTC, Obie had also taught as an adjunct professor at Brooklyn Law School, giving an upper-class seminar in the fall 2007 semester titled "Trading Derivatives." Obie had also gained experience chasing bad guys around the world. If they traded U.S. futures contracts or stole money from U.S. residents, the CFTC was going after them.

When Gensler came aboard, the commission was in need of a big win. The agency was conducting a probe into whether market manipulation had been behind the run-up in crude oil prices to $150 a barrel that had occurred in 2008, and some in Congress were hounding the CFTC for not doing enough to rein in energy market speculators, those who bought and sold not to take delivery of the oil and gas but just to play the prices. Many lawmakers—and the public—blamed speculators for causing record oil and gasoline prices. Yet the agency was one of the few lean operations in the capital. Commodity trading had grown from five hundred *million* trades in 2000 to three *billion* in 2007, while the agency's staff had declined. In some years, Congress failed to fund the agency on time.

The name "LIBOR" had kept cropping up too. Obie had recently been promoted to acting director of enforcement at the

CFTC when he heard the recordings of Barclays traders talking with rate setters about rigging interest rates. Recognizing immediately that this could be something big—maybe that big win the commission sorely needed—Obie shuffled out of his office and replayed the recordings for the new boss, CFTC Chair Gary Gensler, in 2010.

As Gensler later recalled the moment, "I knew we had to pursue this."

It was his chance to change the ending of a story.

The Commodity Futures Trading Commission is housed in a modernist, low-rise redbrick building at 1155 Twenty-first Street Northwest, in the business district of the nation's capital. The entrance looks like a city shopping mall, and on the first floor, facing the street, is Port of Piraeus, a Greek deli playing traditional music. Inside the agency's glass entrance, an X-ray machine and security guards, standard for federal agencies, greet visitors. Unlike other agencies housed in massive edifices, only a modest brass plaque with the letters "CFTC" and the agency's crest graces the entrance.

Gensler arrived each morning from his home in Baltimore wearing the uniform of a banker. He opted for black leather shoes, either penny loafers or lace-ups, blue or white shirt, conservative red silk tie, dark blue or black suit. Gensler's strong jaw, balding pate, and large dark eyes suggested Euro-aristocratic portrait paintings. His office boasted the standard government-issue dark wood desk, blue-and-gold wing chair and sofas, along with photos of his children. His energetic, wiry frame and soft-spoken, professorial style of speaking made listeners lean in and feel included. He was fond of patting his receding hairline with a smile, exclaiming, "I have three daughters!"

At the time Gensler was sworn in as CFTC chair, a Washington veteran suggested he write down one main goal on a Post-it note and keep it in a drawer or on a mirror, a daily reminder of his term's four-year agenda. Gensler did exactly that, as he had derivatives—in particular, swaps trading—fixed squarely in his sights.

"Every day I took a look at that note and asked myself: 'Have I moved that area forward?' Because public service is often about doing the day-to-day that comes 'at' you—from Congress, the media, the rest of the president's administration," he recalled, sitting in his office's standard-issue wing chair.

Although Gensler's stated aim as the head of the CFTC was to bring transparency to the derivatives market, it was LIBOR that, like a storm cloud that never quite burst, hung over him as the questions about LIBOR's credibility remained unanswered. Gensler realized that LIBOR might be his chance to regulate derivatives: If he could prove wrongdoing by the banks rigging interest rates and related derivatives, the case could show once and for all that the CFTC had to start regulating the exotic securities.

LIBOR mattered to most Americans (even if they didn't know it) because so many people had mortgages marked to LIBOR—say, LIBOR plus 3 percent—as well as student loans, credit cards, and lots of things financial that had been marked up according to the rate. As Gensler saw it, for a bank to borrow at LIBOR "was kind of like walking into a jewelry store in the diamond district and paying wholesale."

When he asked Steve Obie to tell him more about LIBOR, Obie did so with alacrity.

"Well, actually, I'm glad you mentioned that," Obie said to Gensler. "We do have an open matter" on the wholesale rates between the banks. That was agency-speak to say that CFTC investigators had already been looking into it.

Gensler perked up. "Really? That's great! I'd be interested in getting a briefing."

Gensler, who had been chair for a matter of months, stood in the foyer to his ninth-floor office as Obie replayed the recording of a conversation between employees at Barclays. The drab offices were quiet, as Gensler's secretary, Deborah, wasn't there and most of the employees had already gone home.

"It was one of those eye-opening tapes where you go, 'What were people thinking?'" Gensler recalls.

Gensler looked at Obie. "Steve, this is bigger than any case that this agency has ever handled. And may be bigger than anything in the next ten or twenty years. It's two-thirds of our market. And there's manipulation right at the center of it!" Indeed, interest rate derivatives represented two-thirds of the contracts the CFTC had been entrusted to oversee for the American people. And it was widely suspected that the banks setting the number were falsely highballing and lowballing that wholesale rate at will.

In simple terms, the CFTC heard the following: Barclays—and possibly a dozen other international banks—had manipulated

LIBOR in three ways. First, it had changed its LIBOR submissions to benefit its own trading positions; second, it had kept its LIBOR number low in order to make itself look better and more creditworthy than it really was; and third, it had tried to induce other banks to change their LIBOR submissions as well.

Tom Hayes, Philippe Moryoussef, and others were far from the only traders rigging the LIBOR: Barclays employees on at least three continents had spent years lying in order to fix benchmark interest rates that help determine the value of about $10 trillion in global debt and $350 trillion in derivatives, mostly swap contracts.

The conversation gave momentum to the investigation. The CFTC sent letters to several banks requesting information. The commission decided it had the authority to act because LIBOR affected the price of commodities, including the futures contracts that traded on mercantile exchanges.

The CFTC's enforcement division can open and close investigations without the respective commissioners ever getting involved, much like the Securities and Exchange Commission or the Federal Trade Commission. There wasn't much to brief Gensler on at that point. Although McGonagle had opened the investigation in April 2008 after reading the piece in the *Journal*, the CFTC still didn't have much evidence even a year later. But then there was that tape.

While Gensler knew this investigation could represent a huge win for one of Washington's smallest regulatory agencies, he soon discovered he would also have to be patient.

One area of particular interest was the Eurodollar contract. Traded heavily on the Chicago Mercantile Exchange, it was the largest futures contract the CFTC oversaw. Traditionally, the agency had started out regulating agricultural contracts like corn and wheat, oil and gas, and precious metals like silver and gold. But the Eurodollar contract had become the largest, the most significant. And in the swaps market, which Gensler had started to work on with Congressman Barney Frank, the biggest contract was the interest rate swaps, pegged to EURIBOR, LIBOR, and other short-term interest rate benchmarks.

Even with a clear objective in sight, however, progress was slow. Every few weeks afterward, as 2010 gave way to early 2011, an impatient Gensler pestered Obie. "Why aren't we getting anything? This is significant," he demanded.

Gensler knew his agency had often wasted time in the past wrangling with the SEC over jurisdiction, and that was a consideration with LIBOR too. But with the passing of the Dodd-Frank Wall Street Reform and Consumer Protection Act of 2010, the CFTC finally had the authority to regulate commodities, futures, and, hopefully, the swaps markets.

Gensler also recognized the need for a powerful player with a prosecutorial instinct to head up the CFTC enforcement division in order to embrace its new, more aggressive regulatory role. He found his legal big gun in David Meister, a former assistant U.S. attorney for the Southern District of New York who had worked with the likes of SEC bigwigs Mary Jo White and Rob Khuzami. In January 2011, Meister joined the CFTC as head of enforcement, arriving from the law firm Skadden, Arps, Slate, Meagher & Flom, where he had been a partner in the firm's white-collar crime group. Gensler needed a "get," and Meister was his man.

During their initial meeting, Meister sat on the blue-and-gold couch across from Gensler. Gensler told him what they knew, told him about the interest rate rigging, and that Meister was "going to be the guy to bring it across the line."

Gensler didn't flinch on tackling senior executives at the banks. "We had to follow the facts of the law wherever it took us, even if it took us to senior levels of these banks. Even if it made it uncomfortable for particular central banks around the globe that might have heard about, known about, seen some of this stuff."

In the year leading up to the 2012 Barclays indictment, Gensler became anxious. He would sit with Obie or with staff attorney Gretchen Lowe and ask, "Why is this taking so long?"

Later, he would recall that there were "times I wanted to go out and give a speech" and let the world know about the shenanigans going on in LIBOR. "I felt like I was head of the police force for a small town, and you're not allowing me to go out and say, 'That part of town is not safe to walk in.' I would say to my press officer, 'You gotta let me give a speech.' They'd say, 'Not yet.'" Not until the CFTC had made its case.

Gensler now had a second bullet point on his Post-it note. It consisted of just one word: "LIBOR."

CHAPTER 8

Barclays and
Other Bad Banks

Sir Mervyn King said, testifying before the Treasury Select Committee, "[LIBOR] is in many ways the rate at which banks do not lend to each other." That was in late November 2008. The credit markets had seized up, and King offered this unhelpful gem.

"It is not clear," King continued, "that it either should or does have significant operational content. I think it is convenient, very often, for people to justify what they do for other reasons, in terms of LIBOR, but it is not a rate at which anyone is actually borrowing. It is hard to see how it can actually have much of an impact."

It wasn't exactly an admission. But King's words went far to explain the continuing permissive climate. It was true that LIBOR was a fiction, but what was he, the head of the British central bank, going to do about it?

Paul Tucker, King's deputy at the Bank of England, had tried to make up for his boss's arm's-length treatment of and disdain for City bankers by cultivating close relationships with top executives. Emails obtained by Labour MP John Mann under the Freedom of Information Act hint at a close relationship between Tucker and former Barclays chief executive Robert Diamond. Tucker's role couldn't be helped; he acted as bagman, doing King's dirty work, communicating with the bankers King despised.

One email, sent to Diamond in May 2008, confirms Tucker had talked to bosses at HSBC and RBS about LIBOR. Tucker wrote to Diamond, "Have spoken to hsbc and rbs, stuart and johnny. Sense similar across all three of you. I encouraged contact amongst Mark Dearlove peer group." Johnny Cameron was head of RBS's investment bank at the time, while Stuart Gulliver was chief executive of HSBC. Dearlove led the Barclays money market desk in 2008.

Then there was that fateful October 2008 phone call Tucker made to Bob Diamond. It would become the subject of parliamentary hearings and send all parties involved scurrying to explain themselves. What actually happened during that call from the Bank of England to Barclays? And why did Bob Diamond write himself and colleagues a note memorializing the conversation?

The three men involved each explained the communication in a way that absolved him from responsibility. Jerry del Missier, co-chief of Barclays Capital, was alleged to have passed an order to lower LIBOR. But Del Missier gave a different account from Diamond's as to how the bank came to lowball LIBOR borrowing submissions in October 2008. Del Missier's account of events also undermined Paul Tucker himself. Diamond's publication of the email that recorded that conversation with Tucker in October 2008, during which the central banker told him that the bank's LIBOR submissions "did not always need to be . . . as high," was widely seen as damaging to Tucker.

Though the email appeared damning, Diamond later told MPs he had not taken Tucker's comments—emailed to Del Missier—as an "instruction" to lower Barclays' LIBOR rates. But Del Missier contradicted Diamond, and later told Parliament that was exactly how the information was passed on to him.

"It was an instruction, yes," Del Missier told MPs. "It did seem an appropriate action given that it came from the Bank of England." He said the instruction had been clear and had come from Diamond in a phone conversation the day before he received the email.

Del Missier explained that he had "passed on the instruction as I received it" to the head of the Barclays money market desk, central to the bank's submission of its LIBOR borrowing rates. He denied that at the time he thought that submitting lowered LIBOR submissions was improper, and he resisted suggestions by MPs that it was also illegal.

Only later did he admit to British parliamentarians that the activity might have been improper. "It didn't strike me as improper in late October 2008. . . . At the time it seemed entirely appropriate. The Bank of England had the expertise."

All the men at the top of Barclays and the Bank of England explained away the LIBOR communication in a way that absolved each of them from responsibility. And everyone came out smiling.

Did Barclays deserve the harsh public rage it would face compared with some of the other banks?

At first, it seemed so. But as the months and years went by, Barclays benefited from the recognition that, though it was the first bank to admit to rigging interest rates, it was far from the last.

To Diamond's credit, he had turned Barclays around financially into what was considered by his employees a masterful profit-making machine. By 2011, Barclays was the sixth largest investment bank globally in terms of revenues from its sales, trading, and investment banking business, and fourth largest in terms of profitability. With the acquisition of Lehman's brokerage business in 2008, Barclays worldwide ranked fourth in fixed income, currencies, and commodities, seventh in investment banking, and ninth in equities.

In 1996, the year before Diamond became its chief executive, Barclays Capital had a balance sheet of £185 billion, split roughly equally between its investment bank BZW and the rest of the group. In 2011, that balance sheet had ballooned, reaching

£1.56 trillion, with the investment bank representing three-quarters of the total. Similarly, the investment bank made pretax profits of just £207 million in 1996, accounting for 9 percent of the company's overall profits of £1.85 billion, according to its annual report. By 2011, pretax profits at Barclays Capital had increased fourteenfold, to £2.97 billion.

Diamond and Del Missier, co-chief of Barclays Capital with Rich Ricci, further changed the shape of the British bank by adding the remnants of Lehman Brothers. Diamond, for his part, was considered the brains behind the operation, while Del Missier and Ricci were thought of by some at the bank as yes-men who traveled in Diamond's wake. "Most people in the bank never understood why Rich and Jerry got as far as they did. They weren't super smart or anything like that," said a former Barclays employee who worked directly with Diamond.

Lingering doubts would remain concerning Del Missier's role in the interest rate rigging scandal. After all, banks were making more money trading in derivatives such as swaps, rather than in traditional lending, and the possibility of making, say, $75,000 per basis point by moving the LIBOR or EURIBOR rates up or down meant more profit to the bank's bottom line. That had been Del Missier's specialty. "The guys making the money are on the swap desk, while the money market desk is just making submissions," said a former money market desk head. "The swap traders have the most to make by rigging rates; Del Missier was a former swaps trader. He was well aware of what goes on in that dark corner."

Behind Del Missier, Ricci, and Diamond—the three men

most renowned for building Barclays into a global powerhouse—
there were long-standing members of the executive team with
less public profiles. French national Eric Bommensath joined
Barclays from Bankers Trust in 1997 as head of derivatives. It's
unknown whether Bommensath knew anything directly about
the rigging, but by October 2008 he had risen to become the
global head of fixed income and a member of the bank's executive committee. He had overall responsibility for the Barclays
derivative counterparty risk management business, so it was on
his watch that the rigging took place.

Ritankar "Ronti" Pal, who oversaw desk trading starting in
2006 after a move from Citigroup, was also implicated in the
rigging, as was Jay V. Merchant. A former Chicago stockbroker,
Merchant had joined Barclays in London in 1998, hired to work
in a group led by Bommensath. Merchant arrived at a time when
the bank was in the early stages of expanding its investment division, including building out a derivatives desk overseen by Bommensath. Merchant moved to the New York interest rate trading
desk in 2006, according to employment records, where he super-
vised several junior traders who later came under scrutiny.

Working at various times on that New York desk was Harry
Harrison, a British banker in charge of dollar-denominated fixed-
income trading. Described as "joyless" and somewhat overbear-
ing, Harrison oversaw Ronti Pal as well as junior traders Alex
Pabon, Dong Kun Lee, and Ryan Reich. Reich, having joined
Barclays in 2006 two years after graduating from Princeton, was
a newbie, schooled by colleagues on how to seek a target LIBOR
to benefit the bank's positions in Eurodollar futures.

As emails from the Justice Department investigation would reveal, by the mid-2000s traders on the New York desk had grown entirely comfortable with the practice of moving interest rates around at will.

Although the majority of Barclays misconduct was believed to have occurred between 2006 and 2009, a report by the UK's Financial Services Authority asserted that efforts to manipulate the LIBOR rate could be dated back to 2005. Specifically, a June 2012 FSA communication details an email exchange between Barclays employees and a Barclays derivative trader from May 27, 2005.

SUBMITTER:

Hi All, Just as an FYI, I will be in noon'ish on Monday

[. . .]

TRADER B:

Noonish? Whos going to put my low fixings in? hehehe

SUBMITTER:

[. . . X or Y] will be here if you have any requests for the fixings.

In a March 2006 exchange, an unidentified trader at Barclays told a colleague he needed a "low" three-month dollar LIBOR "fix" for a position that totaled $8 billion, according to Justice Department and FSA documents. Barclays' trading position at the time was probably an aggregate of interest rate swaps and Eurodollar futures positions. After the colleague confirmed he would produce the requested LIBOR posting, the trader wrote back, "When I retire and write a book about this business your name will be in golden letters."

The colleague responded, "I would prefer this not be in any books!"

What happened to the traders as the LIBOR scandals gained momentum? Reich was fired in 2010 for emails that Barclays said were "inappropriate." Reich then found work as a portfolio manager at WCG Management, a hedge fund specializing in interest rate trading. Pabon resigned from Barclays.

Merchant left Barclays in December 2009 to run an interest rate desk at UBS's trading operation in Stamford, Connecticut. But he left UBS in 2012, around the time federal authorities were scrutinizing him for his work at Barclays. In April 2014, Merchant, together with Reich and Pabon, would face charges of conspiracy to defraud brought by British regulators.

Pal, the interest rate trading boss, was "discharged." Barclays found that he'd "engaged in a communication involving an inappropriate request relating to LIBOR" and that he'd failed to "properly supervise" a trading team making "inappropriate requests relating to LIBOR." This could not have been the outcome Caltech graduate Pal had in mind when he started out in the bond portfolio department of Salomon Brothers in New York in 1993. "I was bored with engineering," said Pal. "Also, the bottom line is it pays really well."

It's conceivable that the entire crew had no idea that what they were doing was illegal; the practice of sending emails to gather information on future LIBOR pricing had gone back to the 1990s at Barclays, long before those young traders joined the firm. "This was systemic at Barclays," one person told Reuters, after news of Reich's cooperation with U.S. federal investigators leaked out.

More likely, the manipulation of interest rates was business as usual. The bosses Harry Harrison and Eric Bommensath remained at Barclays.

Barclays also accepted requests from other banks to submit specific U.S. dollar and EURIBOR interest rates. In particular, traders were gaming the money markets, where mutual firms invest and buy and sell instruments for retail money market funds.

In December 2007, Mark Dearlove, head of Barclays' money market desk, told another executive, Jon Stone, he'd received complaints about the bank's submissions from an employee of J.P. Morgan Chase. In an instant message group among senior traders at banks including Barclays, Citigroup, and RBS, Dearlove wrote, "I don't know what you guys are playing at. We know you're paying 540, why are you setting LIBOR rates at 530?"

Dearlove told Stone that the Barclays submissions were "all wrong"; he appeared to be a somewhat innocent figure in the LIBOR scandal, as he wanted to escalate the rumors about rate rigging to executives above him. Stone was reluctant to move the word up the line, pointing out that all the other banks were submitting artificial LIBOR rates. "I guess the question is, is everybody else, what's happening with everybody else?" Stone replied.

Across the globe, Quan Hui Lee, a Barclays employee in Singapore, asked the bank's LIBOR submitters in London to enter lower rates in order to earn profit for an investment fund run by the bank.

Barclays' Lee emailed colleagues in London instructing them to "go get LIBOR down" and go "LOWER! Go for 3 percent."

Ian Pike, a Barclays employee in London who submitted rates, wrote back to Lee saying, "I'll do my best boss!"

Lee wanted to make a profit and avoid losses at his fund. His submitters followed his orders.

As for traders at other banks, they worked together, within their own companies and with traders outside.

A rates trader at an unnamed major bank in the UK wrote an anonymous account of his days manipulating LIBOR. At a briefing, he reported that a trader had said, "LIBOR was dislocated with itself." This became the standard phrase fed to clients to explain why LIBOR moved without explanation.

As he recalled to the *Telegraph* in 2012, "It sounded so nonsensical that, at first, it just confused everyone, and provoked a little laughter."

Soon, however, the phrase gained currency, not only within the bank but in talking with customers. "What I was explaining was that the bank was manipulating LIBOR," the trader remembered. "Only I didn't see it like that at the time."

Lowering or raising the price a few basis points per day was normal, in their shop and elsewhere. He understood it was generally accepted since there were perhaps two dozen people in the room when the "dislocation" was discussed. There was a sense of at least tacit approval.

"Looking back, I now feel ashamed by my naivety. Had I realized what was going on, I would have blown the whistle. But the openness alone suggested no collusion or secrecy."

Yet LIBOR's "dislocation," he came to understand, was done for good reason—namely, "to hide the true issues within the bank."

At the Royal Bank of Scotland, a broker sent an instant message to a trader reporting on his efforts to help the trader manipulate yen LIBOR in several tenors:

BROKER:

Alright okay, alright, no we've okay just confirming it. We've, so far we've spoke to [Contributing Bank 3]. We've spoke to a couple of people so we'll see where they come in alright. We've spoke, basically . . . basically we spoke to [Contributing Bank 3], [Contributing Bank 4], [Contributing Bank 5], who else did I speak to? [Contributing Bank 6]. There's a couple of other people that the boys have a spoke to but as a team we've basically said we want a bit lower so we'll see where they come in alright?

TRADER:

Cheers.

Todd Morakis was head of trading for emerging markets at RBS. According to allegations in the same suit, he "orally confirmed . . . that 'the practice of requesting to change the rate LIBOR is common in every rate setting environment in the banking industry.'"

Brent Davies was a sterling trader at RBS in London named in Canadian competition law officer Brian Elliott's May 18, 2011, affidavit as one of the traders believed to be involved in the manipulation of yen LIBOR. The intrepid Tom Hayes, then still at UBS, had explained to Davies who his contacts were. Hayes also communicated his trading positions and his desire for certain movement in yen LIBOR, and gave instructions for Davies's trader to get RBS to make yen LIBOR submissions consistent with Hayes's wishes. Davies acknowledged these communications and confirmed that he would follow through. Hayes and Davies also deliberately entered into transactions that aligned their trading interests in regards to yen LIBOR.

Will Hall was a derivatives trader at RBS in London. Hayes also communicated to Hall his trading positions, his desire for a certain movement in yen LIBOR, and instructions to get RBS to make yen LIBOR submissions consistent with his wishes. Hall agreed to do so.

On his last day at RBS in 2013, John Hourican, who was RBS's chief executive of markets and international banking during the financial crisis, issued a statement to his staff admitting to RBS's past LIBOR manipulations. "Although the attempts to influence LIBOR submissions started before I took this job, it continued whilst I was in charge of the division. The continuation of this behavior during the company's darkest hours, when so many of us were fighting to insure its survival, makes it all the more shameful."

At UBS, on August 9, 2007, the head of its asset and liability management group wrote to the manager of the derivatives trading desk that submitted the majority of UBS's LIBOR contributions, among others. "UBS should be submitting LIBORs 'on the low side' relative to other panel banks' submission. . . . It is highly advisable to err on the low side with fixings for the time being to protect our franchise in these sensitive markets. Fixing risk and [profit and loss] thereof is second priority for now."

The next day, UBS dropped its submission by 0.50 percent, or 50 basis points.

On April 9, 2008, UBS submitted a three-month U.S. dollar interest rate that was higher than what it had been paying in the market.

In an electronic chat the following day, a UBS derivatives trader in London stated to a senior manager, "if we are [issuing commercial paper] at 2.81% and that is 3m LIBOR +10 . . . why aren't we putting our 3m rate in at 2.81% for LIBORs[?]."

The senior manager responded, "we should," to which the trader replied, "but then [Group Treasury] will rip our boys a new one for being the highest bank in the poll."

In December 2010, a UBS manager instructed a submitter to

lie when interviewed by UBS attorneys during their investigation into the manipulation. As UBS acknowledged, the manager instructed the submitter to lie about the following: falsely claiming that the UBS yen trading desks did not have any derivative positions with exposure to yen LIBOR; avoiding mentioning the trader in question; falsely indicating that the yen LIBOR submission process did not take into account trading positions; claiming that they never moved the yen LIBOR submissions to benefit the yen trading desks; and claiming that when contributing yen LIBOR submissions, UBS tried to be "as close to the market as possible."

At the very top of UBS sat Marcel Ospel, chair, and Marcel Rohner, CEO. During a 2007 marketing trip to raise equity, Ospel and Rohner gave a presentation regarding the bank's financial state. Ospel was keen to highlight that "structured LIBOR" trading was one of the most profitable divisions at UBS.

In fact, LIBOR traders made millions for UBS in 2007. Ospel said later he didn't know who they were, but on the 2007 road show in London he had praised this division to potential investors. "We have long-established core strength . . . in our flow rates business, government and LIBOR, and in our structured LIBOR business." In 2012 Rohner would reverse himself and testify in front of Parliament that he had no idea how profitable the trade was for his bank.

In a June 18, 2008, electronic chat, UBS employees discussed why it was important for UBS to make submissions that matched those of the other LIBOR banks on the panel:

TRADER:

[A senior manager] wants us to get in line with the competition by Friday . . .

TRADER-SUBMITTER:

. . . if you are too low you get written about for being too low . . . if you are too high you get written about for being too high . . .

TRADER:

middle of the pack there is no issue . . .

Stewart Wiley was a derivatives trader with J.P. Morgan Chase. He too was named in the Canadian affidavit of May 18, 2011, as one of the traders believed to be involved in the manipulation of yen LIBOR. According to the affidavit, an external trader communicated his trading positions to Wiley, along with his desire for a certain movement in yen LIBOR and instructions to get J.P. Morgan Chase to make yen LIBOR submissions consistent with his wishes. Wiley agreed.

Paul Glands was another with whom Tom Hayes worked to manipulate yen LIBOR. Hayes communicated to Glands his trading positions, his desire for a certain movement in yen LIBOR, and instructions to get J.P. Morgan Chase to make yen LIBOR submissions consistent with his wishes; Glands agreed to do so.

J.P. Morgan had plenty of incentive to manipulate the interest rate derivatives market as the largest derivatives dealer in the

United States, one active in markets involving commodities, credit instruments, equities, foreign currencies, and interest rates. Four U.S. banks dominated the U.S. derivatives markets, of which the credit derivatives market is the third largest, representing about 6 percent of all derivatives activities, and J.P. Morgan Chase was the largest U.S. derivatives dealer in the credit markets. For instance, J.P. Morgan at one point had interest rate swaps with a notional value of $49.3 trillion—yes, trillion—and in 2009 the bank acknowledged that a difference of 1 percent (or 100 basis points) would be worth over $500 million to the bank.

According to a former employee, Deutsche Bank "painstakingly constructed a string of trades in hopes of profiting from small changes in various rates" and, as of September 30, 2008, calculated that it could gain or lose as much as €68 million for each basis point of change in the spread between LIBOR and other rates.

A former Federal Reserve examiner said the bets represented "extremely large risk" for Deutsche Bank. The same former employee, who provided documents, told regulators that some employees expressed concerns about the risks of Deutsche Bank's interest rate bets, but that Deutsche Bank officials dismissed those concerns because the bank could influence the rates on which they were betting.

Rabobank started out as a Dutch bank lending to farmers. By the end of the twentieth century, however, Rabobank was heavy into derivatives, and money market traders influenced the lender's submissions to benefit their positions linked to LIBOR.

When Rabobank's behavior became public, it revealed in a telling way how rates traders were colluding with one another, even when they worked at rival banks. Rabobank emerged as one of the worst offenders.

From May 2005 to January 2011, Rabobank traders made more than five hundred attempts to manipulate LIBOR. "Rabobank's misconduct is among the most serious we have identified on LIBOR," said Tracey McDermott, the head of enforcement at the UK's Financial Conduct Authority. "Traders and submitters treated LIBOR submissions as a potential way to make money, with no regard for the integrity of the market."

Thirty current and former employees of the Dutch lender were involved. It was such a common practice that Rabobank placed traders and LIBOR submitters in shared office space, so that requests to manipulate LIBOR could be made quickly and verbally.

On the morning of Monday, August 13, 2007, a U.S. dollar trader messaged a submitter:

TRADER:

High 3s and 6s pls today mate (esp 6mths!!) if u would be so kind. Gotta make money somehow!

SUBMITTER:

cool.

TRADER:

Cheers Every little helps!

That day, Rabobank's three-month U.S. dollar LIBOR submission went down 2 basis points.

On August 14, 2007, a senior Rabobank trader and his supervisor messaged another supervisor, who served as Rabobank's global head of liquidity and finance and who headed its money market desk in London.

TRADER:

any feeling for LIBORs today? specifically, 6mth.

SUBMITTER:

hi 1, 2, 3 month . . . 59, 56, 53.5 . . . 6 month 42, i think thats what [Trader 2] needs.

TRADER:

it's actually me that needs it, but thanks.

SUBMITTER:

ahh, taking all the credit!!

That day, as requested, Rabobank's six-month U.S. dollar LIBOR submission was 5.42, the highest submission of any bank on the contributor panel.

In an exchange on September 16, 2008, a trader wrote to the bank's backup U.S. dollar LIBOR submitter with the subject line: "I don't want to have a row about it but can't understand why you were such an arse this morning?" In the body of the message, the trader pasted the LIBOR submissions for eight banks, including Rabobank.

TRADER:

Before justifying from a cash perspective where the true rate should be etc, I, and you, know that if you were short of 1 month fixing you'd have put in a mid '60's LIBOR. P+L wise I couldn't give a fack but I just can't get my head around why you were being such an arse.

SUBMITTER:

Mate I had no intention to be or desire to be, I have no up-side upseting you or setting the LIBOR too high . . . i honestly thought and still do think 2.78 was fair, obviuosly from ur perspective nearer 2.70 would have helped and I apologise for that . . . i knew you trying to broke me to an extent, but as you know anything lower from me would only have helped by 1-2bp. . . . So I would rather we move on from this, and anything u need torn tell me again and ill try my best.

On October 18, 2010, a trader emailed a replacement as the yen LIBOR submitter.

TRADER:

Why did you put all the Yen LIBORs higher for today without telling me? Where is the team play? You know my position is? I cant believe you did this without telling me. If you had to put them higher for some reason but at least you could have told me in before hand. Im really fukked.

SUBMITTER:

I just saw your email and replied. I fukked up, you gave [the new backup yen LIBOR submitter] new LIBORs last week, didn't save the sheet and today I used my own computer for LIBORs. I fukked up, my mistake, not on perpose mate. I am really sorry. . . . And I would never change LIBORs without consulting you.

On October 20, 2010, another submitter started a conversation.

SUBMITTER:

so whats the reason that you dont put down Rabo JPY LIBOR numbers? just one tick to see what happens? Or is that sort of manipulation and not done? or am I saying something stupid now?

TRADER:

Rabo JPY LIBOR numbers are already one of the lowest four banks among 16 panel banks so even if we put them lower further, it wouldnt give any change on yen LIBOR.

SUBMITTER:

I see.

TRADER:

and i think just keep LIBORs one of the lowest four banks is the good, idea because it isnt obvious so that ppl wouldnt notice, if it is too obvious, ppl could start looking at us manipulating LIBORs.

All these chats and many more were released in October 2013 by the UK Financial Conduct Authority, which found that roughly thirty traders at Rabobank had been involved in rigging interest rates.

With the financial crisis in full swing in 2008, Tom Hayes was still influencing LIBOR and doing backdoor deals with banks such as Lehman Brothers. On June 25, 2008, ICAP's Darrell Read brokered a swap trade between Hayes on behalf of UBS and Lehman with a floating rate referencing the six-month yen LIBOR.

Hayes continued to rank among ICAP's most favored clients. On November 11, 2008, in an electronic chat, Read told Hayes, "Danny . . . will be your point of contact with the cash desk. he has the most influence over Colin and understands the importance of even small moves 'your way.'"

A week or so later, ICAP's Colin Goodman raised his "SUGGESTED LIBORS" for the six-month tenor by 0.11 percent from the previous day to 1.10 percent, but did not move his "SUGGESTED LIBORS" for any other tenor by more than 2 basis points. On that day, two other banks' yen LIBOR submissions increased by 11 basis points, mirroring Goodman's "SUGGESTED LIBORS." That moved the average in Hayes's favor.

On January 20, 2009, Read emailed another broker, "I hope Tom is not being too painful, he has had a storming start and is very happy with the LIBORs Colin and yourselves are managing to fudge for him (as long as he thinks you are trying!)"

In the spring of 2009 RBS agreed to do some fake trades with brokers—called "wash trades"—to generate fees that look like legitimate commissions. In fact, the wash trades were payback for helping to fix the LIBOR and EURIBOR rates. By September 2009 RBS was continuing to help more rigged yen trades, moving LIBOR up and down—like a "whore's drawers," as one RBS employee cracked.

Also in September 2009, ICAP made itself useful when Brent Davies joined the firm. He and Tom Hayes emailed each other to reduce the three-month yen LIBOR. The two men needed a favor from Paul White at RBS, Hayes's old firm, and in March 2010 they got one.

On March 3, 2010, Hayes wrote to a broker, "i really need a low 3m jpy LIBOR into the imm [International Monetary Market date]" and "any favours you can get with the due at [Bank C] would be much appreciated . . . even if he only move 3m down 1bp."

The broker wrote back, "i'll give him a nudge later, see what he can do," and then asked the submitter, "u see 3m jpy LIBOR going anywhere btween now and imm?" noting, "we have a mutual friend who'd love to see it go down, no chance at all?"

The submitter said, "haha TH by chance," and the broker responded, "shhh."

A month later, the CFTC requested RBS start an internal investigation of rate rigging, and by June 2011 RBS agreed to institute some cosmetic changes.

How much did the most senior management at banks including Barclays know about the deliberate misrepresentation in its LIBOR submissions between 2007 and 2009?

Let us set aside the attempts by the likes of Tom Hayes and the derivatives traders to cynically manipulate LIBOR for the benefit of their own trading positions between 2005 and 2008; Barclays has said that as soon as senior management found out about the rate rigging, they reported it to the authorities, and the statements by the FSA and CFTC gave no cause to disagree. Instead, let's look higher, into the communications of those who occupied the executive suites.

On October 13, 2008, the UK government released radical plans to pump billions of pounds of taxpayer money into three major banks, effectively nationalizing RBS, Lloyds TSB, and HBOS. A week later, on October 21 and 22, Paul Tucker and senior government official Sir Jeremy Heywood discussed why LIBOR in the UK was not falling as fast as in the United States despite government action.

Heywood also asked why Barclays' borrowing costs were so high.

"[There's] a lot of speculation in the market over what they are up to," he wrote in an email.

In subsequent evidence to the Treasury Select Committee, Tucker suggested widespread concern at this time that Barclays was "next in line" for emergency government help. Emails also show that Tucker was in regular contact with Bob Diamond.

On October 24, a Barclays employee told a New York Fed official in a telephone call that the LIBOR rate was "absolute rubbish."

On October 29, Paul Tucker and Bob Diamond spoke on the phone. It was the phone call that would change all their fates.

According to Diamond's account of the conversation, emailed to colleagues the next day, Tucker said senior Whitehall officials wanted to know why Barclays was "always at the top end of LIBOR pricing." (Tucker later confirmed that one of the "senior Whitehall figures" referred to in Diamond's now infamous memo was Sir Heywood, who at the time was principal private secretary to Labour prime minister Gordon Brown.)

Tucker said it "did not always need to be the case that we appeared as high as we have recently." Tucker later added that his words gave the "wrong impression" of their conversation and that he had not encouraged Barclays to manipulate its LIBOR submissions. However, following this discussion with the Bank of England, Barclays instructed LIBOR submitters to lower the rate to be "within the pack."

Diamond's detailed note about his conversation with Tucker is worth reading:

FROM: Diamond, Bob: Barclays Capital

SENT: 10/30/2008 14:19:54

TO: Varley, John: Barclays PLC

CC: del Missier, Jerry: Barclays Capital (NYK)

SUBJECT: File note: Bank of England call

Fyi

FILE NOTE: Call to RED from Paul Tucker, Bank of England

Date: 29th October 2008

Further to our last call, Mr Tucker reiterated that he had received calls from a number of senior figures within Whitehall to question why Barclays was always toward the top end of the LIBOR pricing. His response was "you have to pay what you have to pay." I asked if he could relay the reality, that not all banks were providing quotes at the levels that represented real transactions, his response "oh, that would be worse."

I explained again our market rate driven policy and that it had recently meant that we appeared in the top quartile and on occasion the top decile of the pricing. Equally I noted that we continued to see others in the market posting rates at levels that were not representative of where they would actually undertake business. This latter point has on occasion pushed us higher than would otherwise appear to be the case. In fact, we are not having to "pay up" for money at all.

Mr Tucker stated the level of calls he was received from Whitehall were "senior" and that while he was certain we did not need advice, that it did not always need to be the case that we appeared as high as we have recently.

R E D.

There are some other relevant facts. During October 2008, in the wake of the collapse of Lehman Brothers, when liquidity conditions had tightened acutely, Barclays raised its U.S. dollar LIBOR submissions more significantly than other panel members. In that month in particular, Barclays' U.S. dollar LIBOR submissions for three-month maturity were the highest or next highest of the panel on every single day of the month and were therefore excluded from the calculation of LIBOR. Barclays argued it did not understand why other banks were consistently posting lower submissions; Barclays firmly believed that the other panel members were not, in fact, funding at a lower cost than Barclays.

After the BBA circulated guidelines for all contributor banks on setting LIBOR rates in the same manner on November 2, Barclays made no changes to its systems to account for the BBA guidelines.

On November 17, 2008, the BBA issued a draft document about how LIBOR rates should be set and required banks to have their rate submission procedures audited as part of compliance. (The final paper would not be circulated until July 16, 2009.)

In December 2008, Barclays started to improve its systems and controls but ignored the BBA's guidelines. It wasn't until

2009 that the bank constructed a formal wall between the derivatives team and the submitters.

To the question of who knew what when at Barclays, British market expert William Wright discussed three possible scenarios in his blog post called "I Know Nothing. I'm from Barclays . . ." on July 4, 2012*:

#1: While Diamond, chief executive Varley, finance director Chris Lucas, and the Barclays board of directors denied any involvement in the bank's LIBOR submissions and claimed to be unaware of any deliberate manipulation, the CFTC disagreed.

The CFTC reported that in September 2007, senior managers in the Barclays group treasury directed LIBOR submitters to lower their rates. Furthermore, in 2008 Jerry del Missier had passed on the message to Mark Dearlove to artificially lower Barclays' LIBOR numbers, after claiming to have misunderstood a conversation between Bob Diamond and the Bank of England.

Barclays intention was to convince the public that the group treasury instructions in 2007 concerning LIBOR submissions were never addressed with the treasurer, and if they were, never discussed with Varley, Diamond, or Del Missier. Ironically, over a year later, Dearlove would get LIBOR submitters to bring down the bank's LIBOR numbers under the instruction of Del

---

* http://william-wright.com/2012/07/04/a-new-conspiracy-theory-at-barclays/three-scenarios

Missier. No one would acknowledge that this had already occurred in 2007.

No one brought this request to light with the group treasurer, Lucas, or Varley. Varley did not follow up on the memo to reduce LIBOR submissions and Del Missier did not tell Diamond that he in fact had reduced the submissions. At one point, in 2008, the money market team decided to bring Del Missier's instruction to Stephen Morse, the head of compliance. Morse did not address Del Missier's request.

As Wright further explains it, at no point did the instructions to adjust LIBOR come to the attention of treasury department senior managers. This would mean that despite all of the negative press and investigations concerning LIBOR at the bank, no word had reached the executive committee and it did not occur to most senior executives to keep tabs on what was happening with the Barclays submissions.

#2: Under this scenario, Barclays' treasury department might have discussed the decision to lower LIBOR rates with the finance director in September 2007, and Del Missier or Varley might have run the memo by Diamond. The head of compliance might have brought it to the attention of his senior managers.

If Varley showed his finance director the memo, both could have addressed it with Marcus Agius or with the executive committee.

Barclays would say that there is nothing in the reports by the FSA or CFTC to indicate that senior management knew what was going on. However, that is not the same thing as a confirmation by the regulators that the senior management actually didn't know what was happening.

If the first scenario were true, Barclays would have had to have exercised extremely careless management, contrary to its reputation and success. If the second scenario were true, then the higher-ups at Barclays would have been engaged in a cover-up, which would have even more serious implications.

#3: This scenario, William Wright's conspiracy theory, suggests that regulators were complicit in the LIBOR cover-up. Barclays claimed that regulators were not only aware of Del Missier's initial instruction to lower the LIBOR in 2007, but sat back and took no direct action against him. Barclays was aware of this lack of regulatory action over LIBOR, and regulators were wary of setting a precedent for other banks by settling too quickly with Barclays. As a result, they could have struck a deal for a speedy resolution, which did not require the resignation of senior executives, and therefore not attract public scrutiny.

As one member of Parliament would later say to Diamond: "You were either complicit, grossly negligent, or incompetent."

It's still not clear what really happened behind the scenes at Barclays. It stretches credibility to suggest that Barclays was trying to alert regulators to inconsistencies in the LIBOR submissions of other banks yet had no idea about the repeated lowballing of its own submissions during the financial crisis. Barclays would later admit its traders had been lying for years about LIBOR submissions, but the bank's explanation neglects to address who had been aware of the LIBOR manipulation and when.

———

Equally, the Bank of England turned a deaf ear. Given the importance of LIBOR submissions in assessing the banks' health, Bank of England staff were aware of the danger that banks might improperly manipulate their submissions. They noted, "Banks have been subject to the more powerful incentive of avoiding stigma from being seen to submit high rates reflective of what they are actually paying."

However, the staff primarily saw this as a matter for the regulator rather than the Bank of England—except there was no regulator for LIBOR. On November 15, 2007, the Bank of England called a meeting attended by executives from the contributing banks. Also in attendance was John Ewan, the BBA employee who managed LIBOR. He remembered that the members openly discussed that "LIBOR looked artificially low, signaling that banks might be understating their borrowing costs to mask their financial problems."

Tucker later told Parliament's investigative panel that possible clues to dishonesty "did not set alarm bells ringing at the time."

The evidence suggests that the Bank of England was aware of the incentive for banks to behave dishonestly, yet it did not think that dishonesty was occurring. Nor did it appear to have asked the Financial Services Authority to check to see whether such dishonesty was occurring. With hindsight this suggests extraordinary lack of curiosity on the part of the Bank of England.

After all, manipulation was not perpetrated by "a few rogue individuals" but was a "systemic problem," according to British banking regulator Martin Wheatley. For example, at Barclays "there was a web of traders that worked together to try to manipulate LIBOR to benefit one another," Wheatley added. Johnny Cameron characterized LIBOR suppression as "a cartel of people across a number of banks who felt they could fix it."

Rogues were not the problem. As the saying goes: Don't blame the players. Blame the game.

Robert E. Diamond was the first American CEO of Barclays, Britain's second largest bank by assets. Despite pushing the bank to record profitability, Diamond quit in 2012 after the UK institution was fined heavily for manipulating benchmark interest rates like the London Interbank Offered Rate, or LIBOR. *(AP Photo/Jin Lee)*

An American from Nebraska, Rich Ricci ran the corporate and investment bank divisions, known as Barclays Capital. An owner of a string of race horses, including one named Fat Cat in the Hat, the controversial bank boss received £44 million in pay in 2010. *(Rex Features via AP Images)*

Jerry del Missier, COO of Barclays, sent an email message to Diamond and then head of investment banking Rich Ricci in August 2007 hinting they knew the LIBOR rates weren't what they should be. Referring to "the whole LIBOR curve," Del Missier said, "the real story is that these are all fantasy rates." *(AP Photo/Sang Tan)*

Marcus Agius served as chairman of Barclays and of the trade body British Bankers' Association, which oversaw LIBOR. Rivals alleged Agius embroiled himself in a conflict of interest. *(Press Association via AP Images)*

As chairman of the CFTC, Gary Gensler sought to have swaps and other derivatives trade on public exchanges. When his investigators found evidence of LIBOR rate rigging, Gensler turned on Wall Street, where he'd worked, and extracted over $2 billion in fines. *(Bloomberg/Getty Images)*

At Gensler's invitation, David Meister joined the CFTC as director of enforcement and convinced the Department of Justice to go after Wall Street and the banks in the LIBOR cases. *(Daniel Rosenbaum/The New York Times/Redux)*

Golf pro Phil Mickelson signed a multiyear endorsement contract with Barclays in 2008; he was also a multimillionaire client of the bank and close personally with Bob Diamond, whom he said was made a "scapegoat" for the LIBOR scandal. *(Matthew Lewis/Getty Images)*

Bob Diamond's daughter, Nell, a socialite, sent out Twitter messages following her father's ouster: "16yrs building Barclays. Shame to see the mistakes of few tarnish the hard work of so many." *(Kirstin Sinclair/Getty Images)*

British central banker Sir Mervyn King and then New York Federal Reserve bank chief Timothy Geithner met in Switzerland at the height of the financial crisis to discuss strange moves in interest rates. Despite warnings, King denied knowing about outright manipulation. *(AP Photo/Charles Platiau/Pool)*

Academic and economist Rosa Abrantes-Metz read a pivotal 2008 LIBOR article in the *Wall Street Journal* and independently concluded there was widespread manipulation and collusion in interest rates.

British Bankers' Association chief executive Angela Knight defended its interest-rate-setting process during the crisis; the BBA ultimately lost control of LIBOR after the scandal. *(Press Association via AP Images)*

Deutsche Bank cochief executive Anshu Jain discussed a possible global settlement of alleged rigging of interbank lending rates with fellow CEOs at the World Economic Forum in Davos in 2013. *(AP Images/Mario Vedder/dapd)*

Piet Moerland resigned as head of Rabobank, which in 2013 entered into a deferred prosecution agreement with the Department of Justice as part of the LIBOR investigation. *(Bloomberg/Getty Images)*

John Mann, Labour minister of Parliament, released email correspondence between Paul Tucker of the Bank of England and Bob Diamond ahead of hearings that riveted the City of London.

The theft of segregated customer funds by MF Global, a brokerage overseen by Jon Corzine, former New Jersey governor, stained the CFTC. *(AP Photo/Charles Dharapak)*

Michael Spencer was former treasurer for the conservative Tory party. He also founded City brokerage ICAP, which was fined £54 million for fixing the LIBOR rate. *(Bloomberg/Getty Images)*

Trader Tom Hayes hopped from bank to bank as an interest rates trader, successfully making more money. "This goes much higher than me," Hayes said of the LIBOR scandal. *(Rex Features via AP Images)*

"The plan is hatched and sounds sensible," New Zealand's Darrell Read told trader Tom Hayes. Read and his coworkers at ICAP together worked to help traders profit from the rigging of interest rates. *(Bloomberg/Getty Images)*

Colin Goodman distributed a daily email to individuals outside of ICAP, including derivatives traders at banks and those responsible for providing the BBA with LIBOR submissions. Read and Wilkinson, along with Goodman himself, often referred to Goodman as "Lord LIBOR." *(AP Photo/Lefteris Pitarakis)*

Read's supervisor at ICAP was Daniel Wilkinson. The FBI said the trio of Read, Goodman, and Wilkinson would accommodate Hayes's trading positions and requests throughout the day. All three face U.S. charges, while some American traders are facing criminal charges in the UK. *(AP Photo/Matt Dunham)*

CHAPTER 9

Trials, Fines, Justice?

The investigations finally caught up to Robert Diamond. The U.S. Commodity Futures Trading Commission under Gary Gensler as well as the UK Financial Services Authority uncovered too many emails and accumulated too much evidence that Barclays had falsely submitted LIBOR rates. On June 27, 2012, Barclays reached a settlement with those agencies, agreeing to a fine of £290 million ($453 million), and in the following days Barclays chair Marcus Agius and CEO Robert Diamond resigned. The press and public slammed Barclays as representative of the cultural decay in the financial markets, a stain that threatened the Bank of England too.

One insider, writing anonymously in a July 7, 2012, exposé in the *Independent*, offered a revealing and more intimate view of the events that had unfolded over the past decade. "I worked at Barclays for a long time and to begin with it was run by people who cared about individuals."

As CEO, Diamond set policies that filtered down through the executive committee, and then managing directors and directors pushed through the firm. "All of this stuff ultimately comes from the top," the source added. "The way Barclays was run and the way it still is [is] through a culture of fear. You fear for your job and you fear for your bonus."

He went on:

"Barclays operates a culture of escalation. That is endemic. It is almost entombed in the culture of the bank. The purpose of that is that if something goes wrong it gets escalated up the line. I don't know how or why Diamond wasn't questioned more on that point. . . . [At] Barclays, if you don't escalate and it is found that out you haven't, it is grounds for disciplinary action. You will be dismissed."

Back in 2008, this anonymous trader noticed what was going on with LIBOR.

"We were informed on a weekly basis of the rates we were having to charge to clients and the rates at which Barclays was borrowing." But for the insider, after his years at Barclays, he remembered a larger, more intimidating picture.

The writer was also particularly baffled by the MPs' toothless response to Diamond's assertion that he'd found out what his traders were up to only weeks before being asked to testify in front of Parliament. "What I don't understand is why the [members of Parliament] didn't make more of that."

This brings us full circle, and the focus returns to Tom Hayes, who made his first—and much publicized—appearance in a UK courtroom after Diamond's settlement.

When he assumed his seat in the Southwark Crown Court, he sat in what was colloquially known as "the docks." Instead of a holding pen, the modern version of the docks is a glass-walled room constructed in the middle of the courtroom. Hayes wore his wedding ring (his wife did not attend) and bit his fingernails from time to time. A few seats to his left sat Terry Farr and Jim Gilmour, two brokers who had also pled not guilty to charges they had helped rig the interest rates as go-betweens for traders like Hayes. Both wore suits. All three men listened patiently with their arms crossed for most of the day's hearing.

Hayes had hired the best criminal defense lawyer in London, George Carter-Stephenson. A portly, dark-haired, bearded bear of a barrister, he had a reputation for getting high-profile offenders off. He represented famous football players, celebrities, and now bank traders, and was rumored to charge at least £10,000 a day. Like all the other high-level barristers in the court that day, Carter-Stephenson wore a black robe and an old-fashioned white wig woven of Irish horsehair turned into tight curls.

As the Southern District of New York is for Wall Street fraud cases, Southwark Crown Court is the venue for almost all the financial fraud legal proceedings tied to the City. Just across the

Thames from the court, the City is home to most all the major financial firms and some billion-dollar hedge funds. Not unlike Wall Street, the City teems with young men, and a few women, typically in dark suits, leather dress shoes and briefcases, and expense accounts. Most of them arrive at work via the appropriately named Bank station of the subway, emerging out of the dark whoosh of the London underground up onto the streets in front of the Bank of England and the old Royal Exchange, once an open-outcry trading house. It was that culture that created LIBOR and Tom Hayes.

In attendance at Hayes's hearing were some two dozen lawyers and seventy-five or so onlookers, including a ravenous press corps and friends of the defendants in the dock. High Court justice Jeremy Cooke presided, wearing a bright red robe and modern rimless eyeglasses. He too wore the obligatory wig.

The tone for the day, however, was set by the lead prosecutor for the Serious Fraud Office, who dropped a bombshell on the court: Hayes had given the names of at least twenty other people who had helped rig the LIBOR and EURIBOR rates, even though Hayes himself had traded only in yen LIBOR. But now Hayes had abruptly stopped cooperating with prosecutors.

"Your Lordship, he's admitted to conspiring with people across a range of institutions," the lead prosecutor said quietly. A ripple went around the court as everyone asked themselves who the others were and for whom they worked.

The mystery deepened when another wigged lawyer stood up. "His Lordship should know, I represent one of the other co-conspirators, but I can only refer to him as Mr. X." ("Mr. X" hadn't actually been named in a lawsuit by the authorities.) "My client is now in the position of having his name trammeled worldwide—please consider that!"

The attorneys and the crowd began chattering excitedly. Another wig leapt to his feet to counterargue to the judge: "The public has a right to know who was involved in the manipulation of LIBOR generally!"

Hayes had played his hand with the cool of an experienced gambler. As he'd done with LIBOR, Hayes was trading information, only now he was leaking names out slowly and setting tongues wagging about who else was involved. He looked to draw the focus away from him and his own role, naming others with whom he had conspired, all to gain an edge in his legal fight. Hayes would continue to portray himself as one among many traders and high-level bankers playing the rate-rigging game.

Hayes's imputations that his superiors were aware of his alleged tactics all along came with the implication that, when he jumped to Citigroup in late 2009, senior executives there signed off on a plan for the bank to join a Tokyo benchmark rate that Hayes and his boss soon allegedly tried to manipulate. The inside scoop Hayes could have given British investigators could have been top-shelf: Michael Pieri, Hayes's former boss at UBS in Tokyo, was one of the firm's highest-ranking executives. Pieri had once praised the trader's "strong connections with LIBOR setters in London," writing in an email that Hayes was "invaluable for the derivatives books." Among those to whom that email was addressed was Carsten Kengeter, then the head of UBS's non-core division

Hayes may have had more to offer. Former UBS assistant trader Mirhat Alykulov, a Kazakhstan native, had been cooperating with U.S. investigators. In 2011, he phoned Hayes from the Washington headquarters of the FBI, part of an effort to help U.S. prosecutors build a case against Hayes. British prosecutors argued Pieri and Alykulov had helped Hayes with his alleged attempts to rig the LIBOR by asking their UBS colleagues and others to tinker with LIBOR data to benefit their trading positions.

Christopher Cecere, who had been Hayes's boss at Citigroup in Tokyo, was also accused of trying to rig interest rates. Cecere resigned from Citigroup in 2010 at the same time Hayes was fired, then moved to the Geneva office of hedge fund Brevan Howard; he would leave in 2013. A dozen traders at major banks likely feared Hayes would allege that they had also manipulated rates.

A top executive at ICAP knew of an arrangement between the firm and UBS that regulators allege was part of a LIBOR-rigging plot. David Casterton, ICAP's head of global broking, was included in emails between ICAP and UBS as they negotiated a deal designed to reward brokers for helping in the alleged manipulation. Casterton, known to colleagues as "Clumpy," had signed off on a quarterly "fixing service" payment of about $27,000, a bonus of sorts that was spread around among several ICAP employees.

It was unlikely that Tom Hayes was going to simply embrace the role of scapegoat.

"This is just the tip of the iceberg," said MP John Mann at a meeting in his modest office at No. 1 Parliament Street the day after the Hayes revelations. Mann, an unapologetic Liberal in Britain's House of Commons and a self-proclaimed man of the people, didn't wear a tie or a jacket that day, instead opting for a blue button-down-collar shirt and dark suit pants.

Mann had long been successfully bashing capitalism in general and, in particular, the City of London bankers over rigging LIBOR and EURIBOR interest rates, as well as the sale of unnecessary insurance products to small businesses. As a key member of the Treasury Select Committee, Mann had spearheaded the original 2012 LIBOR investigation and hearings in which he grilled Barclays executives Bob Diamond, Jerry del Missier, and Marcus Agius, and Bank of England deputy governor Paul Tucker.

"Everyone was involved," Mann said. "Banks operate as oligarchies. They are competitive in some areas—like mergers and acquisitions—when it suits them. And they're uncompetitive"—colluding to keep profits flowing—when it suited them otherwise. "And the nature of oligarchs is they want more and more—as long as someone else has to lose."

Mann's office in Parliament faced southwest toward the massive white stone British treasury building on Parliament Square, where the Union Jack flies at nearly every official entrance. The rare London sun shone on his face when the clouds cleared as he continued to recount how he had gone after the City of

London's financial wizards and the traders who'd fiddled with LIBOR. Mann had personally called Bob Diamond and Mervyn King to hold them accountable for their failure to spot LIBOR rigging in hearings in front of Parliament.

"LIBOR is straight fraud. And when you create huge financial institutions, some of them will get their hands into other agendas," he added, going on to highlight HSBC's money laundering of drug cartel proceeds and Countrywide's exploitation of subprime mortgage borrowers.

Diamond's own words in 2011 had done him almost as much harm as his firm's behavior. He'd invited the disgust of the public when he remarked to the Treasury Select Committee that it was time for the period of "remorse" for bankers to be over.

He backtracked later. "What I wanted to say is banks need to be better citizens," he told Parliament. But those words came too late: He uttered them a day after being sacked from Barclays.

Diamond had become the "unacceptable face" of banking, in the words of MP Peter Mandelson. And after sixteen successful years, Diamond's era was finished off by LIBOR. More than a dozen banks globally would come under investigation by regulators in the United States, Europe, and Asia.

By 2012, Diamond had become perhaps the most hated man in Britain. The highlight of his Treasury Select Committee hearing was when Mann told Diamond in front of the packed house: "Either you were complicit, grossly negligent, or incompetent."

Diamond skipped a beat. Then he asked, "Is there a question?"

At his grilling in front of British lawmakers, Diamond

returned the politicians' fiery rhetoric, arguing that Barclays wasn't alone in the rate rigging, but that it was an "industry-wide" problem. For once, Diamond was right. Barclays pled guilty first, but UBS, RBS, Rabobank, and others would fall in line and pay billions in fines.

But British lawmakers weren't going to let Diamond off easily. MP Stewart Hosie spoke for the public at large, saying he struggled to understand how it could be that Barclays was raising questions with regulators about how other banks' LIBOR rates were odd without noticing that it was manipulating its own rates.

Mann compared the LIBOR rigging among traders around the world and their hedge fund clients to horse jockeys sharing race day "soft information" with their favorite bettors. "Tips from the jockey give you a better chance of winning."

On both sides of the Atlantic, LIBOR's manipulations drew close attention.

According to an analysis done by New York University scholar Rosa Abrantes-Metz, now with Global Economics Group, only two traders had to collude to move a LIBOR rate around significantly.

Andrew Verstein, now law professor at Wake Forest University, offered a corollary theory, concluding that only *one* trader could move interest rates. Verstein also saw the possibility that corruption was endemic to the system. "I wouldn't be surprised if more banks come out. But the fines they will pay [for rigging the rates] are seen by most bankers as akin to breaking the speed limit—and paying the ticket. It's really just a form of taxation."

Back in the UK, John Mann criticized the U.S. authorities for "only going after the minions and sending them to jail. It's always the drug pusher on the street who's easiest to arrest. Why not jail the dealer and the supplier?"

That said, he doubted senior management at the banks would be implicated or jailed, as they wouldn't have left a trail that could lead back to them. "There never would be a 'gotcha' moment. In the case of Co-op Bank, for instance, the former chief executive said for six years that capital at the bank was spread too thinly. But did he ever write it down? No. He wouldn't self-incriminate."

Instead, Mann chose to focus one step beyond the banks with the rate rigging, turning instead to the people asking for the rigging: namely, London's billion-dollar hedge funds. In particular, he wanted to take a look at Brevan Howard.

Did Mann have any last words on LIBOR and the banks?

"Read *The Prince* by Machiavelli," he said. "It's a manual on how to run a bank—political maneuvering and machinations."

In the States, Gary Gensler had spent his term at CFTC arguing that a tainted interest rate ought to be scrapped. How could the American public have confidence in their mortgages, in their student loans, if the rates were so easily rigged? "It misallocates capital and risk in our economy if it's not based on a real price in the market, between buyers and sellers competing," Gensler complained. "Then all sorts of things in our economy will be distorted."

He had been pursuing every lead.

By the time he appeared in front of Congress for his fiftieth—yes, *fiftieth*—hearing, in 2013, his patience was beginning to grow thin with the members of Congress who didn't even seem to know how to ask their questions. Some were reading questions verbatim from their smartphones under their desks, or taking dictation from their constituents.

Gensler spoke into the microphone, trying to sound conciliatory and educational but not patronizing: "A lot has changed since 1986," he said, pausing and thinking of his wife. "Reagan was president, we were in the midst of the Cold War, and I was dating the wonderful woman I would marry, Francesca.

"And now I have three wonderful daughters, but unfortunately, we lost Francesca. In life, one must adapt to change. Yet LIBOR—embedded in the wiring of our financial system—largely remains the same. This is why international regulators and market participants have begun to discuss transition."

During his LIBOR labors, Gensler met up with David Clark, who, along with Evan Galbraith, had been present at the creation of floating rates decades earlier. Clark had approached Gensler to offer a gentle reprimand after a conference. Gensler didn't have it quite right, Clark said. The LIBOR hadn't been in use since 1986; it had been in use much earlier, Clark explained.

"Everything worked all right for the past fifteen years," he also told Gensler. And LIBOR didn't need to be replaced; it needed to be reformed.

Gensler disagreed, and as the CFTC's regulatory scope was now international, his views were carrying more weight. And he was pondering how to address the transition: When a benchmark is not tied to real trades, it has become unreliable and obsolete.

"Without transactions, the situation is similar to trying to buy a house when your Realtor can't give you comparable transaction prices in the neighborhood—because no houses were sold in the neighborhood in years," Gensler offered. "Given what we know now, it's critical that we move to a more robust framework for financial benchmarks, particularly those for short-term variable interest rates. A reference rate has to be based on facts, not fiction."

Gensler sensed his next remarks would stun regulators across the oceans, so he spoke carefully. He might as well have been talking about recharting the stars.

"I recognize that moving on from LIBOR may be challenging. Today, LIBOR is the reference rate for 70 percent of the U.S. futures market, most of the swaps market, and nearly half of U.S. adjustable-rate mortgages. But as the financier and author Nassim Taleb suggested, it would be best not to accept that LIBOR or any benchmark is too big to replace."

Gensler had fans in Washington, and now he needed them. He had allies, but he also had enemies, particularly the big banks and Wall Street brokerage firms, which felt that he—long one of their own after working at Goldman Sachs for nearly two decades—had betrayed them.

In winter 2013, he stood on the sidelines at yet another

conference, a seemingly endless Capitol Hill circuit of academics, elected politicians, appointed bureaucrats and agency types, lobbyists, and Wall Street suits. He would be speaking to the IMF in Washington to explain how LIBOR had been manipulated during the great financial crisis. Years later it was still rigged, Gensler would point out, and clearly not working amid the Cyprus banking crisis.

More than ever, he saw, the banks just wanted to be left alone to "reform" LIBOR, but not replace it. Imagine the mess it would create, they and their lawyers argued. The millions of contracts with LIBOR embedded in them, the thousands of mortgages. Imagine the billions of dollars it might cost in damages!

For Gensler, this was irrelevant. Later, while in Florida for the 2013 Futures Industry Association conference, he would describe the industry's reliance on LIBOR as "fragile." LIBOR was yesterday's problem *and* tomorrow's.

Gensler then reminded his audience: "LIBOR—central to borrowing, lending, and hedging in our economy—has been readily and pervasively rigged."

Examining the European banks, Gensler showed that the misconduct took place over several years, in offices across multiple countries, and included several—even dozens of—people inside the banks, reaching into senior management. Problems with LIBOR clearly persisted, as publicly available data, such as for credit default swaps pricing, was at odds with LIBOR, which often stayed unchanged for days or even months.

"How is it that in 2012—if we look at the 252 submission days for three-month U.S. dollar LIBOR—the banks didn't change their rate 85 percent of the time?" Gensler asked, incredulous.

"When comparing LIBOR submissions to the same banks' credit default swaps spreads or to the broader markets' currency forward rates, why is there a continuing disconnect between LIBOR and what those other market rates tell us?"

In a different world, the CFTC and the SEC would have been combined into one agency. But so many politicians had a vested interest in keeping the agencies apart that it would never happen. No one in Congress wanted it. Gensler knew the adage about national politics better than anyone: No one gives up power in Washington.

After all, the CFTC was overseen by the House and Senate Agricultural Committees—except for the CFTC budget, which had to be approved by the House and Senate Appropriations Committees. Thus, the agency's overseers were entirely separate from those who approved the CFTC's funding.

Gensler was frustrated that while the swaps market had grown like an invasive species, the CFTC still had not been given full regulatory power to oversee them. And the LIBOR investigations were growing complicated.

Interestingly, while some lenders were harmed because borrowers paid too little interest as a result of LIBOR rigging, borrowers argued that they lost out because they paid too much. A retired San Francisco cable car driver had sued because the benchmark rate on his adjustable-rate mortgage was artificially low; therefore, he was stuck paying an inflated spread over the life of the loan. Annie Bell Adams, age sixty-five, was among the millions of Americans who had their homes repossessed as the U.S. housing market collapsed. Adams was one of the lead plaintiffs in a case pinning blame for higher mortgage payments on the alleged fiddling of LIBOR rates. Her case was the first one brought by an ordinary homeowner, according to her attorney, John Sharbrough.

An artificially high LIBOR also hikes monthly payments for borrowers with private student loans, says Mark Kantrowitz, founder of FinAid, a financial aid Web site. About half of private student loans are pegged to the LIBOR, he says, the rest to the prime rate and the ninety-day T-bill.

But the most outrageous part for Gensler was that LIBOR was still being set by an "honor" system. "Nobody refers to LIBOR because they want to enshrine (or even know) the exact procedure by which it's calculated; they refer to it because they want to get at the underlying concept and they'd rather leave to the BBA the mechanics of getting to that concept," wrote Matt Levine in the *New York Times*. "If BBA LIBOR once represented the unsecured borrowing costs of prime banks—or something else, like the risk-free rate"—and now it doesn't—"then that is a really good reason for contract users to be pissed off."

Gensler wanted to scrap LIBOR. Just get rid of it. But how?

The man Gensler had appointed to be head of the CFTC's Division of Enforcement, David Meister, had a friend at the

Department of Justice. Lanny Breuer and Meister played poker together but, more important, over the course of two years Meister and Breuer, head of the Justice Department's Criminal Division, had marshaled the forces of the DOJ and the CFTC to build the rate-rigging cases. They benefited from support from the new Dodd-Frank regulations, which broadened evidentiary standards for intent to defraud. Goaded by Gensler, they got results.

"Gensler succeeded in bringing home the bacon," explained Michael Greenberger, the University of Maryland law professor and former CFTC commissioner. "To him, manipulation is one of the worst things you can do in the derivatives market."

Not only did Gensler thus open the door on the problem, translating the misdeeds into legal wrongdoing, but his working alliance with the Department of Justice was new too. He prompted the DOJ, which under Eric Holder had for years turned a blind eye to subprime irregularities, to acknowledge that there was such compelling worldwide evidence that it could no longer sidestep the LIBOR case.

Not everyone found Gensler's efforts above criticism. The matter of MF Global would haunt Gensler throughout his tenure.

Jon Corzine joined MF Global as CEO in March 2010 with a plan to transform the firm from a futures broker into a major investment bank. Corzine had been Gensler's superior at Goldman Sachs before leaving Wall Street to run successfully for senator and then governor of New Jersey.

Corzine's strategy at MF Global involved making increasingly risky and larger investments with the firm's money. In the summer and fall of 2011, as MF Global's need for cash was rising and its sources of cash were diminishing, Corzine knew that his firm was relying more and more on proprietary funds that it held alongside customer funds in futures commission merchant (FCM) customer accounts. At some point Corzine made the call to dip into customer money—normally considered untouchable.

By October 2011, MF Global was on the brink of failure and in desperate need of cash to survive. As MF Global's treasurer told the CFO at that time, in one of many recorded phone calls obtained by the CFTC, the firm was "skating on the edge" without "much ice left." Corzine was warned about the firm's liquidity stresses, and he knew that the firm had violated its own policy designed to protect customer funds. The treasurer recommended in a recorded call, "We have to tell Jon that enough is enough. We need to take the keys away from him." Ultimately, massive customer losses resulted, with some $700 million of customer money at MF Global gone missing.

The fact that segregated customer funds, considered holy even by sleazy Wall Street standards, had disappeared under Corzine's watch would damage the credibility of the industry to such an extent that it was almost beyond repair. Since the CFTC was the agency charged with its oversight, MF Global's painful demise was also a black mark against Gensler; it didn't win Gensler any points when he ultimately recused himself from the MF Global case, a move that drew widespread criticism.

James Koutoulas, a hedge fund manager and MF Global customer, remained bitter about Gensler's decision to recuse himself from the investigation of that failed brokerage. "All of MF Global's executives should have been cuffed on day one," Koutoulas added. "The CFTC let the inmates stay in control of the asylum."

Koutoulas, who formed the Commodity Customer Coalition to advocate for the victims of the MF losses, argued that Gensler should have put as much effort into sorting out the mess at MF Global as he did in investigating LIBOR. Koutoulas was dismissive: "[Gensler] is a complete narcissist. He's climbing the rungs of power. He really wanted to be the [Treasury] secretary." Gensler's investigations into derivatives and LIBOR, Koutoulas said, "were all about making himself look good."

Ultimately, the CFTC charged Corzine in 2013, but the recused Gensler wouldn't share in the agency's victory. And the Department of Justice under Lanny Breuer brought no major criminal charges against any executives following the MF Global customer funds theft. (Breuer then resigned to work at Covington & Burling, which represented major banks as clients.)

"To play devil's advocate, he was damned if he did recuse himself and damned if he didn't," said Koutoulas. "But his recusal in effect recused that whole agency."

"The CFTC had some major problems under Gensler's watch," said James Gellert, founder of Rapid Ratings, one of the few independent credit ratings agencies that downgraded MF Global as a public entity. "It was a complete miss from a regulatory standpoint." Under Gensler's tenure, Peregrine, another futures brokerage, failed spectacularly after fudging financial statements for nearly two decades, Gellert pointed out.

Gellert testified in front of Congress regarding MF Global's bankruptcy on October 31, 2011. It was the fifth largest bankruptcy of a financial institution (following Lehman Brothers, Washington Mutual, CIT Group, and Conseco), and the eighth largest bankruptcy of any institution in American history.

Weaknesses in regulatory oversight hurt the CFTC most in the MF Global case. Before the firm's spectacular crash, the CFTC had conducted a review of MF Global's candidacy as a primary dealer, assessing audited financial reports and tax returns in an on-site visit. This clean bill of health led to a memo in January 2011 stating that MF Global "demonstrated a clear ability" to meet the New York Fed's standards, placing MF Global in very exclusive company.

Gellert's firm, on the other hand, downgraded MF Global long before its problems surfaced publicly—and long before the Big Three credit ratings agencies.

The summer of 2012 played out as a huge victory for Gary Gensler, with the resignation of Bob Diamond forced out as CEO over the CFTC-driven investigations into LIBOR. Top executives at Rabobank also were ousted.

More bank CEOs would soon be out of a job as a result of the American regulator's tough tactics, and Gensler was traveling all over the world preaching to anyone who would listen that LIBOR should be scrapped. It was a "fiction," he kept reiterating, based not on real trades but on guesstimates by bookies looking to rig the game and its outcome to their advantage.

By spring 2013, the City of London felt positively funereal during City Week, an international financial services event, as Gensler addressed financial types at the Mermaid conference center in Blackfriars, London. He gave a threatening speech at the April conference, noting that during 2012, a year upended by eurozone instability and war in the Middle East, the LIBOR mostly didn't budge.

"This was during a period when there were a number of uncertainties in the market driven by elections, changing economic outlook, and other events," Gensler scolded. "And yet somehow these banks said they could still borrow at exactly the same rate for four to five months," he added sarcastically. The price of money should have been moving around wildly to reflect uncertainty.

Continuing to support LIBOR and EURIBOR in the name of stability may have the opposite effect, he said. "Using benchmarks that threaten market integrity may create more instability in the long run," he intoned. "It's best that we not fall prey to accepting that LIBOR or any benchmark is 'too big to replace.'"

By the summer of 2013, Gensler was facing the end of his first term as chair of the commission. And he was under attack.

Gensler had earned himself a staggering list of enemies—anyone making money in derivatives up and down the East Coast, in Chicago, London, Tokyo, and especially Washington

D.C. In short, he made enemies by doing what he'd been hired to do: enforce Congress's Dodd-Frank regulations. The CFTC, once a sleepy agency best known for overseeing wheat, soy, and other agricultural futures, saw its powers vastly expanded after the credit collapse as a result of the Dodd-Frank legislation.

The problem was, no one knew what he was fighting for—even Gensler's own family. "My mom—she's eighty-six—still asks me, 'Gary, what's a swap?' "

During Gensler's tenure, banking and futures trading lobbyists logged literally over a thousand visits to the CFTC to plead for a delay in the July 12, 2013, deadline on bringing swaps trading out into the open and on exchanges, like stocks and bonds.

In one meeting in late June 2013, Gensler reminded them of his Wall Street ties. "Guys, I was one of you," he said. "But you're asking us to repeal Dodd-Frank. We're not going to do this."

He summoned into his office a pregnant employee whose due date happened to be July 12. "Tell everyone about that day," Gensler instructed the employee, pointing to her swollen belly. She grinned and answered, "No delay."

Just days prior to the big day, Gensler was called on the carpet by the Treasury secretary. Not his old pal Robert Rubin, nor Timothy Geithner, with whom he'd recently worked closely to help bring American finance back from the brink. No, this confrontation would be with Jacob Lew, President Obama's new Treasury secretary and a former Citigroup banker. Gensler would soon find he was not among friends.

Gensler was about to be subjected to the Brooksley Born treatment, the same rigmarole to which his predecessor had been subjected during her time as CFTC chief. She'd been steamrolled when she tried to regulate derivatives, shunned by colleagues, superiors, then even President Bill Clinton and Gensler himself.

Born had made a name for herself by taking an interest in regulating derivatives, in particular credit default swaps. Greenspan, Rubin and his then deputy Larry Summers, and SEC Chair Arthur Levitt pressed her repeatedly to back off, while Gensler himself had worked with Senator Phil Gramm and Greenspan to exempt credit default swaps from regulation.

When that failed, the "Rubinites," as they came to be known, performed an end run around Born, going to Congress to prohibit her from acting until "more senior regulators" decided what, if anything, to do. That helped precipitate Born's departure.

Twelve years later, Gensler seemed about to accomplish what Born had set out to do. Gensler was making Born's goal a reality by enforcing the new Dodd-Frank legislation and using the CFTC's new power to bring derivatives trading onto exchanges and out of the darkness.

But the Washington spin cycle was now overtaking Gensler. Rumors circulated over the summer that he was facing ouster for his tough position on swaps regulation, which came to a head during the international regulators' meetings starting June 20, 2013. Market watchdogs from Japan, Europe, and the United States regularly hobnobbed to figure out how to harmonize their rules on trading. By July, Gensler had both U.S. and foreign derivatives dealers up in arms about not extending certain exemptions under Dodd-Frank legislation past the July 12 deadline.

Instead, Gensler chose to wait until the last second to decide whether he would grant a delay. "The industry, not having taken the idea seriously that they might not get their way, was now trying every avenue open to them to force Gensler into line," noted Yves Smith, a blogger at NakedCapitalism.com.

The banking industry was pushing for a delay because it was scared that Gensler's powerful reforms might actually come into force. The Dodd-Frank provisions were more stringent than overseas requirements, so they went after Gensler directly, making him out to be a radical egoist acting unilaterally, as opposed to a detached technocrat simply implementing what Congress mandated.

Separately, Gensler faced varying degrees of resistance from three of his four fellow commissioners. International regulators were apparently also unhappy with Gensler's tough stand, to the point where they went over his head, complaining directly to Treasury Secretary Lew.

As Congress recessed for Independence Day, a meeting was quietly arranged between Gensler and Lew.

In financial centers around the world, bankers were howling like stuck pigs because derivatives continued to be a significant profit source. The *International Financing Review* gives an idea of the implications of Gensler's policies: Figures from the Treasury show that U.S. financial institutions reported derivatives trading revenues of $4.4 billion in the fourth quarter of 2012 alone, a 73 percent increase from the previous year.

Wall Street had been brought back from the brink, but the banks were still raking in profits through derivatives, the very instruments that had taken down AIG. But J.P. Morgan, Bank of America, Merrill Lynch, Citigroup, and Goldman Sachs had routed around 50 percent of their derivatives trades overseas, which would mean a sea change for their operations, not to mention their bottom lines, if the exemption was allowed to die.

"U.S. banks simply aren't ready to lose this exemption. It will cost them a considerable amount," whined one derivatives lawyer. "Even just the logistical challenge of reorganizing their trading business will be enormous, and they are likely to lose clients because of it."

Gensler stuck to his guns, again citing the massive taxpayer-funded bailout of AIG: "We Americans bailed them out because they were so interconnected. But eight million Americans lost their jobs, and that cost us six hundred dollars per U.S. citizen. AIG had a large swaps business run overseas. That nearly brought down our economy, so this debate ensured that our laws are not strictly territorial."

In short, Gensler was pushing for the application of U.S. regulations outside the United States. That's what got him into real trouble.

"Risk knows no boundary. If you're an overseas bank of a U.S. bank, you are covered by these reforms," said Gensler. "We have to recall the lessons of the crisis. So many U.S. banks came asunder because of offshore enterprises in the Caymans and elsewhere. If you're guaranteed back here by the mother ship in the U.S., then you need to be covered."

Gensler made the argument as he sat in Treasury Secretary Lew's conference room, with a view of the White House in the distance. The tone of the meeting quickly soured.

Lew became incensed. He insisted that Gensler coordinate better with the SEC, whose new chief, Mary Jo White, was also attending the meeting.

Gensler, already deep into negotiations with his European counterparts, was furious over Lew's demands to back off the overseas regulations. Complying with Lew would gut his whole plan. Gensler snapped. He'd been hearing the same line of reasoning from bank lobbyists aiming to stall the derivatives reform process, and he told the Treasury chief exactly what he thought. Gensler felt as if he were arguing with adversary bankers instead of the secretary of the U.S. Treasury, supposedly an advocate for the taxpayers.

Gensler subsequently apologized to Lew for the outburst. He also softened his rhetoric, cutting a deal with the European Union just one week later.

But having the U.S. Treasury secretary as his antagonist was not a good sign. Lew had suddenly emerged as a fifth column— one of those you think is on your side, dressed in your army colors, but turns out to be fighting for the enemy.

"Lew called him in and said the EU and the Japanese are angry with you and you need to cooperate," explained Michael Greenberger.

Lost in Gensler's stand-down was that he was trying to prevent another "London Whale," the catastrophe that occurred when one of J.P. Morgan trader's $6 billion loss nearly brought down the company in 2013.

"We asked American taxpayers to bail them out, so if U.S. companies make trades abroad, they should be controlled" by a U.S. agency, Greenberger explained. "Gary didn't get the support he needed," he added. "Lew didn't understand what Dodd-Frank was, that credit default swaps caused the crisis. The president didn't understand it either. They just threw [bailout] money at the problem. All they saw was that Gensler seemed to be acting out against our allies."

The Democrats in Congress didn't help either. In the Senate, they viewed him as a troublemaker. "They think Gensler's obstructive," Greenberger added.

Gensler did have a few remaining allies. One was his colorful co-commissioner Bart Chilton. With shocking long white blond hair swept back like Pink Floyd's Roger Waters, Chilton had a penchant for speaking his mind. And together with Gensler, he worked to hold the line against predatory large financial firms.

But their experience revealed how hard serious regulators had to weave and dodge against a well-financed industry just to do their job.

Chilton's quirky parting speech in November 2013 noted that the CFTC was "taking it to the limits one more time," echoing an Eagles song. This was in direct reference to the CFTC's announcement that same day of new, rewritten regulations to establish position limits on speculative commodity futures trading.

Gensler's three other commissioners, especially Mark Wetjen and Jill Sommers, clashed openly with him, saying they were frequently left out of his my-way-or-the-highway rule-making process. Sommers went so far as to fire off a furious email to CFTC staffer Ananda Radhakrishnan after Gensler proposed net capital rules for broker-dealers and futures merchants: "Was this something they worked out with you?" she wrote.

"Actually, Gary [Gensler] asked Jeff Sprecher." Sprecher was head of the Intercontinental Exchange Group, a market exchange that cleared billions of dollars in credit default swaps.

"Thanks," Sommers replied, with heavy sarcasm. "I love the way Gary doesn't even bother to tell the rest of us."

A week after his meeting with Secretary Lew, Gensler won a small victory. Roughly 80 percent of all derivatives would remain unregulated under myriad exemptions, but, as the *New York Times* opined, "Gary Gensler, the reform-minded chairman of the Commodity Futures Trading Commission, got the best deal he could." The commission had voted three to one to approve guidance on how new rules on derivatives would apply internationally, as required under the Dodd-Frank financial reform law.

But the *Times* also recognized the downside. "In the face of unified opposition to strong 'cross-border' regulation—from the big banks; their government allies in both the United States and Europe; and a swing-vote Democrat on the commission, Mark Wetjen—the deal falls short of what's needed to protect American taxpayers and the global economy from the calamitous effects of reckless bank trades."

Chilton called it "the most complicated" piece of Wall Street reform the agency had ever worked on. Massachusetts senator Elizabeth Warren criticized opponents of derivatives rules to foreign subsidiaries of U.S. banks, saying bankers were waiting for Gensler's term to end.

"I think it's a real mistake for commissioners to think they can run out the clock and hold tight until Gary Gensler's term expires. If they try and go in that direction there will be a lot less public support and a lot less credibility in their final product. . . . Three years after Dodd-Frank we can't just say, 'Never mind, guys.' After we spent all the time and energy putting into place real derivatives regulations, we can't just turn around and put into place a Pandora's box abroad."

Warren worried about reports that overseas regulators might "water down" cross-border provisions. "It could create dangerous loopholes in derivatives regulations. The key ones are whether they might roll back or pick apart the definition of guaranteed U.S. affiliates in a way that would escape U.S. regulations or roll back the definition of 'U.S. persons.' Both have the ability to create huge loopholes."

She went on to defend Gensler. "I think Gary is terrific. He really kept the public interest in the forefront. He has been careful and calm but inch by inch he moved this process toward safer and more transparent markets."

Incredibly, Gensler's admonitions to scrap the dirty benchmark that was LIBOR also faced pushback.

His agency made headlines with the joint CFTC-DOJ case

against the LIBOR riggings, and reaped billions of dollars in fines. But by the summer of 2013, the reform momentum had faded, forcing Gensler to backtrack on scrapping LIBOR altogether. Instead, he put forward the option of a real, trade-based benchmark.

Not only did Gensler reverse his earlier calls to scrap LIBOR, but he carefully pledged support for Britain's reforms on how benchmark interest rates would be set. Gensler had learned to play nice with regulators from allied countries; Secretary Lew had slapped his hand once and he didn't want it to happen again.

While Gensler had previously advocated using actual trades as the interest rate benchmark, now he was forced to call for change that would take considerably longer, if it happened at all. "I think it needs to be global," Gensler said from the sidelines of an International Swaps and Derivatives Association conference in September 2013. Translation: I can no longer do this on my own.

He offered a diplomatic solution. "The international community through the Financial Stability Board will find solutions. It doesn't mean that it will happen overnight," he added. "I don't think you can address reform just through governance of LIBOR."

But the Financial Stability Board, the regulatory arm of the Group of 20 leading economies, wasn't due to present a report on LIBOR reforms until June 2014.

And Gary Gensler would be long gone by then. Rumors were already swirling at the White House that President Obama wouldn't nominate him for a second term.

Gensler had faced challenges before. He had run nine marathons and climbed to the top of Mount Kilimanjaro in Africa with one of his daughters. But he had never faced anything like the concerted lobbying effort from U.S. and European bankers—and even the Treasury secretary of the United States—to make him back off reform.

It was a shame. The CFTC's annual budget totaled less than what some big Wall Street banks earn in a week. Yet his enforcement actions had brought in roughly $2 billion in fines, returned to the Treasury.

"Along with Department of Justice with regards to fines on some of these LIBOR cases, we in essence returned in one year the last eighteen years of our funding," Gensler estimated.

On October 1, 2013, Gensler sat alone in his office, phoning around Wall Street firms to monitor the long-awaited launch of electronic trading in swaps, his major goal aside from investigating LIBOR. Gensler didn't have company that day because the federal government had shut down and the "sequestration" budget cuts meant his staffers were furloughed. All the CFTC offices were dark, save his and those of a few key staffers.

In December 2013 he traveled to Penn's Wharton School to address the students. There Professor Steve Sherretta asked the alum, "You talked about a market of $400 trillion. Put that next to the entire U.S. economy, which is about $16 trillion. So it's a big number. Confronted with that, one has to ask, though: How can you possibly regulate something so big and sprawling?

What are some of the fundamental principles that you start out with when you do that? And how did you accomplish what you did?"

Gensler replied: "Here is a market that actually is twenty-five times the size of our economy—the notional amount. The risk is not quite that big. The fundamental principle—going back to basics—is that transparency matters. You can shift information from the few dealers to the broad public and that makes an economy work better. That is true whether it is in automobiles, where we now can go on the Internet and we can see the price of automobiles before we go into the dealership. And it's as true and important in these swaps. . . . AIG and others had fantastic accidents and they took out the bystanders. You could have been a pedestrian, so to speak, on the road and you could have been one of eight million that lost your job—having never heard of a credit default swap."

Sherretta pressed Gensler further about the CFTC's record billion-dollar fines. "Your agency was responsible for bringing in something like almost a billion dollars worth of funds—is that correct—over the last year or so?"

Gensler tried to be modest.

"We're a good investment to the American public because you need cops on the road. You need somebody looking. We're also a good investment, I would contend, to Wall Street, though they don't always agree with what we do. Their brand is wrapped up in the confidence in the markets. Could you imagine, would anybody come to the football games on Sundays if there were no referees? I mean, for a week or two it might be interesting.

But after that it would not. We need referees to ensure that people have confidence in the markets."

Again and again, Gensler shouted from the rooftops to anyone who would listen about how AIG got America into a financial mess and how his reforms would stop that from happening again. "AIG nearly brought down the U.S. economy through its guaranteed affiliate operating under a French bank license in London," he told the Washington D.C. bar association in late 2013.

At the same event, Gensler said, "Lehman Brothers had 3,300 legal entities when it failed. Its main overseas affiliate was guaranteed here in the United States, and it had 130,000 outstanding swap transactions."

But by the end of his term in December 2013, Gensler was giving exit interviews all over town; he was on his way out.

By mid-November President Obama had settled on a successor to head up the CFTC, choosing an under-the-radar Treasury official named Timothy Massad.

Early in his career at law firm Cravath, Swaine & Moore in the 1980s, Massad was involved with the swaps industry's original efforts to write legal documents standardizing these complex contracts. As a senior associate at the firm, he had steered the project, according to former Cravath colleague Dan Cunningham. The agreements and contracts were part of the early documents used by the International Swaps and Derivatives Association, one of the many lobbyist groups that regularly filed into the CFTC offices looking to fight the swaps reforms.

During the financial crisis, Massad worked briefly on a congressional oversight panel for the Troubled Asset Relief Program to help rescue Wall Street. The TARP, which he later oversaw at Treasury, inspired a fierce backlash.

"Nobody ever wants to see TARP repeated. But the fact is, TARP is a program that did its job," Massad told the Brookings Institution in September 2013. "It has worked faster, better, and cheaper than most people ever thought possible." As of November 8, 2013, $421.54 billion had been disbursed under the TARP, while $406.48 billion had been repaid, according to the Treasury.

Massad "was a loyal soldier in Timothy Geithner's administration. Before that, he was a white-shoe corporate lawyer with banks as clients. He worked on the first standards for derivatives for the industry trade group," Jesse Eisinger wrote in the *New York Times*. "Yet he also spent his early years working for both the AFL-CIO and Ralph Nader. Those gigs are expurgated from his Treasury biography, which shows how little Establishment Washington values such experience," Eisinger added.

The CFTC under Massad would now be responsible for writing many of the rules under the 2010 financial reform law, including the contentious "Volcker Rule" that banned banks from making speculative bets with their own money. The Dodd-Frank reform law had vastly increased the agency's responsibilities, leading Gensler to complain to Congress on dozens of occasions that the CFTC's budget was inadequate to implement the law and oversee the massive futures and swaps market.

On his way out the door, Gensler made clear that, given the

CFTC's shortage of resources, he had grave doubts that the agency could implement the Volcker Rule. Speaking at the Futures Industry Association twenty-ninth annual meeting, Gensler said, "At this stage, I'm not confident that the CFTC can effectively enforce this whole package of reforms." The task would involve supervising "about ninety swap dealers, eighteen swap execution facilities, the three swap data repositories, none of which we had any regulatory responsibility for even two years ago," he went on. "All these new responsibilities, and we don't have new staff, new technology."

Gensler had punished Wall Streeters for their financial crimes, but he had been deemed too aggressive by the Obama administration and too much in a hurry by European regulators.

He had also been notably unwilling to maintain the politically necessary facade that the world's most important number should remain in use.

CHAPTER 10

The Victims

Britain's Guardian Care Homes, an operator of nursing homes for the elderly, claimed to have lost millions of pounds from its interest rate deal with the banks. In April 2012, its owner sued Barclays over an interest rate swap deal linked to the LIBOR, saying the company wouldn't have agreed if it had known the benchmark was being rigged. An appeal by Barclays against the LIBOR claims was heard alongside a similar swap case against Deutsche Bank brought by an Indian client, property developer Unitech.

"My swaps have cost me £12 million, so the suggestion that these allegations are irrelevant is fanciful," Gary Hartland, Guardian Care Homes CEO, told the British press.

Guardian sought to tear up the swap deals. Barclays argued Guardian owed £70 million and said the LIBOR claims had no merit. Guardian and Unitech essentially argued the banks had breached a fundamental implied term of the interest rate agreement so that the customer was certain to lose out.

Lawyers for Guardian Care Homes contended Barclays executives, including Diamond, Del Missier, Lucas, and Stone, knew what was happening at the lower trading levels of the bank. And they had evidence to back up their assertions.

"Mr. Lucas doesn't want us to be outside the top end. And apparently they chatted on the whole of the thirty-first floor [the boardroom location]," treasury manager Miles Storey had said to former rate submitter Peter Johnson, according to records from November 2007.

"Mark had a talk with Jon Stone on the phone saying, oh what are you doing with LIBORs? Ya know you're going over the market again. And he said, well that's where they are, in fact they're probably not high enough," said Johnson to two LIBOR submitters in November 2007.

The plaintiffs also cited a damning email from the British Bankers' Association that had been circulated to Varley, Lucas, and Diamond in 2008. It asked them "to do what is necessary within your organization to effect appropriate rates to be set." To the LIBOR watchers in the courtroom, it all began to sound terribly familiar.

Barclays settled with Guardian in the spring of 2014 before a trial could begin.

Similar scenarios would play out over and over, with other businesses and municipalities in both the UK and the United States. But weren't the consumers of these swaps just as guilty for engaging in deals they didn't understand? Weren't they gamblers too?

Perhaps, but in the eyes of the courts, the banks' rigging of the interest rate underlying the deals they struck complicated matters. By way of analogy, someone betting on a horse race is entitled to assume that his or her bookmaker will not fix the outcome.

Large Wall Street banks, including J.P. Morgan and Citigroup, had promoted swaps to government entities, such as municipalities, school districts, and transportation authorities, in cities including San Francisco, Washington D.C., Boston, Chicago, Detroit, and New York City. Baltimore, Houston, Oakland, and Philadelphia would claim they lost out from the rigging of LIBOR, and all of them decided to sue to get out of interest rate deals tied to the scandalized benchmark.

But why did they do the swaps deals in the first place? What were towns and municipalities thinking when they allowed Wall Street to sell them these complicated side bets on interest rates? The thought process in Philadelphia is informative.

The city of Philadelphia took advantage of a 2003 state law approved by then Democratic governor Ed Rendell and Republican legislative leaders. The city agreed to swap interest rate risk on several kinds of borrowings with J.P. Morgan, Goldman Sachs, Wells Fargo, Royal Bank of Canada, Barclays, Wachovia, Merrill Lynch, and Citigroup. These included LIBOR-based swaps contracts.

Rob Dubow, Philadelphia's finance director, worked closely with city treasurer Nancy Winkler, who herself had been a financial consultant to numerous local governments before working for the city. For years, Dubow would defend the use of swaps, insisting that he and Winkler employed "financial professionals" in the structuring of these deals for the city. As officials led their hometown into a financial nightmare, a typical justification was: "We know how to do them and know how to structure them appropriately."

Like any other municipal borrower, Philadelphia issues bonds, and usually pays a fixed interest rate on them. Instead of just sticking with a plain-vanilla loan, officials like Dubow and Winkler decided it would be a good idea to make a side bet on interest rates, entering into a swap with a bank. The city then would pay a floating (presumably decreasing) rate in exchange for a fixed rate from a bank, which would then take the opposite side of the bet, namely that rates would go up. Much as a homeowner would pay a fee to change his or her fixed monthly payment to an adjustable-rate mortgage payment, so would the city. Except instead of just one fee, the city had to pay every month. The swaps were supposed to give the city lower borrowing costs in the near term, plus protection from rising interest rates longer term.

There were some skeptics. "Really?" asked John Coumarianos of Hamilton Research and Management, an investment advisory firm in Northvale, New Jersey. "Philadelphia has hired expert forecasters in interest rate movements? Is the purpose of city government, previously thought to be to educate kids, keep the streets clean and safe, and make buses run on time, now to engage in high finance and interest rate forecasting? Do the taxpayers know that's what they've bargained for?"

Coumarianos thought the Philly folks were completely out of their depth, despite Dubow's insistence that they were "sophisticated." Not sophisticated enough, however. "It becomes difficult to blame Wall Street. They're trying to make a buck," Coumarianos added. "The inability of municipal officials to see how far out of their league they are is really what's staggering."

Once the financial crisis of 2008 hit, the Federal Reserve cut rates in the United States down to near zero and other central banks followed. This was disaster for investors in swaps deals— it meant that Philadelphia, along with everyone else who'd been enticed into swaps deals, was suddenly on the wrong side of the bets they had made with the banks. Philadelphia was suddenly losing money on a bet with a bank on a sum of money not related to the city's actual borrowings. Its side bet, made purely on the direction of interest rates, began losing millions.

How much did Philadelphia lose? City officials were initially vague.

Joe DiStefano of the *Philadelphia Inquirer* later reported that the Pennsylvania Budget and Policy Center had estimated that Philadelphia's swaps losses approached $500 million.

By 2013, the city of Philadelphia decided to sue, having already paid tens of millions of dollars in so-called termination fees to get out of the swaps: $15 million each to J.P. Morgan, Wells Fargo, and Merrill Lynch, along with a whopping $48 million to Citigroup.

Dubow and Winkler, who had consistently sided with Wall Street until the summer of 2013, changed their tune. Because LIBOR was artificially low, payments to the city by the banks were lower than they should have been, the lawsuit alleged. "The systematic suppression of LIBOR, as our attorneys have uncovered, caused financial harm to the City of Philadelphia," Dubow said in a press release.

In the end, the banks got a bailout. All but one of the financial institutions that had engaged in swaps with Philadelphia received more than $160 billion in bailout funds through the TARP.

So where was the bailout for the cities and school districts that had cut these swaps agreements? Peter Shapiro, managing director of Swap Financial Group in South Orange, New Jersey, said Philadelphia's prospects for compensation were good. The city was "receiving a rate that was manipulated lower by what appears to be conspiratorial behavior by a group of banks. They should be paid back what they should have been paid in the first place," Shapiro said.

Elsewhere in the state of Pennsylvania, critics like state auditor general Jack Wagner insisted taxpayer-funded entities had no business doing such complex transactions. But that didn't stop the school district in Bethlehem, a former steel town beset by poverty. Wagner warned that for the borrowers in swaps transactions, the expertise is always on the other side of the table.

"The majority of the time, the winners are the investment bankers and financial service firms," he said. "They never lose."

Judith Dexter remembers the "sharp" financial professionals who sold the Bethlehem Area School District (BASD) on the idea of swap transactions. She trusted their expertise. "We were basically sitting ducks," said Dexter, a former school director.

The risk and exposure of swap transactions, Dexter explained, were not made clear. "We thought we were making better deals for the school district, and most importantly, we did not understand the level of risk there was in the transactions. And I don't think most of these municipalities do."

Cash payments up front were what school districts, water utilities, and other municipal bond borrowers got from banks in exchange for doing swaps deals. But Lucien Calhoun of financial firm Calhoun Baker dubbed deals like the one in Bethlehem "train wreck" swap transactions. Banks that are counterparties to the swap often pay middlemen advisers who shop it around to the cities and schools. "Anytime a counterparty pays the adviser, it creates a conflict of interest," he said.

Dexter recalled that a seemingly "independent adviser" representing the school district also represented another party in the swaps deal. "This was not known to BASD board members when the transaction was discussed."

Dexter said the board was told transactions would generate up-front cash and promised long-term financial management. Then came the financial crash of 2008. For one week, managing one particular swap deal cost the school district $61,000; twenty-one days later, it cost $152,000.

Eventually the school district dug itself out of a negative balance after about $23 million in fees. To do it, the district had to pass several property tax increases, between 2008 and 2011, that went as high as 6 percent.

This scene would be repeated over and over in other cities across America.

A 2012 audit of the Southeastern Pennsylvania Transportation Authority (SEPTA), Philadelphia's public transport system, concluded that swaps had cost taxpayers and transit fare payers $41 million more than if SEPTA had financed debt in 1999 with conventional fixed-rate bonds. The Delaware River Port Authority collected $45 million in up-front payments on swaps in 2000 and 2001, but later paid out $101 million in termination fees.

Philadelphia councilman James Kenney fumed at the banks. "When their bad behavior creates a crisis—that they benefit from—and the taxpayer bails them out, and we're still paying . . . am I supposed to believe it's our bad?" he asked. "That reminds me of the scarecrow pointing in different directions," Kenney added. "But we're still the ones on the hook."

The Massachusetts Bay Transportation Authority, operator of the Boston subway, or T, was an early adopter, long involved in purchasing interest rate swaps to hedge against a rise in rates.

In 2008, the Massachusetts auditor found that, from July 2000 through December 2005 alone, the T had actually increased its debt service costs by $55 million through a number of harmful swaps deals. In other words, the T was losing money on these deals *even before* the economic crisis hit. Since then the T has lost hundreds of millions more. Meanwhile, the riders who can least afford it have been forced to pay for these deals with fare hikes.

As of 2012, the T was losing about $26 million a year on five toxic swaps still outstanding with Deutsche Bank, J.P. Morgan Chase, and UBS. Over the next two decades it could lose another $254 million on these swaps. Meanwhile, it expects to get back $12.6 million—about half of what it's paying to the banks each year—by hiking fares up to 150 percent on riders with disabilities. In other words, half of the T's payments on these toxic swaps deals would be enough to reverse the fare hikes.

In New York City, the Metropolitan Transportation Authority (MTA) has active interest rate swaps with J.P. Morgan Chase, Citigroup, UBS, AIG, Morgan Stanley, BNP Paribas, and Ambac that cost the MTA $113.9 million annually. As of August 2011, the MTA had lost $658 million on these swaps deals since they first went into effect. These payments contributed to the drag on the MTA's budget, which in 2010 led it to lay off more than a thousand MTA workers.

New York subway riders were forced to pay a 7.5 percent fare increase in 2011 and 2013 and they face another in 2015. More than a third of New York area riders make less than $25,000 a year, even though they live in one of the most expensive cities in the world. Ironically, many Wall Street bankers are themselves MTA riders who take the subway to work every day.

The truth was more nuanced than just bankers putting the hard sell on gullible public officials. In fact, consultants had buzzed around like vultures, highlighting the up-front millions the cities and schools would receive in a swap deal.

In Sacramento County, California, a county lawsuit would allege harm in two ways: When the banks conspired to raise LIBOR, the county paid more when it borrowed money; and when the banks worked in concert to drive LIBOR down, the county was robbed of profit.

In Mendocino County, California, the city's total investment pool ranged from $150 million to $220 million, and about 70 percent of that was tied up in LIBOR-related investments. Many of those investments were made on behalf of school districts.

As other towns and cities across the country rallied together, Wall Street had some success in fighting off LIBOR-related lawsuits. In March 2013, federal judge Naomi Buchwald in New York tossed out most of a class-action suit filed by bondholders, the city of Baltimore, and others. Nevertheless, Sacramento County and other California agencies argued they stood on solid legal ground. "We can't be scared away because the New York judge took such a hard-line, narrow approach," said Nanci Nishimura of Cotchett, Pitre & McCarthy, a law firm representing various California government agencies and counties in the fight.

Moreover, the New York legal opinion conflicted directly with what European regulators said was a widespread "cartel" on interest rates.

Joaquín Almunia, vice president of the European Commission in charge of competition policy, explained, "What is shocking about the LIBOR and EURIBOR scandals is not only the manipulation of benchmarks, which is being tackled by financial regulators worldwide, but also the collusion between banks who are supposed to be competing with each other. The Commission is determined to fight and sanction these cartels in the financial sector. Healthy competition and transparency are crucial for financial markets to work properly, at the service of the real economy rather than the interests of a few."

But government officials in some cities accepted bribes as well. J.P. Morgan Chase employee Charles LeCroy had famously said the "key to landing bond deals in Jefferson County, Alabama, was finding out whom to pay off." The entire county was subsequently forced to file bankruptcy because of the J.P. Morgan Chase swap deal, which also resulted in local officials going to jail and the bank paying $722 million in fines.

In Oakland, California, the city council in July 2012 voted unanimously to end a contract with a Goldman Sachs interest rate swap. Protesters from the Oakland Coalition to Stop Goldman Sachs showed up outside the San Francisco office with placards bleating, "Stop the swap!"

"They got bailed out! We got sold out!" the protesters chanted. One protester wore a paper top hat labeled "Mr. Blank Check" and ripped up paper dollars for libraries, firefighters, and city parks.

The über-liberal Oakland had signed the deal with Goldman Sachs in 1998 on the premise it would reduce the costs of its bonds as interest rates were expected to rise. But, again, after the Fed cut interest rates to near zero, Goldman's rate dropped to 0.15 percent, even as it continued to require Oakland to pay a rate of almost 6 percent. The city paid Goldman $3.8 million in 2012 and $16.6 million total from 2008 through 2011. Oakland owed $3.3 million in 2013 and owes $10.7 million total from 2014 through 2021.

Oakland's local Occupy Wall Street movement banded together with city workers and community leaders, warning they wouldn't do business with Goldman Sachs unless they canceled the LIBOR-based swaps contract. Even religious leaders warned against doing business with banks caught up in the LIBOR scandal. At a city council meeting Reverend Daniel Buford, a minister from Allen Temple Baptist Church, said, "You should be concerned about the legality of doing business with a corporation that is being investigated by the FBI, that is being investigated by the Securities and Exchange Commission, and is the subject of at least four different class-action suits filed in United States courts against banks, including Barclays, over the issue of LIBOR fixing."

The reverend had evidently educated himself on LIBOR.

"As we're having this meeting here in the United States, the banks that have conspired to create the LIBOR rate are in turmoil. Check the international headlines right now about what's going on in Britain with Barclays and fifteen other banks, including Goldman Sachs. The flaw in the system is that banks can estimate their own LIBOR rates. You, as the city of Oakland, we, as the city of Oakland, have bought into a synthetic rate that was concocted by LIBOR people who were betting on your failure."

The city ultimately voted to stop doing business with Goldman Sachs unless they ended the swaps contract. As of early 2014, Oakland was still discussing a "debarment" of Goldman Sachs from bidding on any city contracts.

Still, some council members admitted that Goldman Sachs had no duty to tear up the swaps contract simply because it ended up going poorly for Oakland. "The swap deal the city entered into . . . is a legal, enforceable contract," council member Pat Kernighan said. "It is a bad deal, but it's a deal that the city went into with its eyes open. As much as I would like to get out of it, I don't think we have the legal grounds," she told *New York* magazine.

Council member Libby Schaaf opposed kicking Goldman out of town. "We gambled. We lost. That happens all the time, and we have to be grown-up about it."

Of course, what borrowers didn't know was that the interest rate was rigged. Schaaf pointed out that Oakland was at the same time suing roughly twenty other financial institutions over LIBOR.

Why were the banks so intent on selling these interest rate bets to municipalities? Generally, the banks made five times more money on the swaps than on the underwriting of the bond itself. "It was a gold mine," said Andrew Kalotay, a public finance consultant who advises local governments. "The transaction costs up front were horrible, but local officials didn't understand that."

Robert Brooks, a University of Alabama finance professor and an expert on municipal finance reform, echoes Kalotay's perspective. "Investment bankers fly into the county and pitch an idea," he says. "The problem with that is you don't have someone on the county side of the table who can vet the idea. Typically elected municipal officials and their politically appointed staff are just not capable of doing that analysis."

Yet with the passing of the years—as 2014 unfolds and with the arrival of 2015—these swaps deals might actually be worth hanging on to, given that interest rates globally are expected to start rising. Closing out a swap that lost money when interest rates rise could end up throwing good taxpayer money after bad. If rates do rise, cities that stick with their upside-down swaps bets could reduce their long-term costs over the next decade.

Time will tell, but local officials now trying to pay off bad swaps may be getting their analysis wrong all over again.

Epilogue

By 2014, there was no longer any question that the LIBOR story, the one that Carrick Mollenkamp and Mark White-house had broken five and a half years before in the *Wall Street Journal*, had revealed everything they hoped it would. Their discovery had altered the financial landscape.

Nor was there any question about widespread guilt concerning the rigging of interest rates. Nearly all the banks on the LIBOR and EURIBOR panels admitted that their traders, and in some cases top managers and other executives, had messed with interest rates in a systematic fashion over a period of many years. Billions in fines had been paid, resignations demanded, some rules and regulations altered.

The London School of Economics estimated that ten major banks, including the Royal Bank of Scotland, Barclays, and Lloyds, would need to pay £148 billion in fines due to LIBOR and other frauds.

In reality, the fines totaled a fraction of that.

Fines and settlements paid to U.S. authorities alone cost the banks more than $40 billion just in 2013, according to Reuters, led by J.P. Morgan's record $13 billion payout to a number of regulators for misselling mortgage bonds. But even those were nominal within the context of world finance. RBS's penalty for LIBOR, for example, equaled the bank's revenues for just five weeks.

The corruption was breathtakingly widespread.

In addition to its $1.5 billion fine, UBS, Switzerland's largest bank, implicated forty-five employees in rigging interest rates, including eleven managers, with the revelation that Hayes and others had placed almost two thousand requests to manipulate the reporting of interbank borrowing rates for Japanese yen. More than a thousand of those requests had been made by brokers in an attempt to manipulate the rates reported by other banks on the LIBOR panel. But not one person from UBS was indicted.

"How many small businesses and homeowners had any idea that traders from UBS and Barclays were promising rewards to colleagues who agreed to lie about borrowing rates to benefit the banks' trading positions?" asked legal analyst Alison Frankel of Reuters. "And how many of those cheating bankers ever thought about the borrowers who would be affected by their rate rigging?"

Holland's Rabobank paid the second highest fine, €774 million, to U.S., UK, and Dutch regulators over LIBOR and EURIBOR manipulation. Thirty current and former Rabobank employees were implicated. Five were fired, and the majority are still employed there. Sipko Schat, the lender's executive board member responsible for commercial banking, stepped down, while chair Piet Moerland quit a few months before he planned to retire. As at UBS, no employees from Rabobank went to jail.

The victims who came forward to reclaim their losses were many. Though varied, the legal cases put two issues on the table: How to apportion blame? And what would be the calculus of financial damages?

Reaching answers involved yet another question, namely: What should the LIBOR interest rate have been if it hadn't been manipulated? Answering that has proved a particularly intractable problem.

Despite the admissions of guilt, a defense raised early and often by several of the guilty parties in the LIBOR scandal was that, since interest rates were often manipulated *lower* during the crisis, some borrowers benefited. But the opposite was also true. Barclays, UBS, and others also manipulated interest rates *higher*, to help bolster the profits of in-house derivatives trades.

Charles Schwab, which had been among the first to file suit against Wall Street banks, did so in August 2012. The suit accused the banks of setting LIBOR too low, since anyone with a money market fund at Schwab (or other brokerages, like Vanguard, Fidelity, or TD Ameritrade) would be shortchanged when traders pushed the rate too low; by artificially suppressing LIBOR, banks paid lower interest rates on LIBOR-based financial instruments they sold to the Schwab funds. Thus, J.P. Morgan Chase likewise reported significant exposure to interest rates in 2009: The bank stated that if interest rates increased by 1 percent, it would lose over $500 million. It was better to keep rates low on days when the banks were selling paper to money market funds like Schwab.

Lawyers for the discount brokerage made an innovative claim: that the banks rigging LIBOR had acted as a collusive enterprise, violating the Racketeer Influenced and Corrupt Organizations Act, or RICO, statutes.

Federal prosecutors had used RICO statutes against the mafia, drug dealers, and other serious felons, but Schwab decided it applied to the banks as well. "Through their participation together as members of the BBA's U.S. dollar LIBOR panel . . . every member of the enterprise participated in the process of misrepresenting their costs of borrowing."

By submitting false quotes to the BBA to set LIBOR artificially low, banks would win greater profits by making artificially low payments to investors.

The Schwab case is still pending.

Was there a conspiracy afoot in London, New York, Tokyo, and the rest of the global finance network to manipulate interest rates?

NYU's Rosa Abrantes-Metz suspected so and she was the first to give the world real proof.

Rosa, whose friends call her "Romy," grew up in Portugal. Her father had been a professional soccer player, well known in his country. The family lived under the Salazar dictatorship, and her mother encouraged her to leave the country and get an advanced education. "If you can get good grades, you can go to whatever school you want."

Romy fulfilled her mother's expectations, attending the University of Chicago, where she studied economics and earned her PhD studying under famed economists John Cochrane and Robert Lucas, the 1995 Nobel Prize winner. By 2008, she was married and had two children. To the outside world, she had grabbed the golden ticket. With thick dark hair, a taste for brightly colored silk scarves and heavy gold jewelry, Romy looked the part of the glamorous PhD, an adjunct professor at the Leonard N. Stern School of Business at New York University and working full-time in finance at the Global Economics Group.

But all was not quite as perfect as it might have seemed. One of her two sons hadn't spoken until he was almost two years old and had been diagnosed with autism. When her employer couldn't give her a more flexible schedule for her son, she quit and began consulting, working from home. She had heard rumors about LIBOR being a busted market measure in 2007, and in Apirl 2008 was scanning the *Wall Street Journal* Mollenkamp-Whitehouse story on LIBOR interest rates. Could her specialty—crunching data to look for evidence of price fixing—be applied on interest rates like LIBOR?

"I found it exciting," she said. Her younger son told his friends at elementary school, "Mommy catches cheaters."

In August 2008, Abrantes-Metz and three colleagues published a speculative research paper titled "LIBOR Manipulation?" The paper revealed that between January 2, 2007, and August 8, 2007, 95 percent of traders' submissions had an impact on where the rate was set.

The authors' research revealed that to conspire in fixing prices, it helps if you're all acquaintances outside the office. "You have sixteen banks employing people who are eating at the same restaurants, drinking at the same pubs," said coauthor Michael Kraten, an accounting professor at Providence College in Rhode Island. "They look at each other as competitors, but also as friends. It's easy to believe that whether or not they're explicitly talking to each other, they understand each other well and they're implicitly colluding."

After its publication, "LIBOR Manipulation?" was referenced and quoted widely in the press and academia.

Despite the investigations and the fines, rigging and favors spread into other corners of the market. After all, if everyone had made money for themselves rigging LIBOR and EURIBOR, why not other surveyed rates? *Bloomberg Businessweek* helped break another story on April 18, 2013, with an article headlined "Meet ISDAFIX, the Libor Scandal's Sequel."

Brokers influence price setting in a mix of polling situations, among them the daily International Swaps and Derivatives Association benchmark, ISDAFIX. Established in 1998 by the

ISDA in conjunction with Reuters and ICAP, it's a screen service that provides swap rates in a variety of currencies.

ICAP had benefited from a decision in 2002 that put the firm in control of the computer screen used by the industry to price swaps in much of the $379 trillion market. London-based ICAP was the biggest broker of interest rate swaps between banks, paying commissions based on the size of the trades it matched. It brought together dealers over the telephone and then entered the transactions manually into the screen. About six thousand firms on Wall Street and the City of London subscribe to the screen, and prices set daily by the trades ICAP arranges are used by corporate treasurers and money managers around the world to value positions.

ICAP's U.S. interest rate swaps desk, which regulators investigated as part of a price-fixing probe, reportedly paid its brokers as much as $7 million a year at the market's peak, earning the group the nickname "Treasure Island." A team of about twenty people in the company's New Jersey office would make $100 million to $120 million annually for ICAP around 2008 and 2009.

Were they "clean-clean"?

The potential culprits sound familiar—contributors to ISDAFIX being investigated by the CFTC include Bank of America, Barclays, BNP Paribas, Citigroup, Credit Suisse, Deutsche Bank, Goldman Sachs, HSBC, J.P. Morgan Chase, Mizuho, Morgan Stanley, Nomura, RBS, UBS, and Wells Fargo.

The swaption traders told their rate swap colleagues the level at which they needed ISDAFIX to be set each day in order to bolster the value of their derivatives positions before these were settled the next day. The rate swap trader would then tell a broker at ICAP to execute as many trades in interest rate swaps as necessary to move ISDAFIX to the desired level. This would be done just before eleven a.m. in New York, the time when current trades are used to create reference points that help determine the final ISDAFIX rates.

"ISDAFIX, more obscure than LIBOR, has the potential to affect more people's lives," said Jack Chen, a financial consultant in New York, because it's used by pension funds to hedge portfolio risks and by most companies or users of fixed-income derivatives. Chen has written about the swaps benchmark and LIBOR for SFC Associates, a financial consulting firm specializing in litigation matters. Ominously, he added, it "could be potentially bigger than LIBOR in terms of damages."

ICAP in early 2014 gave up administering ISDA's eleven a.m. fix to none other than the ICE, the same outfit that, as we'll see, won the right to oversee LIBOR.

By 2013, Rosa Abrantes-Metz had become something of a minor celebrity. Gary Gensler, then CFTC head, had invited her to speak on an agency panel in Washington D.C.

Her original study had been cited in nearly every plaintiff's lawsuit against the banks; Baltimore and Houston both relied upon her research, as did Schwab.

Agencies underwriting U.S. homeowners would also sue for

damages, claiming the interest rates manipulated by Wall Street and the City of London had cheated anyone with a mortgage linked to LIBOR: Fannie Mae and Freddie Mac, the giant American home mortgage lenders, have filed a massive LIBOR lawsuit claiming $3 billion in damages from banks.

But Abrantes-Metz would turn her attention to the rigging of other markets, including precious metals and energy. She began looking at screening for price rigging in gold, currencies, and even the credit default swaps markets. If nefarious rigging was going on in the foreign exchange market, she believed, "it will be much larger than LIBOR. It's a four-trillion-dollars-a-day market."

In particular, her ability to spot price fixing prompted authorities in Europe and the United States to start looking at other markets that might be manipulated, in particular oil, gold, and currencies. Abrantes-Metz was able to flag unlawful behavior through economic and statistical analyses commonly known as screening. "I am a big fan of screens for conspiracies and manipulations," she explained.

A screen is a statistical test looking for alleged illegal behavior, designed to identify whether collusion, manipulation, or any other type of cheating may be taking place in a particular market, who may be involved, and how long it may have lasted. Screens use commonly available data such as prices, bids, quotes, market shares, volumes, and other data to identify patterns that are anomalous or highly improbable. Abrantes-Metz had previously used screens to flag price fixing in gasoline, pharmaceuticals, and interest rates.

She wasn't the only one looking. Other markets came under

increasing scrutiny as a result of LIBOR. In fact, any market that was set according to an outdated conversational method of a few banks chatting, done over the phone or in a private setting of any kind, was an obvious target for scrutiny. In fact, the LIBOR scandal had raised questions about how all benchmark rates were set.

For example, German banking regulator BaFin had, in 2013, demanded documents from Deutsche Bank as part of a probe into suspected manipulation of benchmark gold and silver prices. According to long-established practice, the price of gold is "fixed" twice a day by teleconference by five institutions: Deutsche Bank, Scotiabank, Barclays, HSBC, and Société Générale. The conversations determine prices for bullion, jewelry, and central bank holdings around the world. In 2014, as investigations opened, Deutsche Bank dropped out of the gold fix, without even bothering to sell its seat.

In the United States, Coca-Cola, along with beverage lobbying groups, pleaded with the Department of Justice to investigate price fixing in aluminum. Initially the DOJ declined. After taking its case to the CFTC, Coca-Cola succeeded in getting a subpoena for one metals warehousing firm, and the DOJ began probing another. Separately, aluminum manufacturers launched class-action lawsuits against the London Metal Exchange.

The concern was whether warehouse companies, many of them owned by Wall Street banks and trading firms like Goldman Sachs or J.P. Morgan Chase, were manipulating prices by controlling how much metal enters and leaves the market.

At Bloomberg, reporters Liam Vaughan and Gavin Finch

were also looking at screens to delve into possible rate rigging in the foreign exchange markets, worth more than $5 trillion a day. In a June 2013 article, Vaughan and Finch first reported the possibility that traders at some of the world's biggest banks were rigging benchmark currency rates. An August 2013 follow-up showed that screening had identified abnormal spikes in these rates around four p.m. London time. Then followed a January 2014 article in which the authors showed that after regulatory bodies and competition authorities had begun investigating the foreign exchange market, the abnormal rates spikes faded. They read that as prima facie evidence consistent with a possible cartel.

Many regulatory bodies have recognized, as Abrantes-Metz and these Bloomberg journalists did, that looking for anomalies in the numbers can be a powerful tool. The SEC has recognized the value of these methods and has implemented screening models for accounting and trading fraud. Authorities in other countries have also used screens very successfully, notably in Mexico and Brazil.

"But some authorities have been less willing to do so," Abrantes-Metz observed. Ironically, those very same agencies are now extremely busy in investigations first flagged by the screens they themselves disregarded and sometimes claimed were useless.

"In my view, the growth in the development and adoption of screens around the world can only increase further. Competition authorities need to realize that a more proactive, rather than reactive, anti-cartel policy needs to be in place, and that screens have an important role to play."

As new manipulations—ISDAFIX and foreign exchange chief

among them—continue to surface, new solutions will be required. "Before LIBOR, people thought benchmarks could be trusted. Now there's a presumption that there's a risk of manipulation," the EU's Joaquín Almunia told the *Financial Times* in November 2013. "Perhaps manipulation is not the exception but the rule."

How has the LIBOR changed? Is it still widely in use? How is it regulated in 2014? This is probably the most essential piece of the story.

The Americans ultimately took the regulation of LIBOR away from the British, and the interest rate is still in wide use. In September 2012, the British government's Wheatley Review identified the need for a new, independent administrator for LIBOR. A division of ICE, a new U.S. exchange, set up ICE Benchmark Administration (IBA) in July 2013 following the Hogg Tendering Advisory Committee, an independent committee established by the UK government to select the new administrator for LIBOR.

The transfer to ICE from BBA LIBOR was completed on February 1, 2014, following authorization by the Financial Conduct Authority. Many of the same players, however, are on the oversight committee: David Clark, Paul Fisher from the Bank of England, UBS benchmark submitter John Hill, Barclays benchmark submitter Brad Hurrell. ICE discloses that the arrangement poses conflicts of interest, for example, if any submitters were to seek to minimize standards of regulation for

ICE LIBOR. It remains to be seen how mightily ICE polices LIBOR.

What LIBOR consists of is also new: Every contributor bank is asked to base its ICE LIBOR submissions on the following question: "At what rate could you borrow funds, were you to do so by asking for and then accepting interbank offers in a reasonable market size just prior to eleven a.m. London time?"

There are now only thirty-five LIBOR interest rates. Every ICE LIBOR rate is calculated using a trimmed arithmetic mean. Once all submissions are received, they are ranked in descending order and then the highest and lowest 25 percent of submissions are thrown out. Submissions are now anonymous and delayed.

Remaining contributions are then arithmetically averaged to create an ICE LIBOR rate. This is repeated for every currency and maturity, producing the thirty-five rates every business day.

In 2014 the FDIC also sued to recover money from the Wall Street banks. So did housing giants Fannie Mae and Freddie Mac. American's national credit unions, which alleged being shortchanged under a rigged LIBOR, filed a similar suit in October 2013, arguing that as a result of the artificially depressed LIBOR they earned less interest income than they should have.

As the LIBOR rigging fallout rolled into 2014, the rates scandal gave way to a currency-fixing scandal. All told, global investment banks could face almost $100 billion in civil settlements from investigations into interest rate and foreign exchange manipulations, analysts at KBW estimated.

At the center of the scandal were instant message groups with names such as "The Cartel," "The Bandits' Club," "One Team, One Dream," and "The Mafia," in which dealers exchanged information on client orders and agreed how to trade at the time of the fix. Vaughan and Finch's Bloomberg stories showed that senior traders who'd participated in "The Cartel" and their banks controlled more than 40 percent of the world's currency trading.

What happened to the traders implicated in LIBOR and EURIBOR scandals? Here are just a few:

Chris Cecere left Brevan Howard in June 2013. In 2011, yen-denominated LIBOR cost was found by Japanese regulators to be maneuvered by two Citigroup personnel; they did not name the traders, but one of them was identified in news reports as Cecere. In 2012 he said that he willingly left Citigroup with a full bonus and denied that he was questioned by the regulators.

Yvan Ducrot was the cohead of UBS's rates business. According to the *Financial Times*, he was suspended by UBS in connection with the LIBOR probes. Holger Seger was the global head of short-term interest rates trading at UBS. According to the *Financial Times*, Seger was suspended by UBS.

Paul White was a principal rate setter for yen LIBOR for RBS. Tan Chi Min was the head of short-term interest rates trading for yen at RBS. According to Bloomberg, White was dismissed from RBS in 2011 as was Tan Chi Min. Tan Chi Min then sued for wrongful termination alleging RBS made him a "scapegoat" for behavior the bank condoned. Ultimately Tan dropped the suit without any payment by RBS to Tan.

Sim Suh-Ting was the executive director and head of regulatory risk and compliance for RBS in Southeast Asia. According to allegations in Tan Chi Min's wrongful termination suit, Ting advised others within RBS that it was acceptable for traders to make requests about the level at which the swap offer rate was set. Todd Morakis was head of trading for emerging markets at RBS. According to allegations in the same suit, Morakis "orally confirmed . . . that 'the practice of requesting to change the rate Libor is common in every rate setting environment in the banking industry.'"

Will Hall was a derivatives trader at RBS in London. He was also named in Brian Elliott's 2001 affidavit as one of the traders believed to be involved in the manipulation of yen LIBOR.

Trader Neil Danziger was dismissed by RBS on October 21, 2011, according to Bloomberg, and now is listed as "inactive" on the FSA's register of people approved to work in the industry. Jezri Mohideen, formerly RBS's head of yen products, was suspended from his position as head of rates trading for Europe and Asia. Paul Walker was RBS's head of money market trading in London. In a January 28, 2013, article in Bloomberg, Walker is implicated in conspiring to manipulate LIBOR with Scott Nygaard. The article quotes Walker as saying, "People are setting to where it suits their book" and "Libor is what you say it is."

Michael Spencer, who in 1986 founded one of the firms that make up today's ICAP, remains one of the richest men in Britain. "We deeply regret and strongly condemn the inexcusable actions of the brokers who sought to assist certain bank traders in their efforts to manipulate yen LIBOR," he said, chalking up the fraud to "very sadly a rotten-apple situation." ICAP paid fines of $87 million.

Barclays' disgraced leader Bob Diamond moved his family back to New York to his $37 million apartment overlooking Central Park West. He invested in an African banking group, Atlas Mara, alongside Ashish Thakkar and in a range of businesses across Africa. The two have invested $20 million in the shell. Thakkar, often described as Africa's youngest billionaire, started his first IT companies in 1995 and is one of the World Economic Forum's young global leaders.

As of 2014, Diamond remains chairman of the board of trustees at Colby College, after having donated millions to his alma mater. Fellow Colby alumni such as Lew Kingsbury are outraged and have helped organize protests to have Diamond ousted. "Why in the world is he still chair of board? Because the board says he's not a criminal. Have they not read the Department of Justice's settlement document with Barclays? He committed crimes just running that place."

Diamond's daughter, Nell, who famously tweeted to British politicians that they should "H.M.D."—or "hold my dick"—in defense of her father, is a socialite and student at Yale School of Management.

Diamond incurred the wrath and indignation of John Mann, Andrew Tyrie, the Treasury Select Committee, and the public at large over LIBOR manipulation. Alison Carnwath, the Barclays board member who tried to block Diamond's million-pound bonuses, was rewarded in 2013 with a title of dame. Under new head Antony Jenkins, in 2014 Barclays began splitting into two banks, to separate its toxic assets from its healthier operations.

In the fall of 2013, Gary Gensler delivered a requiem for his work at the CFTC in front of an audience in Chicago. Asked about progress in turning the Volcker Rule into regulations, Gensler said, "I'm not confident that the CFTC can effectively enforce this whole package of reforms." As the public now knew, multiple banks were "pervasively rigging the world's most important benchmark interest rates," he told the Washington D.C. bar association in late 2013. "I wish I could say that this won't happen again, but I can't. As LIBOR and EURIBOR are not anchored in observable transactions, they are more akin to fiction than fact."

Gensler "accomplished a substantial amount at a heretofore sleepy agency," Wall Street reporter Jesse Eisinger told NPR. "He's managed to put most of these derivatives through something called "clearinghouses" and on exchanges. Even the *National Journal* praised Gensler: "Banks are huger than ever and over-the-counter derivatives are being traded again in the hundreds of trillions—one reason why Gensler, the outgoing head of the Commodity Futures Trading Commission, may be one of the great unsung heroes in Washington thanks to his lonely fight to regulate derivatives internationally."

Paul Tucker, the disgraced Bank of England deputy governor, left to teach at Harvard University.

Jezri Mohideen, who was let go from RBS, later sued contending racial discrimination and unfair dismissal. He reportedly settled out of court with the bank in June 2014.

A few American regulators—and they are the exception—argue that letting off the big Wall Street banks because of LIBOR just isn't right.

SEC commissioner Kara Stein surprised all of Washington when in May 2014 she weighed in strongly against a waiver for Royal Bank of Scotland, citing the bank's "criminal conduct, part of a widespread scheme undertaken by multiple banks to manipulate LIBOR for profit. LIBOR affects in some way nearly every financial market across the globe—consumer and corporate loans, interest rate swaps and derivatives, mortgages, college loans, futures and options. LIBOR rigging impacted millions of American families, businesses, and communities."

She disagreed with SEC Chair Mary Jo White, a former prosecutor whom Obama appointed to clean up financial misdeed. "In the markets the Commission oversees, as well as in global financial markets, this factor weighs strongly against granting a waiver," Stein wrote. "This should be simple. We have a rule that confers a special benefit to issuers that have a good track record. And we have a rule that calls for automatically rescinding that benefit when the issuer misbehaves. Here, the Commission waived that common sense rule despite egregious criminal misconduct. RBS failed to justify why we should do so. In granting this waiver, I believe the Commission has strayed from its mission, and strayed from a careful and prudent course."

More will be revealed with Tom Hayes's trial in January 2015. Expect headlines about how the pawns got rooked as the bishops looked on. Hayes remains a case in point. To hear him tell it, he was an innocent led astray. Rigging LIBOR was, one of his friends told the *Wall Street Journal*, "common industry practice," and certainly UBS made it easy to do what he did, as Hayes found himself seated next to fellow employees who were charged with making the bank's LIBOR submissions.

The LIBOR scandal shares a theme with other great swindles, such as the underwriting of subprime mortgages, the insider trading ring at Raj Rajaratnam's Galleon hedge fund, Enron's collapse, Michael Milken's junk bond empire, and Bernie Madoff's pyramid scam. Most of those began as open secrets in an opaque industry, but ended up costing millions of ordinary investors their life savings, or even their lives.

Alison Frankel of Reuters has offered an observation that applies, one that regulators and journalists and politicians should keep in mind whenever they are tempted to look away from uncomfortable facts, from oddities we don't quite understand, from the evidence of possible cheating or fraud. Perhaps we should call it Frankel's Rule. It goes like this: "Insiders will blithely compromise market integrity for their own profit, and we, the uninformed public, are their dupes."

Acknowledgments

First, I thank my mom and dad, Julie and Richard Arvedlund, who let me read at night by flashlight. I love you!

My amazing sister Maggie Arvedlund, a Wall Street portfolio manager, explained the credit markets and critiqued early drafts. Maggie and her husband, Adam Cassidy, also gave us the gift of their first son, my nephew Svend Joseph Cassidy, in June 2013.

My editors at Penguin, particularly Emily Angell, Brooke Carey, and Adrian Zackheim, proposed this exciting book and shepherded this thorough account of the global interest rate-rigging scandal. Jesse Maeshiro researched photos and other necessary but vital details, and Joel Rickett in London wisely encouraged focusing on consumers in the United Kingdom. My agent Esmond Harmsworth tolerates my many brainstorms; I couldn't survive without his solid counsel at Zachary Schuster Harmsworth.

Ted Knutson acted as jungle guide in Washington and on Capitol Hill. Without him I could not have found my way around congressional hearings or the Dodd-Frank legislation. He introduced me to Dennis Kelleher at BetterMarkets and numerous regulatory agencies. Mimi and Frank Procida opened their home on many overnights and their daughter Eliana also helped "Miss Erin" wake up over breakfast.

Yvonne and Michael Marsh, and their daughter Nicole, invited me to speak at their home and introduced me to PEN America (www.pen.org), which supports freedom of the press and journalists worldwide. I was honored to attend a dinner raising funds for PEN America, hosted by author Salman Rushdie. Alma maters Tufts University and Tufts in Talloires, France, generously invited me to give lectures to students and alumnae, as have my high school Archmere Academy and elementary school Ursuline Academy in Delaware.

My appreciation extends to my adopted home at the *Philadelphia Inquirer*, and editors William Marimow, Brian Toolan, Joanne McLaughlin, and Reid Kanaley. Without their kind permission I would not have completed the book. *Inquirer* staff writer Joe DiStefano is the best "consigliore" out there; Ronnie Polaneczky, *Philadelphia Daily News* columnist, has been a mentor all along. I'm lucky to have them as colleagues and Lewis Katz and H. F. "Gerry" Lenfest as new owners as this book goes to press. My thanks to the CWA (Communication Workers of America), especially Diane Mastrull.

David Schutt at *Barron's* magazine graciously kept me going with assignments, and Eric Uhlfelder with the Top 100 Hedge

Funds. Sandra Ward at *Barron's*, Michael Santoli at *Yahoo!Finance*, and Gregg Wirth at *Wall Street Lawyer* provide moral support and laughs. I thank *Fortune* magazine editors Nicholas Varchaver and Leigh Gallagher for their interest in my work. Brian Portnoy, Phil Gocke, Peter Halloran, Luke Rahbari, David Clark, David Bermingham, and barrister Stephen Rosen translated how Wall Street and the City of London express views on interest rates via trades and how the narrative of whom to blame is often distorted by politics.

Lisette Garcia, J.D., founded the FOIA Resource Center to help reporters such as myself quickly and cost effectively obtain U.S. government records.

To the confidential sources in this book, please accept my everlasting gratitude.

The Tufts 350s, Christina Sonchen, and Joyce Connery remain golden friends; Dixie Tabb Palmer and other members of the Philadelphia "book club" are sterling new friends. I couldn't have completed this without you. John Marchese and Christ Dhimitri, onetime owner of Chris' Jazz Café and current owner of Bliss, introduced me to Philly media circles.

Special credit is due to Leon LaRosa, Ed Liva, Howard Magen, Anne Putney, and the Union League of Philadelphia; to the administrative staff and professors at Villanova Law School's masters in taxation program, who assisted us during a year of loss, especially Professor Harvey, Linda Vines, and Safia Dias.

Among friends and family, my heartfelt appreciation goes to Charlie and Leslie Bensley, Jeni Lofthouse, Cathy Montano, Sujata Rao, Jeanne Whalen, Radhika Jones, and Nell Scott; Jim and Carol Meholic put up with the television cameras; the crew of *Natural Reboot* and Katie Griffin Casting.

To my husband's Marine unit, particularly Peter Rohrman and family, Hetal "Doc" Patel, and the Monaco brothers (Mario and Jessica, Dominic, and Lucy); Kevin Glassco, Ross and Caroline Nowak and his parents, Tracy and Matt Sullivan, Betsy and Eric Flaim, Brett and Peggy Zola, Jim and Paul Gensch and their family, David Lenehan, David Kahn, John Booth, Paul Hawkins, Ray and Day Bank, Bonner Rust, Sarah and Paul MacKenzie, David Rust; Bruce Bromberg, Dr. Paul and Sarah Harris; Mrs. Jane Caughey, Bob Beattie and family, Mrs. William P. Howard; Willis and Kerstin Lefavour; Rev. Patrick G. O'Donovan and Dennis Corcoran of the Church of Christ the King, New Vernon, New Jersey; Dr. Millicent Zacher, Jefferson University Hospital, and Bonnie Schur: All showed us the way forward.

John and Olga Beattie continue to astound with their strength as brother- and sister-in-law, as well as their children Matthew and Hanna, playing hockey for Yale and Williams, respectively. Anna and Gerry Cassidy are a fabulous second set of grandparents to my nephew; Arthur Cassidy is his godfather extraordinaire.

Finally, Anne Beattie and her late husband, John Beattie Jr., gave me their son, my husband Richard Patrick McEwan Beattie. Like your dad, you are a man of integrity who does the right thing, in defending the research and writing of this book and paying a professional price. My life is yours.

Notes

Reports

Treasury Select Committee, UK Parliament, www.publications.parlia
ment.uk/pa/cm201213/cmselect/cmtreasy/481/48102.htm

Wheatley Review, HM Treasury, www.hm-treasury.gov.uk

Settlements

UBS: $1.52 billion, December 2012

Royal Bank of Scotland: $1.14 billion, February 2013 and December
2013

Rabobank: $1.07 billion, October 2013

Deutsche Bank: $983 million, December 2013

Société Générale: $604 million, December 2013

Barclays: $453 million, June 2012

J.P. Morgan: $108 million, December 2013

Citigroup: $95 million, December 2013

ICAP: $87 million, September 2013

RP Martin: $200,000, December 2013

PROLOGUE

2   Hayes had grown up in London: David Enrich, "Rate-Rig Spotlight Falls on 'Rain Man.'" *Wall Street Journal*, http://online.wsj.com/news/articles/SB10001424127887324445904578285810706107442.

2   "incredibly smart geek": Michael Stothard, "Star Trader Was Richly Rewarded," *Financial Times*, December 20, 2012, www.ft.com/intl/cms/s/0/9aa93ade-4ac4-11e2-929d-00144feab49a.html#axzz35HRtoKJK.

3   His new bosses proclaimed him "a star": Enrich, "Rate-Rig Spotlight Falls on 'Rain Man.'"

5   335 out of 738 business days. *United States of America vs. Tom Alexander William Hayes et al.*, Complaint of December 12, 2012, pp. 13–14, www.justice.gov/ag/Hayes-Tom-and-Darin-Roger-Complaint.pdf.

5   "This goes much higher than me": Jean Eaglesham, David Enrich, and Devlin Barret, "ICAP Nears Settlement in Rate Rigging," *Wall Street Journal*, September 23, 2013.

7   "My actions were entirely consistent": David Enrich and Atsuko Fukase, "Libor Rate-Probe Spotlight Shines on Higher-Ups at Citigroup, Other Banks," *Wall Street Journal*, August 28, 2013.

CHAPTER 1

10   Mollenkamp already had: Chris Roush, "Wall Street Reporter Mollenkamp Leaves Reuters," *Talking Biz News*, December 17, 2013.

10   "There is no historic plaque": "Euromoney 30th Anniversary: Capital Market Landmarks," *Euromoney*, June 1999, www

.euromoney.com/Article/1005240/Euromoney-30th-anniversary
-Capital-market-landmarks.html?copyrightInfo=true.

11   **he served as U.S. ambassador:** "Galbraith Named Envoy to France," *American Banker*, October 20, 1981; Dennis Hevesi, "Evan Galbraith, Ambassador, Dies at 79," *New York Times*, January 25, 2008.

12   **I was twenty-two years old:** Author interview with Clark.

14   **The tension had risen:** Martin de Sa'Pinto, "BNP Paribas Suspends Three Funds on ABS Fears," Reuters Hedgeworld, August 9, 2007.

14   **"pour an ocean through a thimble":** "NY Fed's Dudley Sees Limits to What Fed Liquidity Offerings Can Accomplish," AFX News, May 15, 2008.

14   **He'd covered Russian business:** Mark Whitehouse, "Mayor Yury Luzhkov and the Very Big Business of Running Moscow," *Moscow Times*, September 2, 1997.

17   **One solution was to address:** M. S. Mendelsohn, "The Money Shake-Out," *Economist*, March 22, 1975.

18   **Kennedy's tax:** M. S. Mendelsohn, "The Long Historical Lure of Banking in Britain," *American Banker*, July 30, 1986.

18   **Since the 1963 tax:** "Mighty Eurobond Market Celebrates 50th Anniversary," *EuroWeek*, June 28, 2013.

19   **One result was the decision by his successor:** Davis Marquand, "Keynes Was Wrong," *Prospect*, February 22, 2001.

19   **first six months of 1971:** John Browne, "U.S. Trade Surplus Is Trouble Abroad," *Pittsburgh Tribune Review*, October 13, 2013.

19   **Overnight, oil prices quadrupled:** "*Euromoney*'s Richard Ensor on the Profession's Call to Internationalise," *International Financial Law Review*, December 2012.

19   Even the British cabinet: British National Archives, http://
filestore.nationalarchives.gov.uk/pdfs/large/cab-129-173.pdf.

19   "either be a Eurobond issue": John Brooks, "Sixty Years of
American Business: The Pursuit of Happiness Through the Pursuit of Profit," *Forbes*, September 15, 1977.

20   None of the changes moved the dollar: Eugene A. Birnbaum,
"Not So Fast, Mr. Sprinkel," *Forbes*, November 9, 1981.

20   "end of the American banking system": Ron Chernow, *The
House of Morgan: An American Banking Dynasty and the Rise
of Modern Finance* (New York: Grove/Atlantic, 1990).

22   equaled about $45,000: Mark Davis, "One Little Number Can
Pull Many into Credit Crisis," *Kansas City Star*, October 2, 2008.

23   Galbraith may have conceived the idea: Helena Smith, "Banking: System Was Set Up in a More Honest Age, Says Its Inventor," *Guardian*, December 18, 2012.

24   In the early days: Alex Brummer, "How Square Mile Will Win
Tax Skirmish," *Daily Mail*, January 24, 2012.

25   British Bankers' Association: www.bbalibor.com/news-releases/
bba-libor-the-worlds-most-important-number-now-tweets-daily.

25   "At what rate do you think": Sean Farrell, "BBA Fights to Shore
Up Confidence in Libor System," *Independent*, May 30, 2008.

25   explosive growth of Eurodollar business: Armel Cates, "Swap
Financing," *International Lawyer*, Summer 1986.

26   After the initial interest rate "swap": Jonathan Friedland,
"World Bank Polishes Its Image in the Financial Community
with Sophisticated New Funding Techniques," *American
Banker*, September 27, 1983.

27   By 2007, nearly all subprime: Guhan Venkatu and Mark E. Sch-
weitzer, "Alternatives to Libor in Consumer Mortgages," Federal Reserve Bank of Cleveland Economic Commentary, October 11, 2012.

29   In September 2007, Wrightson: Ian McDonald, Alistair MacDonald, Cynthia Koons, and Jon E. Hilsenrath, "Never Heard of the Libor Rate? It Could Hit You in the Wallet," *Wall Street Journal*, September 5, 2007.

30   The prior summer: "Dual Deals for Chrysler Put in Gear," *Credit Investment News*, June 29, 2007.

32   "LIBOR at times no longer": "Is LIBOR Broken?," *EuroWeek*, April 18, 2008.

CHAPTER 2

36   Tom Alexander William Hayes: Federal News Service, Press Conference with U.S. Attorney General Eric Holder; Assistant Attorney General Lanny Breuer, Criminal Division; Deputy Assistant Attorney General Scott Hammond, Antitrust Division; David Meister, Director of Enforcement, Commodities Futures Trading Commission; FBI Associate Deputy Director Kevin Perkins. Subject: International Bank Enforcement Action. Location: Justice Department, Washington D.C., December 19, 2012.

37   Darrell Read worked for ICAP: "Kiwi Libor Scandal: A Plan Is Hatched," *New Zealand Herald*, October 1, 2013.

37   Read's primary responsibility: James O'Toole, "Three Ex-ICAP Employees Indicted in Libor Scandal," CNNMoney.com, September 24, 2013.

37   ICAP: Kirstin Ridley and Clare Hutchison, "ICAP Fined $87 Million Over LIBOR; Three Ex-Staff Charged," Reuters Hedgeworld, September 25, 2013.

37   Colin Goodman also worked: "Former ICAP Brokers in Yen LIBOR-Rigging Case Get Bail," Bloomberg, April 16, 2014.

38   "the market at the moment is so volatile": Matt West, "RBS Among Six Banks Slapped with Record £1.4 Billion in Fines for Interest Rate Rigging," *Daily Mail*, December 4, 2013.

38   **Read and Wilkinson often:** William Alden, "Things Traders Say, ICAP Edition," *New York Times*, September 25, 2013.

39   **Primarily Read was the person:** Jill Treanor and Rajeev Syal, "£55m Libor Fine for City Broking Firm Run by Former Conservative Party Treasurer," *Guardian*, September 26, 2013.

40   **"I get the dribs and drabs":** "Examples of Misconduct from Written Communications," CFTC, www.cftc.gov/ucm/groups/public/@newsroom/documents/file/icapquotes.pdf.

42   **"DAN THIS IS GETTING SERIOUS":** Ibid.

45   **"Oh mate that's so illegal":** Kara Scannell, Caroline Binham, and Philip Stafford, "Court Papers Tell How 'Lord Libor' Wanted More," *Financial Times*, September 25, 2013.

CHAPTER 3

46   **"Over the next two days":** Author interview with Whitehouse.

47   **On April 17:** Carrick Mollenkamp and Laurence Norman, "BBA Inquiry into LIBOR: British Bankers Group Steps Up Review of Widely Used Libor," *Wall Street Journal*, April 17, 2008.

48   **The majority of the banks:** Hearing on Monetary Policy and the State of the Economy, House Committee on Financial Services, Washington D.C., July 18, 2012.

48   **For the rest of April:** Author interview with Abrantes-Metz.

49   **"we can try to keep":** *United States of America vs. Tom Alexander William Hayes et al.*, Complaint of December 12, 2012, p. 12, www.justice.gov/ag/Hayes-Tom-and-Darin-Roger-Complaint.pdf.

49   **One man who got to sit:** Gavin Finch, Liam Vaughan, and Jesse Westbrook, "Tainted Libor Guessing Games Face Replacement by Real Trades," Bloomberg, March 13, 2012.

49   calculation of LIBOR is co-coordinated: Donald MacKenzie, "What's in a Number?," *London Review of Books*, September 25, 2008.

50   "It's the back-up arrangements": Ibid.

51   "It forced people to lie": Author interview with Stone.

51   "After a *Wall Street Journal* article": William C. Dudley, "May You Live in Interesting Times: The Sequel," Remarks at the Federal Reserve Bank of Chicago's 44th Annual Conference on Bank Structure and Competition, Chicago, Illinois, May 15, 2008, www.newyorkfed.org/newsevents/speeches/2008/dud080515 .html.

54   Or were they conspiring: Francesco Giavazzi, "Why Does the Spread Between LIBOR and Expected Future Policy Rates Persist, and Should Central Banks Do Something About It?," June 2, 2008.

54   started by looking at: "Turmoil in the Financial Markets: Capitol Hill Hearing Testimony," Statement of Luigi Zingales, Committee on House Oversight and Government Reform, October 6, 2008.

56   "they were lying": "How Do You Solve a Problem Like Libor?," *Banker*, August 1, 2012.

56   On April 28, 2008: Carrick Mollenkamp, "Fed Knew of Libor Issue in 2007–08, Proposed Reforms," Reuters, July 10, 2012.

57   Geithner's calendar: The "Fixing LIBOR" meeting occurred between two thirty and three p.m. on April 28, 2008, http://s3 .amazonaws.com/nytdocs/docs/119/119.pdf.

57   That morning, the New York Fed: Jo Becker and Gretchen Morgenson, "Geithner, Member and Overseer of Finance Club," *New York Times*, April 26, 2009.

57   Geithner: "The Impact of Dodd-Frank on Customers, Credit, and Job Creators," Hearing of the Capital Markets and

Government Sponsored Enterprises Subcommittee of the House
Financial Services Committee, Washington D.C., July 10, 2012.

58   **daily LIBORs set the wholesale:** www.newyorkfed.org/aboutthefed/.

59   **make matters worse:** David Hou and David Skeie, "LIBOR: Origins,
Economics, Crisis, Scandal, and Reform," Federal Reserve Bank of
New York Staff Reports, Staff Report No. 667, March 2014.

59   **"The banks in the LIBOR panel are suspected":** Jia Lynn Yang,
"Geithner Made Recommendations on Libor in 2008, Documents Show," *Washington Post*, July 12, 2012.

59   **"Figuring out LIBOR":** Felix Salmon, "Defending Libor," *Portfolio*, May 29, 2008.

59   **"made me uneasy":** Author interview with Guttentag.

60   **"always been a fudge factor":** Author interview with Bair.

60   **operated "in a regulatory vacuum":** Author interview with Preece.

60   **email from a Barclays:** New York Fed transcripts, "Supplemen-
tary Information Regarding Barclays Settlement with the Authorities in Respect of Their Investigations into the Submission
of Various Interbank Offered Rates (AMENDED). In Anticipa-
tion of Bob Diamond's Appearance Before the Treasury Committee," July 4, 2012; www.parliament.uk/documents/commons
-committees/treasury/Fixing%20LIBOR%20evidence%202.pdf.

60   **"LIBOR is a different animal":** www.wrightson.com/press
_summary/2007/09/10/default.pdf.

60   **The minutes from one:** "Minutes," Sterling Money Markets Liaison
Group, Bank of England, November 15, 2007, www.bankofeng
land.co.uk/markets/Documents/money/mmlgnov07.pdf.

61   **"a malfunctioning market":** Harry Wilson, "Paul Tucker Denies
Diamond Libor Memo Claims," *Telegraph*, July 9, 2012.

61   **"interbank brokers were a huge part":** Author interview.

62   "source of misreporting incentive": Connan Snider and Thomas
       Youle, "The Fix Is In: Detecting Portfolio Driven Manipulation
       of the LIBOR, December 2012 [First Version: November 2009],
       www.econ.ucdavis.edu/seminars/papers/Snyder57.pdf.

63   "We know that we're not posting": New York Fed transcripts,
       www.newyorkfed.org/newsevents/news/markets/2012/libor/
       April_11_2008_transcript.pdf.

65   "I'm not defending it": Kevin G. Hall, "Ben Bernanke Suggests
       Fraud in Libor Interest Rate," McClatchy Newspapers, July 17,
       2012, www.mcclatchydc.com/2012/07/17/156510/ben-bernanke
       -suggests-fraud-in.html#storylink=cpy.

66   "So, to the extent that": "Appendix A: Statement of Facts," U.S.
       Department of Justice, December 18, 2012, www.justice.gov/
       criminal/vns/docs/2012/12/2012-12-19-UBS-Statement-of
       -Facts.pdf.

66   "We're clean, but we're dirty-clean": Barclays settlement with
       the UK Financial Services Authority, http://online.wsj.com/news/
       interactive/liborfsa0627?ref=SB100014240527023048307045577
       493092589081130.

67   "No conspiracy is required": Author interview with Verstein.

67   "lying premium": Shahien Nasiripour, "Geithner Was Told of
       Libor Fears in 2008," Financial Times, December 18, 2012.

69   Geithner had a passion: Jeff Gerth and Robert O'Harrow Jr.,
       "As Crisis Loomed, Geithner Pressed but Fell Short," Washing-
       ton Post, April 2, 2009.

69   "He never worked a day": William D. Cohan, "Smart Money Is on
       Geithner to Replace Bernanke," Bloomberg, December 16, 2012.

69   son of a railway worker: Chris Giles, "The Court of King
       Mervyn," Financial Times, May 5, 2012.

69   **"We never imagined"**: Honorable Mervyn A. King, Governor of the Bank of England, Economic Club of New York, 427th Meeting, 105th Year, December 10, 2012.

70   **"very intellectual approach"**: "Mervyn King," BBC News Profile, September 20, 2007.

70   **"If you'd asked me the question"**: Ibid.

70   **He had finally married**: Nikki Murfitt, "An Unexpected Phone Call After 30 Years Apart: How Love Repaid Sir Mervyn King's Interest at Last," *Daily Mail*, June 2, 2013.

70   **"I had relationships"**: Hayley Dixon, "Sir Mervyn King Gave Up on Love, Until an Unexpected Phone Call," *Telegraph*, June 2, 2013.

71   **King William III lacked the resources**: Bank of England history, www.bankofengland.co.uk/about/pages/history/default.aspx.

71   **"Mervyn King ruled"**: Alistair Osborne and Louise Armitstead, "Mervyn King Runs Bank of England Like a 'Tyrant,' Says Former MPC Member David Blanchflower," *Telegraph*, April 19, 2012.

71   **"unprepared for the bank run"**: David Blanchflower, "Mervyn King Is a Tyrant, but Who Will Succeed Him at the Bank?," *New Statesman*, April 18, 2012.

72   **Basel . . . 2008**: Robert E. Marks, "Timeline for: Learning Lessons? The Global Financial Crisis Five Years On," *Journal and Proceedings of the Royal Society of New South Wales* 146, nos. 447–448, pp. A1–A43.

73   **"Geithner definitely said something"**: Author interview.

73   **"Recent Concerns Regarding LIBOR's Credibility"**: Samuel Cheun and Matt Raskin, "Recent Concerns Regarding LIBOR's Credibility," Markets Group, Federal Reserve Bank of New York, May 20, 2008, www.newyorkfed.org/newsevents/news/markets/2012/libor/MarketSource_Report_May202008.pdf.

74 memo . . . Bank of England: Bank of England publication, www
.bankofengland.co.uk/publications/Documents/other/treasury
-committee/financialstability/emailchain.pdf.

76 "These individuals report to the head": Yves Smith, "The
Geithner Doctrine Not Only Puts Banks Above the Law, It Also
Serves to Excuse Their Bad Behavior," *Naked Capitalism*, De-
cember 19, 2012.

CHAPTER 4

77 "Banks are hoarding cash": Martin Zimmerman, Maura Reyn-
olds, and Tom Petruno, "Crisis Deepens Amid Fear of Continued Stock Dive," *Los Angeles Times*, September 18, 2008.

78 J.P. Morgan said: "Libor Volatility Due to Poor Liquidity," Reuters, May 16, 2008.

78 "measures we are using": "European, U.S. Bankers Work on
Libor Problems," Reuters, May 16, 2008.

78 "current situation is extraordinary": Tom McGhie, "Angela Knight
Interview: Former Banks' Defender-in-Chief Admits Huge Bonuses
Were Not Always Justified," *Daily Mail*, September 29, 2012.

78 "lots of places where banks": Felix Salmon, "Defending Libor,"
Portfolio, May 29, 2008.

79 That same day Citigroup claimed: Raúl Ilargi Meijer, "LIBOR
Was a Criminal Conspiracy from the Start," *Business Insider*,
July 11, 2012, www.businessinsider.com/libor-was-a-criminal
-conspiracy-from-the-start-2012-7/.

79 HBOS similarly asserted: Ibid.

79 "*Wholly inadequate*": Bank of England memo; "Sir Mervyn
King Called Libor Review 'Wholly Inadequate,' New Emails
Show," *Telegraph*, July 20, 2012.

80 **"Mervyn: We spoke briefly"**: New York Federal Reserve documents, http://news.bbc.co.uk/2/shared/bsp/hi/pdfs/13_07_12 _federalreserve.pdf.

80 **"Whatever the limits"**: Author interview with Carleton.

81 **Richard Bove:** John Detrixhe, "Libor Reported as Rigged in '08 Proving 2012's Revelation," Bloomberg, July 19, 2012.

81 **BIS employee:** Author interview.

81 **"Sir Mervyn King now has serious"**: Rick Dewsbury and James Chapman, "U.S. 'Warned King on Rate-Rigging in 2008': Pressure on Bank of England to Explain," *Daily Mail*, July 13, 2012.

82 **"People told him about the LIBOR issue"**: Mehdi Hasan, "Mervyn King 'Not Interested' in 2008 Libor Rate Warnings, Say Ex-BOE Colleagues," *Huffington Post*, July 16, 2012.

82 **the BBA held:** David Enrich and Max Colchester, "Before Scandal, Clash Over Control of Libor," *Wall Street Journal*, September 11, 2012.

83 **New York Fed briefed U.S. Treasury:** "Recent Developments in Short-Term Funding Markets," Federal Reserve Bank of New York, www.newyorkfed.org/newsevents/news/markets/2012/libor /May_6_2008_Slide_Deck_of_Presentation_to_Treasury.pdf.

84 **"Interbank Rate Fixings During the Recent Turmoil"**: Jacob Gyntelberg and Philip Wooldridge, "Interbank Rate Fixings During the Recent Turmoil," *BIS Quarterly Review*, March 2008, www.bis.org/repofficepubl/arpresearch_dev_200803.02.pdf; and "Fixing LIBOR," UK House of Commons, www.pub lications .parliament.uk/pa/cm201213/cmselect/cmtreasy/481/48105.htm.

84 **"Our treasurer, who takes his responsibilities"**: Gavin Finch and Elliott Gotkine, "Libor Banks Misstated Rates, Bond at Barclays Says," Bloomberg, May 29, 2008.

85 **Knight was known as an industry flack:** Energy UK, www.en ergy-uk.org.uk/about-us/about-our-staff.html.

87 **"For the dollar LIBOR fixing":** Bank of England documents, https://archive.org/details/402835-more-bank-of-england-doc uments-on-libor.

88 **the bank's LIBOR rates:** *United States of America vs. Tom Alexander William Hayes et al.*, Complaint of December 12, 2012, p. 15, www.justice.gov/ag/Hayes-Tom-and-Darin-Roger-Complaint.pdf.

88 **"pretend I'm six feet tall":** Peter Taylor, "Libor Credibility Questioned as Credit Crunch Deepens," *Telegraph*, April 17, 2008.

89 **"get in line with the competition":** "Final Notice, UBS," Financial Services Authority, December 19, 2012, www.fca.org.uk/ static/documents/final-notices/ubs.pdf.

90 **more fictitious than usual:** "Appendix A: Statement of Facts," U.S. Department of Justice, December 18, 2012, www.justice.gov/crimi nal/vns/docs/2012/12/2012-12-19-UBS-Statement-of-Facts.pdf.

91 **"the whole street was doing the same":** "Examples of Misconduct from Written Communications," CFTC, www.cftc.gov/ucm/groups /public/@newsroom/documents/file/misconductwrittencommunica tion.pdf.

91 **masters of the universe:** *The Financial Crisis Inquiry Report: Final Report of the National Commission on the Causes of the Financial and Economic Crisis in the United States, Official Government Edition*, Financial Crisis Inquiry Commission, January 2011.

92 **in October 2008 the British government:** Jon Menon, "RBS, HBOS, Lloyds Get 37 Billion-Pound U.K. Bailout," Bloomberg, October 13, 2008.

93 **"I want to ask you about the LIBOR spread":** Michael Gray, "Fed Transcripts Reveal Early Concern Over Libor," *New York Post*, February 21, 2014; Conference Call of the Federal Open Market

Committee, October 7, 2008, http://federal-reserve.sayit.mysociety
.org/speech/561891.

93   **Dudley didn't say it:** Conference Call of the Federal Open Market Committee, October 7, 2008.

94   **That same month, when the Fed established:** Press release, Board of Governors, Federal Reserve System, April 21, 2009, www.federalreserve.gov/monetarypolicy/20090421b.htm.

94   **Geithner defended his action:** "Timothy Geithner on His Role in Libor Scandal: 'We Were Very Forceful from the Beginning,'" CNBC, July 18, 2012.

94   **"At no stage had":** Mark Scott, "Bank of England Chief Denies New York Fed Gave Warning on Rate-Rigging," *New York Times*, July 17, 2012.

94   **"Looking at those e-mails":** CNBC interview, July 2012, http://video.cnbc.com/gallery/?video=3000104302&play=1.

CHAPTER 5

97   **donated £19,500:** Holly Watt, "Revealed: Tory Donors' Links to the Libor Scandal," *Telegraph*, June 29, 2012.

97   **Liam Fox:** Simon Bowers, "Michael Hintze: Liam Fox Backer Who Helped to Bankroll Foreign Trips," *Guardian*, October 11, 2011, www.theguardian.com/politics/2011/oct/11/michael-hintze-liam-fox-backer.

97   **"asymmetrical outcomes":** Richard Teitelbaum and Tom Cahill, "Brevan Howard Shows Paranoid Survive in Hedge Fund of Time Outs," Bloomberg, March 31, 2009.

97   **Brevan Howard:** Liam Vaughan and Gavin Finch, "Secret Libor Transcripts Expose Trader Rate-Manipulation," *Bloomberg Markets*, December 13, 2012.

97   "Blue, uh, Crest": New York Fed transcripts, www.newyorkfed.org
/newsevents/news/markets/2012/libor/April_11_2008_transcript.pdf.

98   Tan Chi Min: Rachel Armstrong, "Ex-RBS Trader Says Brevan
Howard Sought Libor Rate Change," Reuters, March 30, 2012.

99   "need to bump it way up": Andrea Tan, Gavin Finch, and Liam
Vaughan, "RBS Instant Messages Reveal Traders Skewed Libor," Bloomberg, September 26, 2012.

99   "a dishonest agreement": Kirstin Ridley and Steve Slater, "UK
Prosecutor Says Has 'Vast Amounts' of Documents in Libor
Case," Reuters, March 4, 2014.

100   lawsuit alleged: Andrea Tan and Jesse Westbrook, "Brevan
Howard Asked RBS to Change Libor, Lawsuit Says," Bloomberg, March 30, 2012.

100   "amazing how LIBOR-fixing": Jill Treanor, "RBS Trader Sent
Mocking Messages as He Tried to Rig Libor, Court Told,"
Guardian, September 26, 2012.

101   "an unbelievably large set": "Appendix A: Statement of Facts,"
U.S. Department of Justice Report on Barclays, June 26, 2012.

101   "Dude I owe you big time": Ibid.; Jeffrey Cane, "The Things
Traders Say," New York Times, June 27, 2012.

102   "People are setting": National Credit Union Administration
Board, as Liquidating Agent as Plaintiff, v. Credit Suisse Groupe
AG et al., September 2013.

103   On a conference call: Liam Vaughan and Gavin Finch, "Secret
Libor Transcripts Expose Trader Rate-Manipulation," Bloomberg, December 13, 2012.

103   Danziger to strip clubs: David Enrich and Jean Eaglesham,
"Clubby London Trading Scene Fostered Libor Rate-Fixing
Scandal," Wall Street Journal, May 2, 2013.

104   hired cars transported: Ibid.

104   "We want lower LIBORs": City of Houston, Plaintiff, v. Bank of America Corporation et al., 2013, Texas, No. 13CV02149, July 23, 2013.

104   "Sure, I'm setting": Liam Vaughan, Gavin Finch, and Andrea Tan, "RBS Managers Said to Condone Manipulation of Libor Rates," Bloomberg, September 25, 2012, www.bloomberg .com/news/2012-12-13/rigged-libor-with-police-nearby-shows -flaw-of-light-touch.html.

104   In September 2006: Order Instituting Proceedings Pursuant to Sections 6(c) and 6(d) of the Commodity Exchange Act, Commodity Futures Trading Commission, www.cftc.gov/ucm/ groups/public/@lrenforcementactions/documents/legalplead ing/enfbarclaysorder062712.pdf.

106   Philippe Moryoussef: Rosamund Urwin, "The French Connection: Is Our Banking Crisis a Parisian Problem?," London Evening Standard, May 15, 2014.

107   "cool, calm": Jonathan Prynn and Tom Harper, "London Banker Probed Over Claims He Was at Centre of Europe-wide Rate-Rigging Scandal, London Evening Standard, July 19, 2012.

107   Christian Bittar: Gavin Finch and Liam Vaughan, "Fired Deutsche Bank Trader Loses $53 Million," Bloomberg, January 24, 2013.

108   "bonus of €50 million": Martin Hesse, "Accusations Against Jain: LIBOR Probe Could Cost Deutsche Bank Billions," Der Spiegel, February 4, 2013.

108   Anshu Jain: Nicholas Comfort, "Deutsche Bank Said Set to Weigh Punishing Staff on Libor," Bloomberg, January 8, 2014.

109   "Combining cash and derivatives": Press release, Deutsche Bank, www.db.com/medien/en/content/press_releases_2005_2750.htm.

110   By 2011, Bittar had left: James Hurley, "Trader Loses £30m Bonus Over 'Rigging' at Deutsche," *Telegraph*, January 25, 2013.

110   "not allowed to have those conversations": "RBS and Libor: The Wrong Stuff," *Economist*, February 9, 2013.

CHAPTER 6

111   purse was $1.26 million: "Singh Wins Barclays in Dramatic Playoff That Features a 'Caddyshack' Moment," Associated Press, August 24, 2008, www.golf.com/ap-news/singh-wins-barclays-dramatic-playoff-features-caddyshack-moment#ixzz 31jhHp2Gy.

111   Mickelson was exactly the type: "World's 100 Highest-Paid Athletes," *Forbes*, www.forbes.com/pictures/mli45igdi/7-phil-mickelson.

112   PGA Tour: Ryan Ballengee, "Mickelson 'Crushed' Over Barclays CEO Resignation," *Golf News*, July 4, 2012.

112   £15 million pay package: Jill Treanor, "Big Hitter, Bob Diamond, Chief Executive, Barclays Capital," *Guardian*, August 5, 2005.

113   "It's done": Ibid.

113   Diamond first went to London: Chad Bray and Michael J. de la Merced, "After Barclays, a Former Chief Strives to Revive His Reputation in Africa," *New York Times*, May 8, 2014.

113   At Colby College: Gerry Boyle, "The Natural," *Colby Magazine*, September 11, 2007.

113   low-paying job at U.S. Surgical: Ibid.

114   When he left Morgan Stanley: John Plender, "How Traders Trumped Quakers," *Financial Times*, July 6, 2012.

114   "considered public enemy number one": Alexander Crossman, "'Coach' Proud of His Trading Floor Origins," *Financial News*, December 4, 2000.

114   **Allen Wheat:** Author interview with Wheat.

114   **Barclays de Zoete Wedd:** Salz Review, Barclays, www.euro money.com/downloads/2013/Barclays-Salz-review.pdf.

115   **"hotshot newcomer":** "Barclays CEO Resigns," *Daily Beast*, July 3, 2012, www.thedailybeast.com/articles/2012/07/03/barclays -ceo-resigns-scandal-links-to-bank-of-england.html.

116   **"touch his golden sleeve":** Martin Vander Weyer, "Banking Crisis: Why Robert Diamond Is Not the Only One to Blame," *Telegraph*, July 1, 2012.

116   **"just like English tea":** Stephanie Baker and Jon Menon, "Diamond Parries Attacks on Pay with Vow to Earn Public Trust," Bloomberg, November 30, 2010.

117   **"Friends of Bob":** Ibid.

117   **In 2001, Diamond poached:** Helen Dunne, "Barclays Capital Wins Team from Deutsche," *Telegraph*, May 17, 2001.

117   **Four of his traders famously:** Suzanne Kapner, "Five Bankers Fired from Barclays Over $62,700 Spent at Meal," *New York Times*, February 26, 2002.

118   **"I'm not disappointed":** Heather Timmons, "Barclays Shuffles Managers and Names Its Next Chief," *New York Times*, October 10, 2003.

119   **"We created a monster":** Interview with Bill Moyers, http://bill moyers.com/episode/full-show-how-big-banks-are-rewriting-the -rules-of-our-economy/.

119   **"Bobtimistic":** Bess Levin, "Bob Diamond's One-Man Cheering Squad Has Not Gone Unnoticed," *Dealbreaker*, November 30, 2010.

120   **"Mayor's Best Friend":** "Diamond: 'Unacceptable Face of Banking' Who Showed No Remorse," *Independent*, July 4, 2012.

120   **five-year pay package:** Hugo Duncan, "Backlash Over Barclays' £70m Man," *Daily Mail*, September 8, 2010.

122   "three asset classes": Ed Blount, "Breaking Away," *ABA Banking Journal* 97, no. 10.

123   "Find the place": Penelope Overton, "Different Path Leads to Milestone, UConn Holds Largest Midyear Graduation," *Hartford Courant*, December 18, 2006.

124   "roll of the dice": Julia Werdigier, "With ABN Amro in Play, Chief of Barclays Capital Savors a New Test," *New York Times*, June 22, 2007.

124   Diamonds would maintain: Mira Bar-Hillel and Jonathan Prynn, "Barclays Bank Chief Makes £15 Million by Selling His House," *London Evening Standard*, June 4, 2008.

125   Barclays had gone "berserk": Ibid.

125   "If there were another leg down": Alan S. Blinder, *After the Music Stopped: The Financial Crisis, the Response, and the Work Ahead* (New York: Penguin, 2013).

126   Steel at U.S. Treasury: Shawn Tully, "The Death of Bob Diamond's Dream for Barclays," *Fortune*, July 30, 2012.

127   "Barclays acted like": Abigail Hofman, "The Loser List," *Euromoney*, November 2008, www.euromoney.com/Article/2038377/Abigail-Hofman-The-loser-list.html?copyrightInfo=true.

128   Asia and the Middle East: Jill Treanor, "Barclays Under Fire for Middle Eastern Fundraising," *Guardian*, October 31, 2008.

128   More than four hundred: Sara Schaefer Muñoz, "A Payday for Barclays's Diamond," *Wall Street Journal*, June 13, 2009.

129   "send the message": Hugo Dixon, "What If Barclays Hadn't Lowered Libor Submissions?," Reuters, July 4, 2012.

129   central bank had "received calls": Ed Monk, "The Phone Call That 'Led to Rate-Rigging,'" *Daily Mail*, July 3, 2012, www.dailymail.co.uk/news/article-2168242/Barclays-release-details-Bank-England-man-says-led-Libor-rigging.html#ixzz31jwiM2Xm.

130   **"Well done, man":** Claire Jones and Norma Cohen, "Emails Add to Pressure on Tucker," *Financial Times*, July 17, 2012.

CHAPTER 7

132   **Gensler's father had installed:** Remarks of Chairman Gary Gensler Before the Maret Business Club, October 28, 2013.

132   **ran for class treasurer:** Paul West, "Marylander Gensler to Head Commodity Futures Trading Commission," *Baltimore Sun*, December 19, 2008.

132   **Goldman Sachs:** Kambiz Foroohar, "Gensler, Evolving in Derivatives War, Sees No Deed Go Unpunished," Bloomberg, June 21, 2011.

133   **National Football League:** "Gary Gensler, Commissioner of the Commodity Futures Trading Commission," *Washington Post*, May 2009.

133   **Government service:** Ibid.

134   **"We took them all through":** Author interview with Rickards.

135   **At that time, Brooksley Born:** Author interview with Greenberger.

136   **McGonagle had just finished signing:** Press release, CFTC, www.cftc.gov/PressRoom/PressReleases/pr5481-08.

139   **profile in the *New Republic*:** Noam Scheiber, "Beating the Street," *New Republic*, May 2010.

139   **"There's not a day":** Ibid.

142   **"I knew we had to pursue this":** Author interview with Gensler.

145   **Eurodollar contract:** Carrick Mollenkamp, Jennifer Ablan, and Matthew Goldstein, "How Gaming Libor Became Business as Usual," Reuters, November 20, 2012.

147   **that Meister was:** Oversight of the Swaps and Futures Markets, Committee on Agriculture, U.S. House of Representatives, July 25, 2012.

CHAPTER 8

148   **Mervyn King:** Remarks of Chairman Gary Gensler Before the Institute of International Bankers, March 4, 2013.

149   **Emails obtained by Labour MP:** Bank of England documents, www.bankofengland.co.uk/publications/Documents/foi/disc170712b.pdf.

150   **"It was an instruction, yes":** Victoria Bischoff, "Del Missier: Diamond Told Me to Order Libor Fixing," Citywire.co.uk, July 16, 2012.

152   **profits of just £207 million:** Kevin Crowley and Howard Mustoe, "Barclays Names Consumer Chief Jenkins CEO After Diamond," Bloomberg, August 30, 2012, www.bloomberg.com/news/2012-08-30/barclays-names-antony-jenkins-bank-s-group-chief-executive.html.

152   **"The swap traders have the most":** Author interview with former Barclays employee.

153   **Eric Bommensath:** Peter Lee, "Barclays Capital: Big Risks Remain in FICC," *Euromoney*, www.euromoney.com/Article/2861134/Barclays-Capital-Big-risks-remain-in-FICC.html?copyrightInfo =true.

153   **Ritankar "Ronti" Pal:** Carrick Mollenkamp, Jennifer Ablan, and Matthew Goldstein, "How Gaming Libor Became Business as Usual," Reuters, November 20, 2012.

154   **June 2012 FSA communication:** "Final Notice, Barclays Bank," Financial Services Authority, June 27, 2012, www.fsa.gov.uk/static/pubs/final/barclays-jun12.pdf.

155   **"When I retire":** "Appendix A: Statement of Facts," U.S. Department of Justice Report on Barclays, June 26, 2012.

155   **In April 2014, Merchant:** Suzi Ring, "N.Y. Barclays Libor Traders Said to Face U.K. Charges," Bloomberg, February 28, 2014.

155   **"Also, the bottom line":** Renee Tawa, "Caltech Grads Discover the Lure of Wall Street," *Los Angeles Times*, June 10, 1993.

156   **"I don't know what you guys":** Kit Chellel, "Barclays Executives Knew of Libor Lowballing, Guardian Claims," Bloomberg, October 17, 2013.

157   **Quan Hui Lee:** Jill Treanor, "Barclays Facing New Libor Allegations in Appeal Court," *Guardian*, October 17, 2013.

157   **"LIBOR was dislocated with itself":** Anonymous, "Libor Scandal: How I Manipulated the Bank Borrowing Rate," *Telegraph*, July 1, 2012.

158   **Royal Bank of Scotland:** United States of America Before the Commodity Futures Trading Commission. Order Instituting Proceedings, The Royal Bank of Scotland plc and RBS Securities Japan Limited, February 6, 2013.

159   **"orally confirmed":** Affidavit, Canadian competition law officer Brian Elliott, May 18, 2011, http://clients.oakbridgeins.com/clients/blog/libor86.pdf.

159   **Brent Davies was a sterling trader:** Ibid.

160   **At UBS:** "Appendix A: Statement of Facts," U.S. Department of Justice, December 18, 2012, www.justice.gov/criminal/vns/docs/2012/12/2012-12-19-UBS-Statement-of-Facts.pdf.

160   **"if we are [issuing commercial paper]":** "Examples of Misconduct from Written Communications," CFTC, www.cftc.gov/ucm/groups/public/@newsroom/documents/file/misconductwrittencommunication.pdf.

160   **In December 2010, a UBS manager:** Statement of Facts, U.S. Department of Justice. "We have long-established core": UBS presentation, www.justice.gov/opa/pr/2012/December/12-ag-1522.html.

162   "middle of the pack": "Final Notice, UBS," Financial Services Authority, December 19, 2012, www.fca.org.uk/static/documents/final-notices/ubs.pdf.

162   Paul Glands was another: Jean Eaglesham and David Enrich, "Libor Probe Expands to Bank Traders," *Wall Street Journal*, July 24, 2012.

163   Deutsche Bank: Jean Eaglesham, "Bank Made Huge Bet, and Profit, on Libor," *Wall Street Journal*, January 10, 2013.

163   Rabobank started out: Press release, Financial Conduct Authority, October 29, 2013, www.fca.org.uk/news/the-fca-fines-rabobank-105-million-for-serious-libor-related-misconduct.

164   U.S. dollar trader messaged: "Attachment A: Statement of Facts," U.S. Department of Justice, October 29, 2013, www.justice.gov/iso/opa/resources/645201310298755805528.pdf.

166   "Mate I had no": Ibid.

166   "Why did you put all the Yen LIBORS": "The Things Traders Say, Dutch Bank Edition," Dealbook, *New York Times*, October 29, 2013.

168   "Danny . . . will be your": United States of America v. Darrell Read, Daniel Wilkinson, and Colin Goodman, Defendants, www.justice.gov/iso/opa/resources/838201392583237891746.pdf.

171   "a lot of speculation": *Fixing LIBOR: Some Preliminary Findings, Second Report of Session 2012–13*, UK House of Commons, Treasury Committee.

171   "senior Whitehall figures": Ibid.

173   Lehman Brothers: Ibid.

174   when at Barclays: William Wright, "I Know Nothing. I'm from Barclays . . . ," william-wright.com, July 4, 2012.

177   "Banks have been subject": Bank of England documents, www.bankofengland.co.uk/publications/Documents/other/treasury-committee/financialstability/emailchain.pdf.

178   "systemic problem": Wheatley Review Final Report, September 28, 2012.

CHAPTER 9

179   "I worked at Barclays": "Whistleblower: 'The Culture Ultimately Comes from the Top,'" *Independent*, July 7, 2012.

182   "His Lordship should know": Cassell Bryan-Low and Jenny Strasburg, "Judge Allows Publication of Names in Libor Case," *Wall Street Journal*, October 21, 2013.

183   "strong connections": David Enrich, "Pieri: Rate-Rig Spotlight Falls on 'Rain Man,'" *Wall Street Journal*, February 8, 2013.

184   Mirhat Alykulov: Caroline Binham, "SFO Narrows Libor Charges," *Financial Times*, October 21, 2013.

184   Christopher Cecere: David Enrich and Jenny Strasburg, "U.K. Expected to Name Alleged Co-Conspirators in Libor Scandal," *Wall Street Journal*, October 17, 2013.

185   "just the tip of the iceberg": Author interview with Mann.

186   "better citizens": Bob Diamond, "Banks Will Be Good Citizens," *Guardian*, November 3, 2011.

187   According to an analysis: Author interview with Abrantes-Metz.

187   "wouldn't be surprised if more banks": Author interview with Verstein.

189   Gensler complained: Gensler interview, WBUR Radio.

189   "A lot has changed since 1986": Remarks of Chairman Gary Gensler on Libor Before the Global Financial Markets Association's Future of Global Benchmarks Conference, February 28, 2013.

191   reliance on LIBOR as "fragile": Remarks of Chairman Gary Gensler Before the FIA's 2013 38th Annual International Futures Industry Conference, March 13, 2013.

191   "How is it that in 2012": Ibid.

192   San Francisco cable car driver: Jean Eaglesham, "Banks Face Key Hurdle in Libor Fight," *Wall Street Journal*, February 25, 2013.

194   "Gensler succeeded in bringing": Author interview with Greenberger.

194   Corzine joined MF Global: Press release, CFTC, June 27, 2013, www.cftc.gov/PressRoom/PressReleases/pr6626-13.

196   "All of MF Global's executives": Author interview with Koutoulas.

196   "CFTC had some major problems": Author interview with Gellert.

198   City Week: Author interview with Gensler in London.

198   "Using benchmarks that threaten": Remarks of Chairman Gary Gensler at London City Week on Benchmark Interest Rates, April 22, 2013.

199   "No delay": Ben Protess, "Deadline on Trading Rules Abroad Splits an Agency," *New York Times*, July 2, 2013.

199   confrontation would be with Jacob Lew: Silla Brush and Robert Schmidt, "How the Bank Lobby Loosened U.S. Reins on Derivatives," Bloomberg, September 4, 2013.

201   *International Financing Review*: "Closing Loophole Could Cost US Banks Millions," *International Financing Review*, June 22–28, 2013.

202   "U.S. banks simply aren't ready": Yves Smith, "Gensler Staring Down Administration and Banks on Derivatives Reform," *Naked Capitalism*, June 25, 2013.

202   "We Americans bailed them out": Gary Gensler, Chairman, Commodity Futures Trading Commission, Before the U.S. Senate Committee on Agriculture, Nutrition and Forestry, Washington D.C., July 17, 2012.

202   **"We have to recall the lessons"**: Chairman Gary Gensler's Keynote Address on the Cross-Border Application of Swaps Market Reform at Sandler O'Neill Conference, June 6, 2013.

203   **"Lew called him in and said"**: Author interview with Greenberger.

205   **"Was this something they"**: FOIA: "Sommers went so far as to fire off a furious email to CFTC staffer Ananda Radhakrishnan." Refers to FOIA request of emails between Steve A. Linick, Inspector General, and Edward DeMarco, Acting Director, Office of Inspector General, Federal Housing Finance Agency. Subject: Effect of Possible LIBOR Manipulations on FHFA Regulated Entities. Courtesy, Lisette Garica.

206   **"It could create dangerous"**: Ben White, "Warren Hits Gensler Opponents," *Politico*, June 25, 2013.

207   **"international community"**: Huw Jones, "CFTC's Gensler Says Libor Overhaul Will Take Time," Reuters, September 19, 2013.

208   **In December 2013, he traveled**: http://knowledge.wharton.upenn .edu/article/can-anyone-regulate-400-trillion-market-gary-gensler/.

211   **Massad told the Brookings Institution**: "Wrapping Up the TARP: What Will Be Its Legacy?" Brookings Institution, September 30, 2013.

211   **"a loyal soldier"**: Jesse Eisinger, "In Obama's Pick to Lead a Financial Regulator, an Enigma," *New York Times*, November 20, 2013.

212   **"I'm not confident"**: Bill Sokolis, "US CFTC's Gensler: 'Not Confident' CFTC Up to Dodd Frank," MNI News, November 6, 2013.

CHAPTER 10

213   **"swaps have cost me £12 million"**: Kit Chellel, "Barclays Executives Knew of Libor Lowballing, Guardian Claims," Bloomberg, October 17, 2013.

214 thirty-first floor: Tim Wallace, "New Libor Claims Hit Barclays," *City A.M.*, October 18, 2013.

216 employed "financial professionals": Romy Varghese, "Philadelphia Can't Explain Its Swaps Yet Fights Ban," Bloomberg, April 4, 2013.

216 The swaps were supposed to give: Joseph N. DiStefano, "PhillyDeals: City Looks Into Its Losses Gambling on Rising Rates," *Philadelphia Inquirer*, October 21, 2012.

218 changed their tune: Harold Brubaker, "Philadelphia Sues Big Banks Over Swaps Losses," *Philadelphia Inquirer*, July 31, 2013.

218 city was "receiving a rate": Ibid.

219 "basically sitting ducks": Melissa Daniels, "Under PA Proposals, It's the Financial Consultants Who Would Pay," *PA Independent*, via Watchdog.org, September 10, 2013.

219 Lucien Calhoun: Ibid.

220 2012 audit: "Performance Audit: Southeastern Pennsylvania Transportation Authority," www.auditorgen.state.pa.us/Reports/Performance/SO/stoSEPTA081712.pdf.

220 "When their bad behavior": DiStefano, "City Looks Into Its Losses Gambling on Rising Rates."

221 Metropolitan Transportation Authority: "Riding the Gravy Train: How Wall Street Is Bankrupting Our Public Transit Agencies by Profiteering Off of Toxic Swap Deals," Refund Transit Coalition, 2012, refundtransit.org.

221 New York subway riders: Ibid.

222 "We can't be scared": "Sacramento County Sues Big Banks, Alleging Rate Manipulation," Global Association of Risk Professionals, July 24, 2013.

223 "What is shocking": "Antitrust: Commission Fines Banks €1.71 Billion for Participating in Cartels in the Interest Rate Derivatives

Industry," press release, European Commission, Brussels, December 4, 2013.

223   **"key to landing bond deals"**: William Selway and Martin Z. Braun, "JPMorgan Proves Bond Deal Death in Jefferson County No Bar to New Business," Bloomberg, August 12, 2011.

223   **In Oakland:** Alison Vekshin and Darrell Preston, "Oakland Nears Firing Goldman as Swap Burdens City: Muni Credit," Bloomberg, January 3, 2013.

224   **"You should be concerned"**: "Reverend Daniel Buford Testifying Tuesday Before the Oakland City Council," Democracy Now, July 3, 2012.

225   **"The swap deal the city"**: Kevin Roose, "How Do You Run Goldman Sachs Out of Town?," *New York*, April 11, 2013.

225   **"We gambled. We lost"**: Ibid.

225   **"It was a gold mine"**: John W. Schoen, "Damage to City Budgets: Some Was Self-Inflicted," CNBC, November 18, 2013.

226   **"Investment bankers fly"**: Ibid.

EPILOGUE

245   **"common industry practice"**: David Enrich and Atsuko Fukase, "Libor Rate-Probe Spotlight Shines on Higher-Ups at Citigroup, Other Banks," *Wall Street Journal*, August 28, 2013.

Index

279